THE CONFUSION OF THE CHURCHES

THE CONFUSION OF THE CHURCHES

A Survey of the Problem of Reunion

BY THE
REV. KENNETH D. MACKENZIE, M.A.
FORMERLY FELLOW AND DEAN OF PEMBROKE COLLEGE, OXFORD

Si la vérité a ses droits, la charité a ses devoirs.
CARDINAL MERCIER, *Archbishop of Malines.*

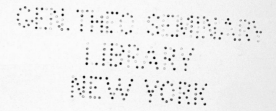

EDWIN S. GORHAM
NEW YORK

First published in 1925

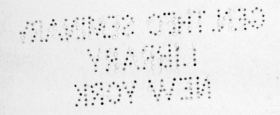
PRINTED IN GREAT BRITAIN BY ROBERT MACLEHOSE AND CO. LTD.
THE UNIVERSITY PRESS, GLASGOW.

PREFACE

THE writer desires to express his great indebtedness, first to Professor Claude Jenkins, D.D., for remarkable kindness in reading through the whole of this book in typescript, for his many and severe criticisms, and for numberless valuable suggestions; secondly, to the Rev. N. P. Williams, for an illuminating conversation which supplied the outline of such groundplan as the book possesses; also to the Dean of Christ Church, the Dean of Canterbury, Canon E. F. Spanton, Canon F. A. Douglas, Ph.D., the Rev. C. E. Douglas, the Rev. W. R. Corbould, the Rev. H. J. Fynes-Clinton, the Rev. F. W. Green, the Rev. G. E. W. Holmes, the Rev. E. Lorimer Thomas, the Rev. P. Usher, and M. Zs. de Szász, who have all in various ways showed him remarkable kindness, and without whose help this study would have been incomplete indeed.

Much use has also been made of Canon Ollard's volume entitled *Reunion* in the series of *Handbooks of Catholic Faith and Practice;* some use also of articles in *The Commonwealth* on "The Household of the Faith," by the Rev. M. Donovan.

CONTENTS

DOMINE JESU CHRISTE, QUI DIXISTI APOSTOLIS TUIS :
PACEM RELINQUO VOBIS, PACEM MEAM DO VOBIS : NE
RESPICIAS PECCATA MEA, SED FIDEM ECCLESIAE TUAE :
EAMQUE SECUNDUM VOLUNTATEM TUAM PACIFICARE
ET COADUNARE DIGNERIS : QUI VIVIS ET REGNAS DEUS
PER OMNIA SAECULA SAECULORUM. AMEN.

Missale Romanum.

I

THE NEED FOR REUNION

It has rightly been said [1] that the one unpardonable sin to-day is to have a closed mind. If that is true in general, its force is multiplied when we are dealing with the concerns of religion. For there is no department of the mind in which closure more readily takes place, or has more disastrous consequences. A certain conservatism seems to be necessary in religion if it is to have coherence and stability ; but the temptation and the ruin of the religious conservative is to let himself degenerate into a sheer, stonewall, religious Tory. He may retire to the backwoods, and forget the existence of all but his compeers in religion, or he may rush to the assault and break a lance on behalf of truth as he has always known it : the one thing he cannot do is to look at anything afresh. If he is a writer, he leaves behind him a dreary trail of theological works, either virulently controversial or blandly oblivious of anything controvertible ; if he is a preacher, his own traditions are the only thing which he can conceive of as important ; and either way he only succeeds in making us feel that he is pleading a case, and that his work is useless except as ammunition, or else as a target.

Now when we touch the problem of Reunion we are in contact at once with all the power of entrenched conservatism in its strongest form. Many of us have all our lives heard religion presented controversially, and have unconsci-

---

[1] The Bishop of Winchester, *Diocesan Magazine*, Jan. 1925.

ously been led to think that other people's ways and thoughts are all more or less wrong. Religious emotion, which is part of the primitive stuff of our nature, if anything is, normally arises in response to a particular stimulus. And this stimulus is not as a rule the unmediated and unmingled touch of the Divine Spirit Himself. We are accustomed to receive religious excitation along a particular channel, and all our deepest rooted and least rational instincts are in revolt when it arrives along an unfamiliar one. In the presence of a fresh presentation of external religion one whole stratum of our psychical nature behaves like a child with a new nurse. An irrational hatred of the unfamiliar is only too common a characteristic of popular religion, and these hatreds operate chiefly on the level of external things. Theologians may be arguing about fundamentals ; but what the natural man is afraid of is that some unfamiliar stimulus is going to be applied to him instead of the one which he expects : in the sixteenth century Matins instead of Mass ; in the nineteenth or twentieth Mass perhaps instead of Matins. Hence arises an emotional antipathy and dislike which soon deepens into distrust, and may then be " rationalised " into an insurmountable obstacle.

One of our first objects, then, in approaching this matter of Reunion must be to transcend the merely instinctive religious dislike which we have of one another's ways, and begin to think kindly and sympathetically of one another. " Le rapprochement des cœurs," as Cardinal Mercier says, " n'est pas l'unité dans la Foi, mais il y dispose." As regards externals, we can say quite frankly that we like certain ways : incense, Matins at eleven, extempory prayer ; even in a sense we " believe in them," because they are of a piece with our dearest convictions, and symbolise the presence of God to us, with our preconceptions, as no other ways could ever do. But it has never surely entered any sane man's head at this time of day to attempt to impose on all Christians external uniformity. If Reunion comes to pass it will

certainly mean that there will have to be a great deal of
mutual forbearance about externals. For, more often than
we know, our divisions are mainly external : if we could only
come to an agreement on externals the doctrinal and disciplinary divisions would prove less intractable. They would
indeed remain, but in an atmosphere in which there was
some chance of their ultimate disappearance. As long as
we think that Reunion means that our religious practice has
got to be conformed to someone else's, or else his to ours,
the will to union will be lacking, and no progress can be made.

Having fixed it then in our minds that any scheme of
Reunion, even if successful, is going to leave our actual
religious practice almost unchanged, we have next to ask
what Christian Reunion would mean, and why we should
wish to have it.

Essentially it would mean (if it ever became complete)
that all Christians would recognise that they belonged to the
same holy, world-wide, international society, the Church of
Jesus Christ. They would almost altogether give up speaking
of " The Churches," and substitute " The Church " : they
could, either more or less freely, frequent any Christian
church building they liked, without feeling that they were
changing their allegiance : they could make their Communions at Westminster Cathedral or at the Central Hall
without feeling that there was any difference in what they
received or in the certainty that they were receiving it.[1]
All Christians would recognise all others as indeed brethren
in the Lord's family. In particular, it would be impossible

[1] How far they would do this in practice would be a matter partly of
taste, but partly also of discipline. On the one hand, it is not very
probable that apart from emergencies many people would desire to vary
their religious observance in this way. On the other hand, in churches
where discipline is enforced, permission to an individual to vary his rite
would not be readily given. It must not be supposed, e.g., that there is
free intercommunion between Latins and Uniates in the churches of the
Papal obedience to-day. They are held together (a) by unity in the
faith, (b) by common allegiance to the Pope. But they do not frequent
each others' churches. Still less is any priest at liberty to vary his rite.

to raise any further questions as to the position of any priest or minister : all who exercised any ministry in the reunited Church would be in possession of such authority as would be beyond dispute.

Such a picture may seem fantastic : certainly there is no sign that any such state of affairs is actually on the way. It may, of course, be said that it is a mirage, and that it can only distract us from simpler and more practical schemes of reunion, yet it is difficult to see how we could be permanently satisfied with anything less than this. Any form of reunion which interfered with the ultimate possibility of communion with the holy and apostolic see of Rome would leave many of us cold. So also would any scheme which would obscure the vision of unity with the great national churches of the East. So also reunion would be incomplete indeed if it did not include that vast host of Christians who are separated from historic Catholic Christianity.

Granting then that any such reunion as this is not yet appearing on the horizon, it still remains worth asking whether it is in itself desirable, and worth aspiring after and working for.

Now, of course, it must be assumed in any such vision that the uniting bodies have so far composed their real differences as to make it true that they really profess the same religion : in other words, that they have the same general conception of God, of religious duty, and of the method of salvation. We cannot imagine that a Unitarian and a Trinitarian could ever rightly belong to the same religious body : nor a polygamist and a believer in mono-gamy : nor a sacramentalist and a member of the Society of Friends (as at present it makes its profession of faith). But supposing such adjustment to have taken place, can it be doubted that the world would be a better, and indeed a safer place to live in ?

It can hardly be an exaggeration to say that the statesmen of the world must be living in a horror of the possibility of

another war. The War which was to end war has but left
the stage set for a conflict before which the terrors of 1914-
1918 may seem but child's play. Frenchmen and Germans,
Serbs and Croats, Rumanians and Hungarians, yellow races
and Europeans, are glowering at one another across, or more
dangerously within, natural or artificial frontiers. India,
Egypt, South Africa each has its racial question. The Turk
and the Bolshevik are not yet at the end of their schemes for
the extermination of Christians. If the world of 1914 was
like a well-ordered and carefully guarded powder-magazine,
the world of 1925 resembles a bomb-factory in the middle
of a crowded street. The explosion, if it comes, will spare
no one this time. Another war would go far towards getting
rid of civilisation altogether. And between ourselves and
this explosion there is interposed nothing but the League
of Nations and the rapidly evaporating memories of our
recent struggle. These memories will soon be gone, and
all that will then be left to link the nations together will be
the League, that foundling of American ancestry, left on a
European doorstep on the chance that kind-hearted statesmen might adopt it. While it would be impossible to
exaggerate the importance of keeping the League alive, as
the only human hope for world peace, it can hardly be denied
that it is a sickly infant, and in great danger of perishing
through sheer lack of affection. It must inspire more love
if it is to thrive. Without minimising for a moment the
great work which the League has accomplished and the
actual successes which stand to its credit, it would be difficult
to say that it inspires anyone with great confidence in its
power to prevent the catastrophe of war. What we want is
a real brotherhood, in the heart, not merely on paper ; in
the spirit, not in the letter, as S. Paul would say ; and this
brotherhood could be most completely and most happily
found in the sphere of religion, that is to say in a *de facto*
world-church.

It is easy to point to the fact that members of the church

which approaches most nearly to the ideal of a world-church were fighting against each other in the late war : the Catholics of France and Italy were fighting against those of Germany and Austria : that of course is perfectly true. But it must be remembered that France and Italy, although their populations are mostly Roman Catholic, are both in their traditional politics ranged against the Papacy, and *as states* probably feel little sense of religious brotherhood with Austria. And it remains true that the main facts of the outbreak of the war were an attack by Catholic Austria on Orthodox Serbia, and an attack by (predominantly) Protestant Germany on Catholic France and Belgium. It is almost impossible to conceive that events would have been pushed to their dreadful conclusion with the same precipitancy if the vast bulk of the inhabitants of the protagonist nations on either side had belonged to the same religious brotherhood as those on the other.

Nationalism unrestrained is the great force which makes for strife. So it has always been. War feeds on national antipathies. Imagined self-interest may strike the light, but the sentiment of national antipathy is the fuel without which any war will soon burn itself out. The solemn singing to order of a hymn of hate was but the practical recognition of this fact by a very logical and sentimental people with little sense of humour.

Sentiment must be fought with sentiment, and it seems to follow that there is desperate need of some binding force between the nations with a stronger appeal to the heart than the League of Nations has shown itself to possess if we are to be delivered from the terror which is ours to-day. That force ought to be supplied by religion, the strongest of all emotional forces. At present religion is dominated by national feeling, and is a dividing factor in the world. If we could but replace the national ideal by the Catholic, we should have enlisted religion on the side of peace.

It is often said that it was the Papacy which held Europe

together and prevented the collapse of civilisation during the dark ages. It might be truer to say that the Papacy along with the Holy Roman Empire gave all Christians the sense that in the end they were one brotherhood, and that their common Christianity was a civil as well as a religious bond. " Christendom," says Gierke, " which in destiny is identical with mankind, is set before us as a single universal Community, founded and governed by God Himself."[1] And the great and recurring problem of the period is the relationship between the spiritual and temporal powers, both alike ordained of God. Their failure to adjust their respective spheres led to exaggerated claims on this side and on that, and finally to the chaos which was the result of trying to govern the world by means of an ecclesiastical autocracy.

No doubt every Western mediaevalist would have supposed that this unity depended on autocratic and coercive authority, both in the religious and in the civil domain. But if we are right in supposing that Catholicism need not imply Papalism, it may also be true that Christendom might feel itself a civil unity without in any way tampering with valid national rights. We do not need an Emperor ; but a united Christendom would have once more its civil expression as well as its religious one. We are not dreaming of a single world state ; but unity of religion would have brought us nearer to the federation of the many states of the world.

And would not religious unity have some contribution to make to industrial peace ? Here again the problems at issue are the nightmare of statesmen. There are not wanting those who are deliberately working day and night for social upheaval ; nor is it possible to forget the existence of those lives of vicious or idle luxury which tempt men to say that the only way to clear the air is to declare war on parasites. Flaunting luxury is an incitement to civil strife, and this incitement is going on all the time.

Now Church unity is not going to remove the causes of

[1] *Political Theories of the Middle Age*, ed. Maitland, p. 10.

possible revolution ; too many of those who would be willing
or unwilling factors in a revolution have little use for a church,
united or otherwise ; but any enlargement of the sphere in
which men can feel that they are brethren in the Lord is a
step towards charitable and equitable dealings with political
opponents. And it must be remembered that in England
our ecclesiastical divisions correspond far too closely to our
social and political ones : the definition of the Church of
England as the Conservative party at prayer has still just
enough truth in it to carry a tiny sting.

Now supposing that all those Labour men and Liberals
who had any religion at all were acutely conscious that they
belonged to the one religious brotherhood, would it not make
all the difference to the methods of the General Strike, when
and if it arrives ? If the railway director and the strike
picket recognised each other as fellow-communicants it would
be far more likely that they would show mutual sympathy
and tolerance.

Humanity, it seems then, needs a single Church, even for
purposes outside the strictly spiritual sphere. But much
more do we as Christians need union. Something must
surely be wrong somewhere. To put the matter at its
lowest the present system is absurdly wasteful. We build
half a dozen competitive buildings where one or two ought
to be enough : and correspondingly we have to multiply
all our organisations as though there were no one but ourselves doing the work, when all the time to a very large
extent it is the *same* work that all these different bodies are
doing. We spend time and money in opposing each other
which had far better be spent on the objects we all agree
about. We dissipate interest on domestic points of controversy when we might all be fighting the common foe.
We make ourselves a bye-word for narrowness and jealousy.
We cannot be thoroughly enthusiastic even over our own
sectional presentation of the faith : it is too obviously
sectional sometimes. " Church of England " has ceased to

be a name to conjure with. As Mazzini said, "Men will not die to reform Naples : they will die to save Italy." A certain amount of wholesome competition may be all to the good ; but that is no reason for all the competitors running on different tracks.

If we look to the mission field the need for unity stares us in the face. In some places our disunion has already done damage which seems irreparable. In Japan for instance there was once a promising young Christian church, organised by the matchless missionary zeal of S. Francis Xavier. Differences began to declare themselves and the Japanese in disgust rejected Christianity altogether for centuries.

In other places the native Church is threatening to take a short way with European quarrels, which were none of their making and have no interest for them. They are showing signs of reuniting without waiting for the consent of anyone but their own people. It is obvious that here is a great danger of creating a new schism in mending an old one.

In other places there is yet a third result, in some ways the most pathetic of all. The recent negotiations for combining Anglican missions in East Africa into a single East African (Anglican) Province were brought to nothing by the African vote in the Synod or Diocesan Conference. The Baganda had learnt to take a side in our unhappy divisions only too well, and were not going to enter into closer fellowship than they could help with the "Popish" U.M.C.A. "Bananas," they said, "fall into two classes, good and bad. How can we good bananas join ourselves to the bad ones ? "

If we look higher we see but more clearly the need for unity. The whole conception of a Body which is no less than Christ's own Body becomes meaningless if we are content with the present confusion. Christ and the Church S. Thomas would have us see as *quasi una persona mystica*, and his words go not a jot beyond S. Paul's conception.   If the visible Church is to be Christ's Body it must of necessity be one.

Few scholars will be found to-day to maintain the thesis that the Catholic Church was formed by the coalescing of separated and independent bodies.   The Congregationalists themselves would not put the matter quite like that.   The original conception of the Church of Christ was precisely the conception of the one Church of God, heir to the covenant with Abraham, Isaac and Jacob, but differentiated from the ancient Israel by the fact that national barriers were thrown down.   The Church that had been national had become universal.   But it is clear that there cannot in the nature of things be more than one *universal* Church.   Unity is demanded by our very name.   As Dr. Carnegie Simpson says, " The Church is not just a club. . . .   The idea of the Church has more than authority : it has necessity."

And to look higher still, the intention of our Lord claims unity for His disciples.   With almost His dying breath He prayed for unity, analogous to and depending on that unity which reigns between Himself and the Eternal Father.

Moreover, we feel that ultimately, not only is our aim the same, but our attainment, such as it is, is the same. What of course is quite *un*true is that we are all going the same way : that is precisely what we are not doing.   But our aim and our attainment are no less than God in Christ : and in that we are one.   This too was well put by Dr. Carnegie Simpson at Mürren last year.   After quoting S. Bernard,

Quam bonus te quaerentibus !
Sed quid invenientibus !

he went on : " As *quaerentes* we differ.   Individuals differ, ages differ, Churches differ, and the true differences may be far from unimportant.   But they are not final.   For as *invenientes*—if so be we know God in Christ and are known of Him—we are at one."

We may well be ashamed of our divisions. That we *are* ashamed is the most hopeful fact in the situation. If that is so it is certainly time to see whether something cannot be done to end them. But if so, what ?

II

CATHOLICISM, NATIONALISM, SECTARIANISM

ALL Christians are agreed that we ought to be united, and the man in the street may well be excused if he asks us why then we are not. What is the difficulty? Of course different men will always differ to some extent; but if there is such a thing as a common Christianity how has it come about that it has been too weak to maintain unity? And what is the difficulty about reuniting on this basis? Would it not be possible to find out what there is that all Christians believe, and form a great society, or at least a federation of societies, consisting of all who hold these views, and get that group generally recognised as " The Church," or, if you like, " The Catholic Church " ?

Before we are in a position to answer that question we shall have to make one or two long excursions into historical and doctrinal fields. It is no good trying to think intelligently about religious differences unless we have been at the pains to discover what is their significance, and how they actually arose. But, as a preliminary to this enquiry, it is worth while to draw attention to three tendencies observable throughout Church History. For it is to the interaction between these tendencies that most of our divisions are actually due.

The first is Catholicism.

What exactly does " Catholic " mean? It is first applied to the Church by S. Ignatius, to whom it seems to mean the Church *as a whole*, but already there is to be detected the secondary meaning of the *true* Church. " Wherever Jesus Christ is," he says, " *there* is the Catholic Church." And of this presence of Christ and the Catholic Church the Bishop is the pledge.   That is to say, if we are linked with the Bishop we are linked with something greater than a mere local gathering : we are linked with the universal Church, and so with Christ Himself.

In S. Cyprian the word has come to be almost equivalent to " orthodox."   In S. Augustine we find it both in its natural meaning of " world-wide " and in the secondary sense of " orthodox."   The local church, in his teaching, must compare its doctrine with that which is universally held.   If it is really universal, it is true.   *Securus judicat orbis terrarum.*

Thus with the arising of strongly defined national groups it has come to mean something like supra-national, or international.   Further, with the rise of new forms of belief, and new Christian sects, there comes into it a temporal meaning. The Catholic Church is the historic Church.   Only, as in Ignatius himself, there is always in the background the sense that this universal Church is not only supra-national, but supernatural and authoritative.   Thus it is fit to stand as an article in the Creed.

But when we speak of Catholicism as a *tendency* we are not using the word in this mystical sense.   By " Catholic " we shall simply mean " world-wide " as opposed to local, and, as national divisions become accentuated, " supranational " as opposed to national.

Now it is obvious that to speak of the Church as *Catholic*, when it consisted of about two hundred Jews in one city, is only justifiable if we mean that the germ and potentiality of Catholicism was present.   From this small nucleus of the Jerusalem Church Christianity spread and grew.   From the very first all life and authority in local churches was derived from membership in the one Church, now rapidly becoming world-wide. Doctrine, Ministry and rules of conduct depended for them on the fact that they belonged to the

Catholic society. "We have no such custom, neither the churches of God "[1] is a clinching and decisive argument. "Was it from you that the word of God went forth ? or came it unto you alone ? "[2] are questions to which only one answer is conceivable. During the lifetime of the Apostles there is a world-wide ministry to which the local ministry is always and obviously in subjection. The ultimate government of the local churches, that is to say, is in the hands of the universal, or " Catholic," authority.

After the passing away of the Apostolic form of jurisdiction the vital difference between " Bishop " and " Presbyter " is that the Bishop, though limited in the exercise of his ministry to a particular see, has none the less succeeded to the position of an Apostle in this respect, that he is a member of the world-wide episcopate and represents the whole Church to all who are under his authority. He is in communication with his fellow-bishops, and his union with them forms the bond which unites his local church with the whole body of the Great Church throughout the world. So it seems to have been from the beginning, and so it was increasingly through all the early ages of the Church's life.[3]

Of formal Church organisation there is naturally little in the earliest days ; but all our scanty information goes to show that there was an extraordinary amount of communication between different local churches even in the first two centuries, both by letter and by personal visits. The sense that the Church as a whole is one body in Christ is vivid and obvious at every stage. In no respect is this more clear than in the universal acceptance of the four Gospels by every part of the Church almost simultaneously. Even the Epistles sent to particular churches seem to have been con-

[1] 1 Cor. xi. 16.   [2] 1 Cor. xiv. 36 (R.V.).

[3] We must not of course imagine that the presbyter is a local or congregational official : he is a " pastor of the Universal Church," a " Catholic priest " ; but it is through the bishop that his ministry has this universal character.

sidered the property of the whole body almost as soon as they were received.[1]

The idea of a Diocese, still more of a congregation, having a life independent of the rest of the Church is one which never emerges anywhere. The tendency is almost entirely the other way. More and more the Church became grouped round those great sees which from the fifth century were recognised as " patriarchal " : and more and more the Roman Bishop established his see as a centre which seemed to unite the whole body. The ultimate triumph of this principle of international Catholicism (unfortunately to the exclusion of other considerations), is to be looked for in the Roman Catholic Church of the present day. Down to the eighteenth century there were still clearly marked national groups within the Roman Church. Gallicanism was not the only nationalist movement at that period. Even in 1870 the divisions of opinion among the Bishops attending the Vatican Council seem to have been more or less on national lines. But since the Council of Trent the policy of the Vatican has been to crush out, little by little, all manifestations of local patriotism in religious matters.[2]

The second tendency is Nationalism. It must be obvious from the beginning that the national spirit is going to be the chief difficulty in realising the ideal of a Catholic Church. For undiluted Catholicism ought obviously to mean the subjugation of national to supra-national feeling. And when the supra-national Church falls before the temptation to assimilate herself to a secular state, there is a serious danger that it should work out in practice to the exaltation of one nation over all others ; and from this point of view it is

[1] The Canon of the New Testament was not finally settled for many years ; but the testimony of S. Irenaeus proves the universal acceptance of the four Gospels by the latter part of the second century.

[2] It is fair to say that this only applies to the West. There has been plenty of Latinization among the Eastern Churches in communion with Rome ; but no settled policy of destroying national peculiarities.

not without significance that this complete and exclusive Catholicism has only been attained at the price of making the government of the Roman Catholic Church predominantly Italian. Extremes meet. Ultramontane Romanism turns out to be Nationalism *in excelsis*, the world-wide domination of the Papal City-State.

This primary and obvious difficulty of making room for Nationalism within the Catholic Church hardly made itself felt in the earliest days of Christianity, for the natural reason that the spirit of Nationalism was in abeyance. The Roman Empire was co-terminous with civilisation, and Christian missionaries were not slow to use its organisation for the permeation of the world with Christian principles.

But Nationalism is a spirit which cannot be destroyed. With the signs of the weakening of the grip of the imperial power it reappears : and wherever it is found in the sphere of religion it inevitably creates its own characteristic danger of schism. Even before the beginning of the dissolution of the Empire we can discern the influence of national, or at any rate racial, feeling in the great schisms which disturbed the peace of the Church. Marcionism was anti-Semitic : Montanism in its earlier form was deeply tinged with the characteristic Asiatic fanaticism : Donatism was African rather than European, and betrays its origin. It is idle even at this early date to think of a heresy as the result of cool, detached ratiocination. It is a mass movement, a group phenomenon, and the group is always more or less defined by national or racial characteristics. Donatism was not a heresy at all : nor was Montanism, though it tended in that direction.

So, when the Western Empire at last went under, the great danger of Arianism was not in the theological schools of Alexandria so much as in the fact that it was professed by the Goths ; and they were for the moment the lords of the world, prepared to impose Arianism as their national form of Christianity.

Arianism has not survived, but two of the other great Christological heresies have left their mark on the state of the Christian world to-day.   There is a Nestorian Church, and there are two Monophysite Churches.   In both cases they represent a particular *local* tendency of theological thought, combined with a resentment against imperial, *i.e.* supra-national, domination.   There seems to be no tangible divergence from orthodoxy in modern Nestorians, Jacobites, or Copts.   The schisms have been continued almost entirely because they are bound up with national feeling of one kind or another.

So, when we come to the great schism between East and West, it would hardly be possible to exaggerate the influence of national feeling on both sides.   " There was," says Dr. Hearnshaw, " a radical difference of genius between the Greek and the Latin.   They were divided not only by language but by a fundamental antagonism of ideas.   The one was metaphysical, speculative, disputatious, aesthetic, ritualistic, emotional ; the other was legal, practical, authoritarian, averse from controversy, ready for compromise, eager for conquest, zealous in missionary enterprise, masterly in organisation and government." [1]   At the last moment the exasperation of the Greeks at the idea of a Northern barbarian presuming to call himself Emperor, and ruling half Europe with the aid of savage hordes, was only equalled by the scorn of the new race of Germanised Latins for the effete civilisation on the shores of the Bosphorus.   Racial repulsion, far more than *odium theologicum*, was responsible for the tragic cleavage of East and West ; while it was the national memories of the Fourth Crusade which more than anything else caused the failure of subsequent attempts to heal the breach.

The later history of the Eastern Orthodox Churches has been chiefly concerned with the problem of how to combine Nationalism with the international Catholic spirit ; and

[1] *Mediaeval Contributions to Modern Civilisation*, p. 29.

indeed they have achieved a unique success in the establishment of national churches without serious breaches of
Catholic unity.   But they too, as we shall see, have had their
Phanariote difficulty, the Eastern counterpart of Ultramontanism, and it has not always been too easy to bring
about a *modus vivendi* between Greek and Slav.   At the
present moment there is a situation which in some ways
cannot but remind us of the " Babylonish captivity " of the
Papacy at Avignon.   At that period the Popes were exposed
to French political influence to an extent which very seriously
diminished their prestige ; and in like manner to-day we see
the Patriarchate of Constantinople faced with the difficulty
of how to fill up her sacred Synod and maintain its authority,
when the Turkish authorities insist that not only the
Patriarch but all the Metropolitans who constitute the
Synod must be Turkish subjects.

In the Reformation period we shall find the same thing.
Some states are seized with the reforming fever ; some are
not : and the course of the Reformation itself runs on purely
national lines.   The original driving force throughout is
national resentment against the Papacy.   That was very
obviously the case in this country, but is also true of every
state in which the Reformation proved itself to have any
permanent power.   It was an assertion of national feeling,
a wedge driven into the solid trunk of the Western Church,
and destined to destroy her external unity.

The third of these tendencies from the interplay of which
our modern divisions take their rise may be called Sectarianism, or, from another point of view, the critical spirit.
It is obvious that the natural opposition between Catholicism
and Nationalism does not account for all the facts.   Otherwise we should have the nations of Christendom each showing
a clear and united religious front to the world ; or at most
divided into two sections, according as the claims of Catholicism or Nationalism in religion had had most weight with
individuals.

In many countries this, or something like it, is actually the case. In the countries of Northern Europe generally it would be true to say that Christians are divided into Nationalists and Catholics, and that the Nationalists in religion all belonged to one religious body, which is in some sense a national Church. We see this very clearly in Germany, where since the times of Frederic I. of Prussia it has seemed intolerable that there should be two fully organised Protestant bodies going on side by side, both claiming, as Lutherans and Calvinists in different forms did claim, that the State should give them its protection and support. Thus we have, over against the solid front of Catholicism, another solid front of the Evangelical State Church. All other religious organisations are frowned on : even the Salvation Army has serious difficulties in obtaining more than the barest toleration. Much the same position is found in Scandinavia and Denmark : if a man is not a Catholic he [is a nationalist in religion, *i.e.* in those countries a Lutheran. In Holland or Hungary he would be a Calvinist : so he would in France, where Protestants, though a small minority, do represent national history. The same has been true of Scotland in the past and will soon be so again.[1]

But in countries where the Catholic trend has proved stronger than the national—Spain, Italy, and the Orthodox countries of the Near East—Protestantism takes a sectarian rather than a nationalist form. Those who dissent on points of doctrine or practice from the Catholic or Orthodox Church, not being numerous enough to embody the spirit of patriotism, have to rest the whole weight of their schism on intellectual or doctrinal grounds. They may justify their separation either on the Lutheran theory that the true Church is invisible, or on the Congregationalist principle that every Christian group is a Church, or they may take their stand

---

[1] The position in Scotland is complicated by the fact that there is in existence the Scottish Episcopal Church which combines Catholicism with Nationalism.

simply on the freedom of the individual conscience. They disagree with the rest of their countrymen, and their schism is anti-national and dissenting : commonly an affair of the *intelligentsia*. The Russian sect of " Old Believers " were a curious exception to this rule. They were a sect and not a national Church, but owed their separate existence (as did the " Wee Frees " in Scotland) to the fact that they exhibited the national characteristics of their own Church in a form more intense than their fellow-churchmen could tolerate. But usually the rule holds good that in countries where Nationalism has created for itself an ecclesiastical form it attracts to itself all that is anti-Catholic ; but when the national spirit has surrendered itself to Catholicism, or, having revolted from Catholicism, has failed to find a separate form of religious self-expression, then the sectarian type of Protestant arises.

But to this rule England forms a very notable exception. It has, and has always had, a national Church ; but it is very far from being the truth that all English Protestants find therein a natural and congenial home. Not only the nationalist but also the sectarian spirit has had free play among us, and the result is the unexampled confusion of religious status which prevails. This is to be accounted for in two ways. The Church of England, though much more strongly nationalist since the Reformation than she was before that period, does still retain her hold on Catholic principle. It is only a completely nationalised Church which absorbs into itself all the anti-Catholic feeling of a nation, and the Church of England has always professed to be a part of a wider whole ; she has never altogether forgotten that the Church is an international and historic body, and that that is a fact which profoundly affects both doctrine and practice. Consequently the thorough-going anti-Catholic has never felt quite at home within her borders. Moreover, regimentation is always a difficulty in dealing with Englishmen. They have to be very thoroughly convinced of the Divine authority of the Church before they will consider it a duty to submit or even belong to her.   Apart from such a conviction the Englishman generally shows himself a strong individualistic conservative in religion, and is determined to worship and believe as he chooses, and as his father and mother chose, and in no other way.   The Church of England has always stood for an authoritative religion, something *given*, not merely chosen : and that is not a conception which appeals to the " natural man " in this country.

As regards the United States of America we must remember that many of the original settlers took with them some very definite forms of religious conviction, fashioned under English or Dutch skies, and coloured accordingly.[1] Something in the American climate seems to tend towards extremes, and we need not be surprised therefore if the sects who went to America developed their religions there in their most extreme form.   These first settlers were Calvinists, and Calvinism held strongly to the idea of a visible and very much established Church. Those, therefore, who in England had been sectarians, on getting a free hand became religious Nationalists of the most uncompromising type.   The Puritans in New England set up a Calvinist *régime* as strict as that of Geneva and as intolerant.   But with the infiltration of many races and many forms of faith religion ceased to have a national expression, and sectarianism revived.   Thus it is now the case that throughout North America, except among Catholics, Roman or Anglican, the individualistic, sectarian spirit is probably more rife than in any other country in the world.

It would probably not be untrue to say that a place must be found for all three elements if the Church is to know peace once more.   The Roman Church of to-day is the best example of a Catholicism which aims at excluding altogether the other two tendencies ; for exclusive Nationalism we may

---

[1] With the exception of Maryland, founded in 1632 as a home for Roman Catholics when they found themselves excluded from Virginia.

look to the German State Church (though it must be confessed that the English Church of Elizabethan times ran it
very close) ; while for the purely individualistic and sectarian
spirit we had better go to America. From an unprejudiced
point of view none of these expressions of religion seems
entirely satisfactory. The Roman plan of suppressing all
national and individual characteristics seems to produce a
certain hardness and a feeling of a great machine rather than
of a living body. But even so it gives a far truer sense of
religion than the ghastly unreality of a really Erastian Church,
founded and organised as a department of the State ; while,
as compared with sectarianism, it has this immense advantage
that it has a definite and authoritative religion to preach, and
is in no danger of blurring Christian theology until it ceases
to have any recognisable outline at all.

There remains the Anglican Church. It is difficult to be
unprejudiced where one's own whole-hearted allegiance is
concerned. Certainly the propagation of Anglicanism in all
its present confusion is not an ideal to live for. But it is not
only Anglicans, but even some outside the borders of our Communion, who believe that the Anglican *ideal* is the true one ;
and that it can be so held as to be truly and primarily Catholic,
and yet give room for all that is rightly demanded in the
name of national character, individual freedom, and honest
criticism.

III

THE RISE OF THE PAPACY

IT is time to consider the way in which the interaction of the forces we have been thinking of actually produced the condition of Christendom as we know it now. " However did it happen ? " is our first instinctive question when we see the results of a great disaster, and we shall never begin to understand the divisions of the Empire of our Lord until we have been at the pains to read some history.

Here then we must begin our little " History of Schism and its Causes." Would that it were possible to write, " Its Cause and Cure ! " but before we have finished we may perhaps be able to get a glimpse of the direction from which we may expect our healing to arise. Our immediate task is simpler : it is merely to tell the story of the Church according to the waxing and waning phases of Catholicism, Nationalism, and Sectarianism.

If we say that the first part of this history is simply that of the rise of the Papal power, this is not meant controversially. It is very far from being the case that the aggrandisement of the Papacy was altogether unjustified. On the contrary it was to a very large extent inevitable, beneficial, and apparently providential. It is quite true that the extreme claims which are made for the Pope have as a matter of history caused a terrible amount of disunion ; but it cannot be denied that they have also proved themselves a very powerful cement. The action of the Papacy in history has been like that of a snow-plough on a narrow mountain path : the one

23

half of those whom it touches are hurled away into the abyss, or may we not say on to another ledge ? the other half are pressed the closer against the rock. This in itself is not unlike what we should expect to happen if the Pope *is* Christ's Vicar ; but then we cannot help asking, Is he ? There is no inherent impossibility about the idea that our Lord did ordain that primacy, or supremacy, of the Popes which gradually showed itself in the history of the Church : the only question is, Did He ?

If He did not it is still open to us to see in the development of the Papacy a logical outcome of the idea of Catholicism. The argument that the Church must have an earthly head because it is an earthly body is probably fallacious in more ways than one ; but it is not too much to say that if the Church on earth is really international, it must have a clearing house somewhere, and some sort of localised executive ; even the League of Nations has Geneva ; and further, that if this international Church is really the earthly embodiment of Christ Himself, then even a clearing house and an executive must partake of the august holiness of the Church's Head. But, in the absence of a " divinely revealed dogma," it is also open to us to say that in pressing to the utmost the logical results of one quality of the Church, the Popes and their helpers failed to allow for two permanent characteristics of human nature—patriotism and the critical spirit.

The origin of the Roman Church is lost in obscurity. All that we know for certain is that there were already Christians in Rome when S. Paul wrote his epistle to that city (56 or 58 A.D.). There does not seem to be any early tradition which would justify us in believing that the faith was brought there by an Apostle in the first instance. The tradition of S. Peter's twenty-five years' episcopate in Rome cannot be traced further back than S. Jerome, and conflicts with the earlier belief, which always assigned the foundation of the Roman Church to S. Peter *and* S. Paul. This is, perhaps, implied by Clement and Ignatius, and definitely asserted as the common knowledge of his time by Irenæus. It seems probable that the early introduction of Christianity into Rome was due to travelling Jews, who might well have found their way to Jerusalem during the first twenty years of the existence of the Christian Church, and accepted Christianity before returning home. We know from Acts ii. that there were Roman Jews in Jerusalem on the Day of Pentecost, and there is no improbability in other such Jews of the Dispersion coming into touch with Christianity. The decree of Claudius expelling the Jews from Rome was issued in 49 A.D., but Aquila and Priscilla, and therefore presumably other victims of the edict, were in Rome again when S. Paul wrote the epistle to the Roman Church.

What we do know without any shadow of doubt is that S. Paul attached great importance to his own presence in Rome (Acts xix. 21, xxiii. 11), as apparently the crown of all his Apostolate, and that S. Luke, whatever intentions he may have had of publishing a sequel to Acts, was as a fact content to bring his second volume to a close when he had conducted his hero to the Imperial City.

S. Paul was twice in captivity in Rome, and it is almost certain that S. Peter was also there before his death. There is little reason for doubting the invariable tradition that both Apostles ennobled the city by their martyrdom, and the local traditions of that city seem to imply some considerable residence on the part of S. Peter.[1]

From the first the Roman Church appears to have been ready to adopt an authoritative tone in dealing with her neighbours. The letter of S. Clement to the Church of Corinth (probably not later than 95 A.D.)[2] is evidence for that, and we should observe that, so far from resenting the

---

[1] Dr. E. T. Merrill in *Chapters in Early Christian History* maintains that the whole story of the joint foundation of the Roman Church by SS. Peter and Paul is the invention of Hegesippus ; but he seems almost the only modern scholar who disbelieves the tradition.

[2] Dr. Merrill dates it in the middle of the second century, and denies the existence of " Clement."

interference of Rome in the affairs of another Apostle-founded Church, the Corinthians proceeded to enshrine the Clementine letter in the Liturgy, along with the Epistles of S. Paul himself. It has, however, often been pointed out that the authority which is so obvious in the letter is that of the Church rather than of the Bishop. It is not even quite certain that Clement was Bishop at the date of the letter (it *may* be considerably earlier than 95), and in any case he never mentions himself or his own authority from beginning to end.

A very early witness to the eminence of Rome among the Churches is S. Ignatius. On his way to martyrdom he wrote letters to various Churches, and it is certainly true that he almost exhausts language in his efforts to find words meet for the " God-worthy " Church " that hath the presidency in the country of the region of the Romans " ; but unfortunately the true interpretation of the crucial word " presidency," twice repeated, is far from clear.

About 160 A.D. we find S. Polycarp paying a visit to the Roman Bishop Anicetus to consult about the date of Easter, concerning which the Oriental tradition differed from that of the West. No agreement was come to, but perfect harmony prevailed. The adverse bearing of this incident on the theory that the Roman Bishop has always claimed supremacy is obvious ; but we should also notice that to enter into conference with Rome is, even at this early date, the natural course for an important Bishop of the East to take, even though he was apparently convinced that he had Apostolic authority for his own customs. We should perhaps also notice, for what it is worth, that in this as in so many other instances it was only a question of time before the Roman custom gained the day.

Our next evidence is a famous passage in S. Irenæus (125-205 A.D.), though unfortunately we have only a rather vague Latin translation of a Greek original, containing no less than three phrases which are ambiguous to the last degree. Irenæus is an important witness as uniting in himself the testimony of East and West. A pupil of Polycarp, who had been a personal disciple of S. John, he had migrated westward and had been appointed Bishop of Lyons. This is what he seems to have said : " To this Church, on account of her pre-eminence, all other Churches must resort (*convenire*), the faithful from every quarter, inasmuch as the Apostolic tradition is always preserved in her by men from all parts." The words are a testimony to the pre-eminence of Rome, to her fidelity to the Apostolic tradition, and to her central position ; everyone goes to Rome from time to time, so her testimonies are of exceptional value. In other words, in S. Irenæus' view Rome stood for continuity of tradition and universal consent.

" Papalist " writers invariably translate *convenire* " agree with " rather than " resort to " : this is possible, but in the context does not seem to make such good sense. But this would not justify the assertion of Dom Chapman (*Revue Benedictine*, Ann. xii. p. 364), that Irenæus teaches that Rome is the centre of the Church and the infallible throne of truth. " Centre of the Church " perhaps ; but " infallible " is a word which is supposed to have a very definite meaning, and ought not to be lightly used in this controversy.

Our next mile-stone belongs to the year 196, and is again concerned with the Paschal controversy. It is a good example of the way in which, as has been said, " the inclination of the Roman Church to give advice becomes a tendency of the Roman Bishop to give orders," or, as the late Professor Gwatkin put it, " The voice of counsel slowly passed into that of command." [1] Victor, in striking contrast to the methods of Anicetus, went so far as to excommunicate the Easterns on account of their custom of keeping Easter on what they believed to be the Johannine date. His action was widely reprobated and drew down on him in particular the condemnation of S. Irenæus. No one paid any attention to the excommunication, and in the end he had to withdraw

[1] *Early Church History*, vol. i. p. 214.

it. The matter, owing no doubt in part to Victor's ill-considered act, remained unsettled till the Council of Arles, 314 A.D. That is one side of the matter. But, as Professor Harnack pointed out, there is another. If excommunication was intolerable as a means of furthering unity, no one suggested that it was *not* the place of the Roman Bishop to take the initiative in a matter of this sort. Rome and its Bishop are not beyond criticism, but they are most emphatically the centre of unity, and the core of the developing conception of Catholicity.

We come to the third century. It is not an age of great Popes; but we can trace a growing influence of the Roman see. Rome is still the one capital of the world : the Apostolic City also *par excellence* ; and on the whole the most faithful custodian of the Apostolic faith. It is curious, however, to find in the early years of this century a furious attack on the Roman Bishop from one of his own immediate subordinates, S. Hippolytus, on the ground of heretical sympathies ; and it is at this date also that we hear from the lips of the same Pope, Callixtus, a claim based on the words, *Tu es Petrus.* The claim, however, in this case is not to universal authority, but to the episcopal power of remitting sins in Christ's name.

The third century also saw the beginning of the first Rigorist schism : that of Novatian. We may consider it as the first exhibition of the *sectarian* spirit. Neither Nationalism nor heresy is concerned. It is a quarrel between two rival bishops, both claiming to be Bishops of Rome. Cornelius was the canonically elected bishop : Novatian allowed himself to be consecrated in opposition purely on disciplinary grounds. Cornelius was accused of laxity. In other words, he was prepared to allow a place of repentance to those who had failed under trial of persecution. The matter was decided by the Council of Carthage, but Novatian declined to give way, and for three hundred years there was a Novatianist schism, rigidly orthodox and rigidly puritanical.

It was in connexion with Novatianism that S. Cyprian wrote the famous treatise *De Unitate Catholicae Ecclesiae*, in which he developed his theory of the Episcopate as the guarantee of unity.   It is clear that he regards the Pope as the leading bishop : unfortunately the extent to which he looks on him as S. Peter's successor is not quite certain. But the main point of the treatise is that the unity of the general body of bishops constitutes the unity of the Church. Our Lord gave supreme authority to S. Peter first, in order to make it clear that the Bishops are to act as one man. (This seems to be the meaning of the passage.)   But the same authority is afterwards assigned to the Apostles as a body, and is inherited by the bishops.   It is the bishops' task to maintain unity, " for it resides in the episcopate which is one, and a whole in which each enjoys full possession."

In practice S. Cyprian certainly looked to the Pope as the natural leader of the bishops of the world, the person who ought to act for the rest of the " College."   He wrote to Stephen I. asserting that he ought to have already excommunicated Marcian, the Novatianist Bishop of Arles, and asking him to do so now and to nominate his successor.

Cyprian's whole attitude suggests a transition stage.   He considers that the Pope occupies the same position as S. Peter. But that seems to amount to no more than that the Church must have a centre of unity, and that that is to be found in Rome, " the chief church whence has arisen sacerdotal unity " (in Cyprian's idiom this means " episcopal ").   But Cyprian was quite ready to act independently of the Pope, and did so in the matter of heretical Baptism : though here, as usual, the Pope turned out in the end to have been right. But the theory that no one can be a Catholic who is not in communion with the Pope was certainly not held in Cyprian's day.   Stephen had excluded from communion all who failed to follow the Roman custom of acknowledging heretical Baptism as valid.   Cyprian wrote to inform Firmilian, the Bishop of Caesarea, who in his answer thus apostrophised the Pope : " How great a sin hast thou heaped up, when thou didst cut thyself off from so many flocks ! For while thou thinkest all may be excommunicated by thee, thou hast excommunicated thyself from all."

The contradiction between this position and that of the letter in the Marcian case is mitigated when we remember that the excommunication of one bishop by another is not in its essence disciplinary action on the part of a ruler towards a subject, but merely a declaration on the part of the excommunicating bishop that he for his part will hold no further communion with the other. How much effect this will have depends on the action of the rest of the Episcopate : and that in turn depends partly on the rights of the case, partly on the prestige of the bishop who first takes action. We can all remember an occasion when a Bishop of Zanzibar excommunicated a Bishop of Hereford.[1] The other bishops did not take the situation seriously, and no one was a penny the worse. The matter would have been very different if the excommunicator had been the Archbishop of Canterbury.

It is characteristic of Stephen that from him we hear for the first time the now familiar claim that the Pope succeeds to the chair of Peter. The great claims which came to be built on *Tu es Petrus* lead henceforward to the disappearance of S. Paul as co-founder of the local church of Rome.

The fourth century sees two historical events which at once changed the face of the world. The first is the conversion of the Roman Emperor Constantine to Christianity in A.D. 312, and the second is the removal of the residence of the Emperor from Rome to " New Rome," or Constantinople, in A. D. 327. The motive of this action is variously stated. The resentment of the Roman populace against him because of what was said to be the judicial murder of his wife and son is assigned as a reason ; so on the other hand is the desire to make a Christian capital. The effect of his action can hardly be exaggerated. To begin with, it universalised

[1] The rights of the case do not concern us here.

the idea of "Rome." Henceforward "Rome" meant two cities instead of one ; and in losing the clear outline of the concrete and historical the word came to stand for the abstract unity of civilisation. And the new civilisation was to be Christian. "Christianity," says Bryce, " as well as civilisation, became coterminous with the Roman Empire. To be a Roman was to be a Christian ; and this idea soon passed into the converse : to be a Christian was to be a Roman." [1]

The fourth century inaugurates the age of the Oecumenical Councils, but we can only touch on the history of these assemblies in so far as they affect our subject. We have to notice then in the first place that there is as yet no sign that the Pope as such has any power to call an Oecumenical Council, or to preside at it, nor is it even clear that his ratification of its decrees was considered necessary, though in fact the decrees of all the Oecumenical Councils did ultimately receive the formal approval of the Pope.

In connexion with the Council of Nicaea, and the Arian controversy to solve which the Council was called, there are several points which seem germane to our subject. We should notice that, although the Pope, S. Sylvester, had representatives at the Nicene Council, there is no real evidence to show who did actually preside.[2] On the other hand the custom of appealing to Rome is growing. Although the dispute arose in Alexandria, outside the immediate and natural sphere of Roman influence,[3] the enemies of S. Athanasius send a deputation to Rome to complain of him.

[1] *Holy Roman Empire*, pp. 12, 13. This " converse," however, did not come to pass until the time of Justinian (the sixth century).

[2] Hosius, Bishop of Cordova, was the Emperor's confidant, and perhaps suggested to him the idea of summoning the Council. His signature stands first, and is followed by those of the Pope's legates, who were *priests*. It seems that the Pope was the only bishop who was represented by proxy. See Burn, *The Council of Nicaea*, pp. 20, 21.

[3] It would be an anachronism to speak of the " Patriarchate " of Alexandria. But the Bishop of Alexandria had a position which differed but little from the recognised " Patriarchate " of the fifth century.

Athanasius puts himself under the protection of Pope Julius, who decides for him against the Arians, and moreover complains that his deposition had not been notified at Rome, or submitted to him for approval. This is the first indication we have of any such custom : it would be interesting to know how long it had obtained. About the same time we find the Council of Sardica, or rather those Western bishops who attended it, assigning to the Roman see a regular appellate jurisdiction : a grant which was again made, from the civil side, in the year 380, by the Emperors Gratian and Valentinian.

Julius' successor, Liberius, appears to have signed under duress a decree which was semi-Arian, and he excommunicated Athanasius ; one of the few exceptions to the general rule that in all the early centuries Rome and orthodox faith are inseparably connected. In 366 we find that a contested election to the Papacy is the cause of strife and rioting in Rome, and, as the pagan historian Ammianus Marcellinus notices, it was a prize worth fighting for, such was the wealth and dignity which went with it. On one day, he tells us, one hundred and thirty-seven bodies were found. The bishopric is the only great elective office in ancient Rome, and in the absence of the Emperor the Bishop is coming to be the greatest man in the city.

The contest resulted in the election of Damasus, and it was during his pontificate that the Second General Council, that of Constantinople, was held (381 A.D.). This Council at first was actually under the presidency of a bishop out of communion with the Roman see (though now canonised as a saint), Meletius : he was Bishop of Antioch, or at least was recognised as such throughout the East. The proceedings of the Council are somewhat obscure ; but one result was a decree recognising the primacy of Rome, but assigning the second place to Constantinople, "because it is the new Rome."

In the following year, in a Western Council, Pope Damasus made a definite pronouncement of the primacy of Rome, basing it directly on the promise of Christ to S. Peter. It may help us to keep our minds clear and balanced if we remember that it was at the same Council that the Canon of scripture was first settled for the West. We shall have to criticise the development and definition of the Papal claims ; but we must not condemn them on the mere ground that they *were* developed and defined.

We must notice in the same decade a curious example of the wild talk which has from the beginning confused the issues in this matter. In 376 S. Jerome wrote to S. Damasus an extravagant letter, in which he professed himself ready to accept from the Pope any doctrinal statement he likes to issue, a new creed, if he likes, to supersede that of Nicaea. But a very few years later, disappointed perhaps at not being made Pope himself, he turns against ecclesiastical Rome altogether, and with equal violence asserts that one bishop is as good as another.

At first sight S. Jerome's language in this letter seems as exaggerated on one side as that of his former one does on the other. Dom Chapman points out, however,[1] that he is merely saying that *as bishops* all bishops are equal, and for the matter of that (according to Jerome's own belief) there is no essential difference between priest and bishop. Therefore, he says, it is as absurd for a deacon to claim precedence over a priest (as the great Roman deacons, the predecessors of the Cardinal Deacons of to-day, were in the habit of doing) as it would be for them to claim it over any bishop, even the greatest. Still it is difficult to resist the conclusion that Jerome is rather pointedly counting in the Pope as one among many bishops.

From the Papacy of Damasus then we may say that the first definition of Papal powers may be dated. Hitherto all that we can observe is, as Mgr. Batiffol acknowledges, the solicitude of the Roman Church for all the churches, the authority given her by the deposit of the Apostolic

---

[1] *Bishop Gore and the Catholic Claims*, p. 78.

faith, and her recognised power of correction over other churches, when necessary. Mgr. Batiffol's language may perhaps be thought to go beyond the evidence, but from Pope Damasus onwards we begin to know where we are. There is no doubt henceforth as to the Pope's *claims* to universal obedience, though no doubt there is considerable difference in their acceptability to the Church at large.

Thus in the immediately succeeding Pelagian controversy we find Popes Innocent I. and Zosimus claiming almost infallibility ; but the Church in Africa, independent as in the days of Cyprian, is by no means ready to accept his pretensions at their face value. " Is it held," wrote the Council of Carthage (A.D. 424) to the Pope, " that the illumination of the Holy Spirit has been reserved for a single person ? " It is of this period that Mgr. Duchesne writes : " There was not a guiding power, an effective expression of Christian unity. The Papacy, as the West knew it later on, was still to be born."

But the great and famous African Church was near its end : the Vandals swept across North Africa, and it was gone ; and with it the last obstacle to Papal domination in the West.[1] For the Empire, as far as the West was concerned, was practically extinct. Since the time when Constantine lorded it over the whole civilised world the Empire had been sometimes united under a single head, but during most of the period there had been two Emperors, an Eastern reigning at Constantinople, and a Western with his nominal capital in Rome. But Rome had been sacked by Alaric in 410, and the Western Emperor was no more than a puppet during the sixty-six years which had still to run before the abdication of Romulus Augustulus and the final abandonment of the theory of a dual Empire. To the dignity and much of the

---

[1] The teaching of S. Augustine, the greatest of the North African bishops, prepared the way for the extension of centralised hierarchical rule. His identification of the Church with the " Kingdom of Christ " provided ecclesiastical statesmanship with powerful suggestions. See Robertson, *Regnum Dei*, Lecture iv.

power of the Emperor the Bishop of the Imperial City was residuary legatee.

We come to the Council of Ephesus, A.D. 431. With the Nestorian controversy in itself we are not concerned, only with some of its circumstances and results.

An important theological dispute had arisen between Cyril, Bishop of Alexandria, and Nestorius, Bishop of Constantinople. Both sides appealed to Pope Celestine, who readily took the matter up. He held a local council, condemned Nestorius, and threatened him with deposition. Nestorius appealed to a General Council, which the Eastern Emperor proceeded to summon. An extraordinary story of confusion follows. The Council met in a hurry without the presence either of the Roman delegation or the Antiochene bishops. Nestorius was duly condemned and deposed. Then enter John of Antioch and his suffragans. Cyril is condemned and deposed likewise. The Roman legates now appear, and naturally side with the first Council. The Emperor is appealed to, and promptly arrests both the disputants, and proposes that both had better be deposed. At last, however, he hears the case afresh himself, and decides in favour of Cyril and of Rome. As a result the Eastern half of the Patriarchate of Antioch, i.e. that part which lay outside the borders of the " Roman " Empire, went into schism, inserting the name of Nestorius in the Canon of their liturgy. They became a great missionary Church, and took the Christian faith right through Persia and as far as China, but failed to withstand the assaults of Mohammedanism. All that now remains of them is the Assyrian Church, a scanty homeless remnant of 50,000, pitiful survivors of the Great War, with a handful of " Syro-Chaldeans " in Malabar, who seceded from Rome in 1880, and obtained Episcopal Orders from the Assyrians.

Next comes Leo the Great and the Council of Chalcedon. The history is curiously like that of Ephesus. The heresiarch in this case was Eutyches. Condemned by a local

Council at Constantinople he appealed to the three great sees of Rome, Alexandria and Jerusalem. Dioscorus, Bishop of Alexandria, was Eutyches' supporter, and saw his opportunity to assert himself against the upstart see of Constantinople. He contrived that the Eastern Emperor should call a council at Ephesus : this was the famous " Latrocinium " or " Robber Council." Dioscorus took the chair, and Eutyches was duly reinstated. But the Pope had determined to take a hand, which indeed he did with some effect. He had not long to wait for a more favourable civil situation. The Eastern Emperor Theodosius died suddenly, and a new Council was summoned in the name of both Emperors, not indeed, as Leo had wished, in Italy, but at Chalcedon (451 A.D.). Now at last a Pope does through his legates preside at a General Council. The result was a foregone conclusion. Leo's famous and magnificent theological treatise, The Tome, was produced, and carried all before it. As the bishops in their subsequent letter to Leo stated, " You directed us as the head directs the members." Nothing could exceed the enthusiasm exhibited for S. Leo, both in his own person and as " interpreter of the voice of Blessed Peter." But, as Professor Clement Rogers points out, " After they had heard " The Tome read out " they said, ' Peter hath spoken by Leo.' They did not say, ' Let us hear and obey what Peter will say by Leo.' That is, they acknowledged its authority because they thought he was right ; they did not think he was right because they acknowledged his authority." [1]

But Leo had effectually asserted his claim over the East, and presided at a Council within the realm of the Eastern Emperor. Six years before he had secured an imperial mandate from the Emperor of the West giving him authority either to forbid or to sanction any ecclesiastical innovations in Gaul and over the Western Empire generally. Chalcedon marks the high-water mark of the acceptance of the Papacy.

[1] *Rome and the Early Church*, p. 49.

Its claims were intensified in later centuries, but never accepted over a wider area. " Leo," Dr. Kidd actually goes so far as to say, " exercised an authority, vaguer indeed but not less real than that of a Bishop in his diocese, over the Catholic Church as a whole." [1]

Leo's action in view of the famous 28th Canon of Chalcedon is characteristic. This canon merely repeated what had already been settled at the Council of Constantinople, that Constantinople should take the second place after Rome, on the ground that the privileges of the elder Rome rested on the fact that she was the imperial city, and that it was just that the other imperial city should have precedence after her. This canon moved Leo to the greatest indignation, but whether because of the reason assigned for the Roman primacy, or because he considered it an infringement of the rights of the older sees of Antioch and Alexandria is not quite clear.[2] Leo was perhaps the first to see how grave a danger to unity might be constituted by the rise of the see of Constantinople, and was correspondingly anxious to do all he could to keep the leadership for the see of Peter. The College of Bishops must, as he clearly saw, have its president, and his theory seems to have been that neither could the College act lawfully without its president nor he without it.

Like the Council of Ephesus that of Chalcedon led straight to a schism on a wide scale. There was in fact no general and immediate acceptance of the Chalcedonian decrees in the East. Egypt, Syria, Armenia and Palestine refused assent, and for a century the Eastern Church was as much Monophysite as Catholic. Within the Church the heresy was suppressed by Justinian (527-565), but the Monophysite party promptly nominated Patriarchs of their own in Antioch and Alexandria, and the East was henceforth split into two halves. It is the Monophysite schism which

---

[1] *History of the Christian Church*, vol. iii. p. 390.

[2] In any case it must be remembered that the canons of an Oecumenical Council have not the authority which attaches to its definitions ; they deal with the contingent : the definitions with the eternal.

is responsible for the Coptic Church of Egypt and the Jacobite church of Antioch, together with the Armenian and Abyssinian Churches. The so-called " Orthodox Syrian " Church of Malabar, claiming S. Thomas the Apostle as founder, also looks to the Jacobite Patriarch of Antioch as its head. As with the Nestorians, the feeling which prompted this schism was far more national than theological : hatred of Byzantinism as personified in Justinian had more to do with it than any special distaste for the Chalcedonian decrees.

We return to the date of the Council. It was the year of Attila's invasion of Western Europe and the beginning of two centuries during which Italy was to be the cockpit of Europe. During those two centuries the Church and the Church alone gave continuity to civilisation. And the Church meant the Papacy. From the day when Leo went out to meet Attila and subdued him by the mere spell of his presence the Roman Bishopric was the one authority which did not rest on brute force. Certainly the Papacy had its vicissitudes, including the astonishing tergiversations of Vigilius, who at last was anathematised and excommunicated by a General Council. But on the whole the Popes of the fifth and sixth centuries maintained the position asserted by Leo, and the next truly great Pontiff, S. Gregory, found all things ready for a fresh consolidation of the power of his see.

Gregory certainly succeeded in riveting his authority very firmly on the Bishops of the Western Church. He seems to have been the first to use the " pallium " as a definite token of delegated authority. This ornament, which in more ancient times had been merely a complimentary gift, was shortly to become the definite sign of metropolitical jurisdiction, which thus came to be absolutely dependent on the pleasure of the Pope. S. Gregory's usage marks a long step towards this practice. Since the time of Pope Siricius (A.D. 384) the experiment had been tried of appointing Papal Vicars in various parts of the world, as a means of extending the influence of the Roman see, or as a mere compliment to an important bishopric. In the case of the Bishop of Arles this appointment had been connected with the gift of the pallium. S. Gregory extended the custom, and made the pallium a definite mark of office.

By force of circumstances, too, Gregory may be considered as the founder of the temporal power of the Papacy. Northern Italy was by now practically lost to the Empire. There was an imperial " Exarch " quartered at Ravenna, but his authority was non-existent, and the whole country was in possession of the Lombards. Only in the city of Rome was there ordered civil government, and there it was the Pope's writ, not the Emperor's, that ran. Nominally still the Emperor's subject, and needing his confirmation of his appointment, the Pope was rapidly becoming the independent ruler of the ancient imperial city ; and an Emperor who could give no succour to one of his own capitals could not be surprised if its *de facto* governor used his position to promote ideals other than imperial.

Our subject is Reunion, and we cannot forget that it was during the Pontificate of Gregory that our own country first made contact with Roman Christianity. The South of England, to speak generally, was converted from Rome : the North from Ireland by way of the Scotic monastery of Iona. The ancient British Church had been driven West by heathen invaders into Wales and Cornwall, and took no part in the reconversion of England. The fact that the North of England was converted from Ireland is significant. Ireland was the only civilised or semi-civilised country, with the partial exception of Armenia, which had never formed part of the Roman Empire. Equally, almost consequently, it was true that the coercive authority of the Roman Bishop was also unknown in the Churches of Irish foundation.

Naturally the two Christian streams coalesced with difficulty, and strong action had to be taken to avoid a schism. The history of what may be called the catholicising of the

opportunity, and at once secured his election or appointment to Lichfield.   But first, Bede tells us, " Theodore completed his consecration afresh in the Catholic manner."   What exactly this means is by no means clear, but it would be impossible to exaggerate the importance of the incident as unimpeachable precedent for the case of a bishop whose consecration might seem indisputable, yet is in fact disputed.[1]

Wilfrid returned to York.   But he also, in the tenure of his see, was to furnish precedents of a far-reaching order. Wilfrid's appeal to Pope Agatho against the division of his Diocese was the first of a long series which at last exasperated the patience of the English people.   His own utter confidence in the Papal decision, and the fury with which it was received in England, seem to recapitulate beforehand eight centuries of history.   " The Roman decree," says Bright, " duly drawn up, with its leaden *bullae*, and its ' apostolic ' seal, was in his eyes a ' banner of victory ' : he never reflected that to others it might be a provocation and an insult." [2]

The Church during this period was exercised over the last great Christological heresy, that of the Monothelites. For our present purpose it is only necessary to notice one of the rare cases in which the theological judgment of the Roman see was at fault.   The Pope Honorius wrote in favour of the heresy, and was duly condemned and anathematised at the third General Council of Constantinople, 680-681.   The record of the anathema actually remained in the Roman breviary till the sixteenth century.   The Council itself, however, was a great Papal success ; Agatho swayed it by his legates as Leo had done that of Chalcedon, and it is noteworthy that from this date onwards the Pope adopts the very title which Gregory had rebuked the Bishop

---

[1] In spite of S. Augustine's great authority (see pp. 264-266) the line between validity and regularity in the case of Holy Orders does not seem to have yet been drawn so sharply as it was by the theologians of the thirteenth century.   The Popes and Anti-popes of the tenth century regularly re-ordained the clergy upon whom their rivals had laid hands.

[2] Bright, *Early English Church History*, p. 298.

of Constantinople for assuming : that of " Universal
Bishop." The verbal dispute is symbolic of the real point
at issue : it is not possible to have two universal Bishops ;
and we have now to trace the steps which led to the final
alienation of the Sovereign Pontiff from the Oecumenical
Patriarch, and the greatest schism which has ever afflicted
the Church.

It would be a mistake to think of the schism between East
and West as one great and sudden catastrophe which at once
and for ever changed the face of the ecclesiastical world.
There are few such dates in history ; and certainly 1054 is
not one of them. Of the five hundred years which followed
the death of the Emperor Constantine almost one half saw
Rome and Constantinople as much out of communion with
each other as they are to-day : and no less than nineteen
Patriarchs of Constantinople, as compared with two, or at
most three, Popes, were heretical. The fact was that the
Eastern Patriarch never had anything like the independence
enjoyed by the Pope. He had to speak with the same voice
as the Emperor, or it would be the worse for him. This is
the system which, not unjustly, is called Caesaro-Papism.

Already at the end of the fifth century the Emperor Zeno
and the Patriarch Acacius had been in league for the setting
up of an imperial church of the East. The jurisdiction of
Alexandria and Antioch had been infringed, and the West
had been deliberately ignored. The imperial city was now
Constantinople : the very pretence of an Emperor had
vanished from Rome. Let theories correspond to facts, and
the ecclesiastical world be governed from the same centre
as the civil.

A vigorous Pope could hardly fail to act. Acacius had
upset an arrangement to which a former Pope (Leo the
Great) had been a party. He had compromised himself
with the Monophysite party and given active support to a
usurping Patriarch at Alexandria. He had paid no attention
to the Papal protests, and finally had first imprisoned and

then deceived his legates.   Pope Felix passed a solemn
sentence of deposition on the Patriarch, and despatched
messengers to serve it upon him.   This they contrived to
do by pinning it on to his back while he was conducting a
service ! As a result there was schism between the West
and the *whole* East (not merely Constantinople) for thirty-
five years.

Until the eighth century the Patriarch had claimed no
jurisdiction further West than Illyricum. In 733 the
Emperor Leo the Isaurian was excommunicated by the
Pope. He promptly retaliated by a fresh assertion of the
principle that *his* Patriarch must have a jurisdiction corresponding with that of the ecclesiastical head of Old Rome.
There was no longer a Western Empire ; therefore the
whole Roman Empire, so far as its sway was effective at all,
must come within the Patriarchate. This meant that
Illyricum and Southern Italy, together with a part of the
ancient Patriarchate of Antioch, were added to the ecclesiastical domain of a Patriarch whose title of " Oecumenical "
was now beginning to justify itself indeed. It might have
seemed that the sun of Rome had set. An ecclesiastical
Magna Grecia had sprung up in a night as a challenge to her
supremacy. The sacred city itself was in constant danger
from the fierce and violently Arian and anti-clerical Lombards who had occupied Northern Italy for the greater part
of two centuries. The Pope's counter-stroke was pregnant
with the subsequent history of the world. In 741 he sent
the keys of the Tombs of the Apostles to Charles Martel, the
virtual ruler of the new great league, or nation, of the Franks,
and claimed his help. Alone among the Teutonic nations
the Franks were Catholic, and it was in their support that the
Popes saw their last hope of succour. Charles Martel died
almost immediately, but was succeeded as Mayor of the
Palace by his son Pipin. The Pope pronounced the deposition of Pipin's nominal sovereign, the Frankish King, and
appointed, and anointed, Pipin to take his place. Pipin, in

answer to a letter purporting to come from no less a person
than S. Peter himself, brought his forces southwards,
defeated the Lombards, and bestowed upon the Pope, as a
temporal sovereign, that territory in Northern Italy of which
the Lombards had been for almost two centuries the *de facto*
possessors. It was the birthday of the Papal States.

Obviously the territory was hardly Pipin's to give. In
theory it was still claimed by the Emperor, and ruled from
Ravenna by his Exarch. But the Apostolic letter had been
accompanied by that remarkable fabrication known as the
" Donation of Constantine," in which we have a detailed
account of how Constantine forsook Rome for his new capital
on the Bosphorus in order that the spiritual government
might have a free hand, and how he gave to Pope Sylvester
and his successors sovereignty over Italy and all the West.
Thus the bounty of Pipin was made to bear the character
of a restoration rather than a new gift.[1]

[1] The " Donation " was afterwards included in the still more famous
collection of documents known as the " Forged Decretals." These
purported to be a set of Decretals issued by the early Popes, and collected
by Isidore of Seville, who died in 636 A.D. The author of these forgeries
is not known. Their provenance seems to be one of the ecclesiastical
provinces of Mayence, Reims, or Tours—certainly neither Seville nor
Rome. They were composed in the middle of the ninth century and
brought to Rome about the year 862. The primary object of the fabrication is to uphold the authority of the individual Bishop against that of
his Metropolitan and Comprovincials, as well as against the civil power.
But the natural protector of an oppressed bishop was the Pope. Thus
it comes about incidentally that these " Decretals " are a storehouse of
proof-texts for the Papal prerogatives. The early Popes are made to
claim for themselves in very definite terms the position of Supreme Head,
Lawgiver, and Judge of the Church.

Pope Nicholas I. employed them in settling a dispute between the
Archbishop of Reims and one of his suffragans, the Bishop of Soissons,
and unfortunately committed himself to the statement that they were
contained in the archives of his see. It is only charitable to suppose
that the Pope's fault did not go beyond a failure to verify his authority,
though indeed from the comparatively slight use that he makes of the
forgeries it may be thought that he himself entertained some suspicion
of them. As a matter of fact they do not carry the claims of the Holy See
very much further than they had been pushed already, and the statements
of Döllinger and others that they created the Papal monarchy seem
exaggerated. But what the " Decretals " did only too effectually was to
tangle the web of ecclesiastical history by antedating the establishment

The course of events was leading straight towards the establishment of a rival empire of which Rome itself should be once more the centre.

In 797 the Byzantine throne was usurped by a woman. The Pope saw and seized his opportunity. On Christmas Day, 800, Charles the Great was crowned Roman Emperor in S. Peter's by Leo III. Henceforth it is not a case of one Empire in two parts: there are two Empires, and two supreme monarchs, each in theory denying the existence of the other.

All seems ready for the final ecclesiastical separation of East and West, now for ever politically separate.

Theologically they had long been drifting apart. Ever since Chalcedon Pope and Emperor had been as often as not in violent opposition; and almost always the Pope was solidly orthodox and kept the whole of his ecclesiastical world in right paths, while the Patriarch, under the iron hand of theologically minded Emperors, was practically abdicating the teaching office of the Episcopate. Even at this moment the outward aspect of the churches in the East bore witness to the unchecked power of the image-breakers. Most sinister sign of all, there were at last two opposing secular heads.

We have still to wait for the final great quarrel which was to issue in schism. But the ninth century did produce its plentiful crop of ecclesiastical disputes. In the first half of the century the iconoclastic controversy was still raging: in the second the Photian schism distracted the Church.

In 857 Ignatius, Bishop of Constantinople, refused Communion to the incestuous Bardas, the Emperor's uncle. The Emperor, in the authentic Byzantine manner, deposed

---

of the autocracy of the Pope. They proved a convenient instrument in the hand of Gregory VII. (Hildebrand), and deceived S. Thomas and all the mediaeval canonists. The forgery was not discovered until the fifteenth century, and the influence of these documents was so great, and their authority so undoubted, that it may be questioned whether the full claims of the Papacy could ever have asserted themselves successfully without their help. See Fournier in the *Revue d'Histoire ecclesiastique*, 1906, 1907.

the bishop, and contrived that a successor, Photius, should be consecrated to fill his place. Photius, though owing his consecration to an irregular bishop, and his see to the interests of immorality, actually appealed to Pope Nicholas I. for support. Nicholas had the satisfaction of exercising, in the most striking manner possible, the dazzling prerogatives of the pseudo-Isidorian Decretals. He was judging the case of the Oecumenical Patriarch, and actually at the request of the *de facto* holder of the rival see. He was not slow to " depose " the intruder.[1] Then Photius made the *riposte* which he no doubt had planned. Flinging out a general accusation of heresy and schism against Western Christianity in general he proceeded to depose the Pope. The Westerns had interpolated a word into the Nicene Creed [2] : they presumed to fast on Saturdays : the monks had their tonsures shaved all wrong : their secular clergy were not married. It seems obvious to the modern mind that most of these complaints are quite beneath contempt as occasions for schism between two great parts of the Catholic Church. The only serious charge was at the time an unjust one. The word *Filioque* was *not* yet in general use as part of the Creed, certainly not in Rome (though Nicholas did defend the interpolation). On the whole the Papal influence had been exercised hitherto against it. Fifty years earlier Leo III. had declined to support the Latin monks of Jerusalem who were using it, and had the authentic Creed inscribed on silver tablets and fastened to the doors of S. Peter's.

Of course Photius was really piling up charges as counterweights to the characteristically Oriental subservience to the

[1] A.D. 863.

[2] The " Nicene " Creed as ratified at Chalcedon stated that the Holy Ghost " proceedeth from the Father." The words " and the Son " were first added in Spain after the conversion of the Goths from Arianism, and gradually spread over the West. There is no ultimate difference between Eastern and Western *doctrine* on the point. But the Easterns consider that the disputed words suggest a twofold source of Godhead, whereas to the Latin mind they seem to guard the Deity of the Second and Third Persons of the Trinity.

quite a long time before churchmen on both sides realised what had happened. Communication between different parts of the world was not what it had been in sub-Apostolic days, when information could pass from one end of the Church to the other in no longer time than the conditions of travel demanded. In those times of confusion and disorder news did not travel at all. A century and a half later, however, the fact that a schism existed was brought home to the Easterns in a very practical way by the behaviour of the French and Venetian bravos of the Fourth Crusade. Instead of attacking the infidel they turned their attention to an easier prey. Constantinople was sacked, and a Latin Empire organised there, with its counterpart of a Latin Patriarch in opposition to the occupant of the historic " Oecumenical " throne. The Eastern court retired to Nicaea : and the memories of the Crusade abode and rankled.

IV

THE BEGINNINGS OF CHRISTIANITY OUTSIDE THE EMPIRE

HITHERTO we have confined our attention to the Church as it organised itself within the Empire ; and we have seen the Church split into two halves, the one Latin and German, the other Greek. These two halves correspond to the two great Patriarchates of Rome and Constantinople. The other patriarchates have practically disappeared. All alike have fallen into Moslem hands and have been almost destroyed : and what Christianity is left is, mostly at any rate, heretical, and out of communion with the Orthodox Church.

But in order to complete our picture it is necessary to glance outside the imperial borders at the nascent Christianity of the younger races which have been pressing into the Church.

The migration of Slavonic tribes within the sphere of the Roman Empire began in the seventh century, when the Emperor Heraclius gave a home to the ancestors of the Serbs and the Croats. A certain amount of missionary effort was devoted to them by missionaries from Rome, and at the same time they began to enter into commercial and other relationships with their new neighbours the Byzantine Greeks. But little progress was made, and very soon the whole Balkan area was again thrown into a ferment by the invasion of the Bulgars, a non-Slavonic, Turanian race, who carved out for themselves a country in land that had been settled by the earlier Slav invaders. Yet in the end the Bulgars were the first to accept Christianity.

The date of Prince Boris' baptism is 865, just when the quarrel between Nicholas and Photius was at its height. It is not surprising that both sides were anxious for the access of power which the conversion of the fierce young Bulgarian nation would bring them. Boris was not slow to play off Pope and Patriarch against each other. What he really wanted was to be an independent Emperor with a Patriarch of his own. Neither Rome nor Constantinople was likely to grant this, and Boris finally chose Photius in preference to Nicholas. For a time the Bulgars had to submit to bishops of Greek race chosen and consecrated by the Patriarch. In 917 the victory of the Bulgarian arms against the imperial forces enabled the Bulgarian prince to set up a Patriarchate, but before long the fortune of war inclined in the opposite direction, and the Bulgarian Church became once more subject to Constantinople.

The Serbs also accepted Christianity in an Eastern dress, and found themselves within the Patriarchate of Constantinople.

Russia was evangelised partly by the Greeks, partly by the newly Christianised Slavonic nations, and her Church has never swerved from the strictest form of Eastern Orthodoxy.

The Rumanians are noteworthy as the only people of the Latin civilisation which has accepted the Eastern form of Christianity. They represent a Roman colony settled in Dacia in the very early days of the Empire, as a protection to the imperial frontier formed by the Danube, and in consequence are of mingled ancestry : in any case they are non-Slavonic.

The Poles and Bohemians on the other hand, dwelling under the shadow of the Western Empire, were converted by Roman missionaries, and remained faithful to the Western types; while the wilder Czechs and Hungarians, as they were tamed by the Western Emperors, naturally gave their allegiance to the Pope. The Romanism of the modern Croats is to be accounted for in the same way.

V

FIRST ATTEMPTS AT REUNION

IT will be worth our while to pause for a moment and consider the part which the three great ecclesiastical tendencies have so far played in our story.

The spirit of untempered Catholicism, as represented by Rome, has begun to stand out in high relief. One by one her rivals have disappeared. More and more the Church has become centralised. Order, authority, discipline, have been gradually evolved. True, there have been periods when the theory of the Papacy has seemed no better than a nightmare, terrifying and ridiculous. But each great Pope seems able to join hands with the last of his predecessors who was worthy of the name, and to receive from him the reins of government tangled but unbroken. Almost before we realise it he has advanced a further claim, yet always with the characteristic pontifical air of a growing institution rather than an exceptional personality.

But already the nations of modern Europe are being born. Since the sixth century different languages have been spoken in the two great imperial capitals. Since the seventh century the great Slavonic race has begun to differentiate itself into nations. And through all the ten or twelve centuries with which we have been concerned there has been the constant phenomenon of new, wild tribes urged to attack a moribund civilisation, yet in the end grafting themselves into the root and fatness of the ancient stock, and receiving its culture in exchange for their own rude strength.

Nor has the critical spirit, with its tendency to issue in sectarianism, been idle. For seven centuries the whole Orient was seething with theological thought. A whole series of one-sided, coldly logical systems of thought were propounded and enjoyed an ephemeral success. Rome and the West looked on almost impassively ; sometimes, it is true, intervening with decisive effect, but more often allowing the heresy to work out its own contradiction, always provided that the honour of the Roman see was not impugned. The result on the East was remarkable. Preoccupation with doctrine had a stabilising effect on theological thought, and at the same time led the Easterns to think of Christianity as primarily a doctrinal system. All the obvious forms of heterodoxy having been tried and rejected, the East settles down to be that part of the Church whose Christianity consists in the fact that they are *orthodox*. Their Catholicism is doctrinal rather than institutional.

If the Catholicism of Rome is the opposite of nationalism, that of the East is the opposite of sectarianism. Both Rome and the Eastern churches are both Catholic and Orthodox ; but the names by which they choose to be called are significant of their general attitude.[1] Unfortunately the Orthodox desire to make everything a matter of orthodoxy led them to treat their own local customs as though they were universally binding. Not content with upholding the cause of the sacred images, in which the whole Church supported them, nor with protesting against arbitrary Papalism, in which they were

---

[1] " The Latin Church, still permeated by the practical instincts of Rome . . . could not think of the Christian people except in the form of a body of worshippers, organized under a government, and a government with an autocratic head. Thus she created the Pope. . . . But to the Eastern Christians, occupied as they had been with determining the nature of God and Christ, the Christian people appeared in the form of a body of worshippers professing exactly the same life-giving dogmas." Bryce, *Holy Roman Empire*, p. 345.

" L'Orient inclinait à croire que l'orthodoxie suffit à tout, et Sainte Sophie a été son sanctuaire de prédilection. L'Occident, dévot au tombeau de Saint Pierre, demandait à Rome l'ordre dans la foi et dans la discipline." Batiffol, *Siège Apostolique*, Intr. p. vii.

amply justified, they put themselves in the wrong by championing clerical marriage and leavened bread as though they were articles of faith.

During those dark centuries, the eighth to the eleventh, the critical spirit seems dead all through the Church, and it is in the West that at last it is to be reborn. Arnold of Brescia, Dante, Marsilius, Ockham, bring it again into the ecclesiastical area, and when once Wycliffe, Huss and Jerome of Prague have applied it to doctrinal matters, the Western Reformation is near at hand.

To find the first attempts at Reunion we must go back to a date just before the Fourth Crusade. Since the fatal day of separation in 1054 the Popes had occupied themselves chiefly with the great struggle which now began with the civil power as represented by the Western Emperor. The part which the Emperor had the right to play in the election of a Pope is a matter of dispute. Certainly he had long had a prescriptive right of confirming the appointment made by the clergy and populace of Rome. A strong Emperor would do a good deal more than confirm. Doubtless some interference by the civil power was very necessary, for every Papal election was the signal for an orgy of electioneering. More than once during the tenth century two rival Popes had contrived to get themselves elected, and neither would give way to the other.

In 1046 Henry III. had taken the strong step of having the Pope deposed, a measure which seems more than any other to have effected a permanent reformation in the morals of the Papacy. In 1047 Henry appointed a new Pope himself, but not without protest from the Church. In 1048 it is said that the Roman clergy and people actually asked him to make an appointment, and accepted it when made ; but there are various accounts of the proceeding, and we cannot be certain of the truth.[1] But in 1059, under the influence of the Archdeacon Hildebrand, Pope Nicholas II. proved strong enough

[1] See A. J. Carlyle, *Mediaeval Political Theory in the West*, vol. iv. c. ii.

to make an effective protest against the whole custom of the
Emperor or any other layman having anything to do with the
appointment of a Pope.   For the first time we hear of the
College of Cardinals as the electoral body.

This famous and exalted company of ecclesiastical princes
has, like so many of the institutions of the Church, a beginning which is almost commonplace.   They are in theory,
as in origin, the bishops of the dioceses immediately sur-
rounding Rome, together with the parish priests of the
ancient and original parishes in Rome itself, and the seven
deacons in immediate attendance on the Pope.   But their
importance at this date is that they are a body of *ecclesiastics*,
and if only the appointment to the Papacy can be kept in
ecclesiastical hands the Pope is master of the world.   Hildebrand himself ascended the Pontifical throne in 1073 as
Gregory VII.[1] and carried the same policy a step farther by
declaring that an ecclesiastic receiving any spiritual charge
from a layman under conditions was guilty of the sin of
simony.   This seemed to destroy at a blow the whole feudal
system in so far as it concerned the relationship of clergy to
lay overlords, and it was bitterly resented.   The whole
famous " Investitures " quarrel of the twelfth century, which
raged so fiercely in our own country was but a part of the
same dispute.   At first it seemed that the Pope had won a
decisive victory after a short struggle.   In 1077 at the castle
of Canossa the Emperor stood for three days in the snow
waiting the pleasure of the Pope, till at last he was admitted
to do penance at his feet.   But the fight was not over :
it was a full century more before the two great powers were
reconciled by the sudden submission of the Emperor Barbarossa to the Pope in the porch of S. Mark's at Venice
(A.D. 1177).

The first attempts at Reunion then date from a period when
the prestige of the Papacy was at its height.

[1] The restriction of the title of " Pope " to the Bishop of Rome dates
from an ordinance of Gregory VII.

The quarrel of Rome was primarily with Constantinople, not with the East generally, and she has never relaxed her efforts after reconciliation with the separated Eastern Churches one by one.   Often a semi-political situation has proved a bridge for at least a temporary reunion.   So it was in the present case.   Two new nations, as we have seen, had arisen in the East, both desiring recognition, Serbia and Bulgaria.

Recognition meant coronation, and it is probable that neither of the princes cared very much whether he received the crown from Pope or from Patriarch.   But the Patriarch was the Eastern Emperor's puppet, and the Emperor stood to lose by the emergence of new kingdoms in what had been imperial territory.   The Pope on the other hand welcomed nothing so much as the exercise of his power to act as the Providence by whom kings reigned.   If at the same time he was able to reconcile schismatics to the Holy Roman Church, that was an added attraction.   Legates therefore were sent to both Serbia and Bulgaria, and found the princes ready to promise almost anything on behalf of their subjects in return for the crown.   For a few years the whole of the Serbian and Bulgarian churches were Uniate, *i.e.* acknowledged the supremacy of Rome, while maintaining their national character.

But the sack of Constantinople altered the situation.   The East was profoundly shocked.   The Bulgarians, attacked by the usurping Latin Emperor, Baldwin, flew to arms, and actually took the Emperor prisoner.   The Serbians saw a chance to have not only a crowned king but an independent national Church.   The Orthodox Patriarch in exile was more compliant than in the day of his power.   While not granting autonomy, he, with the Emperor, consented to a native Archbishop being appointed, owning no allegiance except to the Patriarch himself.   This was a great improvement on the previous position in which, before the short-lived reconciliation with Rome, all Serbia had been under the jurisdiction of a Greek sent from Constantinople to be Bishop of the Bulgarian see of Ochrida.

But the establishment of a Latin Empire with an Emperor and a Patriarch of its own at Constantinople naturally led to plans for Reunion on a wider scale.   In 1215 the Fourth Lateran Council was summoned by Innocent III.   The Latin Patriarchs who had ousted the Orthodox ones not only from Constantinople but also from the already somewhat shadowy jurisdictions of Antioch, Alexandria and Jerusalem, sent their legates to Rome and made a formal submission on behalf of their Patriarchates ; and for forty-six years the Church was at one again in theory.[1]   In practice, however, the Easterns continued to look to the Orthodox Patriarch as their head : so much so that during this very period when, according to the Papal theory, Constantinople and Rome are supposed to be united, we find the Pope engaged with Prince Daniel of Galicia in a bargain of the kind with which the example of Serbia and Bulgaria has already made us familiar. A Uniate Church was actually set up, but, the Coronation safely accomplished, the Union disappeared.

In 1261 the Greek Emperor, Michael Palaeologus, was restored, and with the return of the Orthodox Patriarch to Constantinople the nominal union came to an end.   The Emperor himself, however, was now desperately anxious for reconciliation.   Another French army seemed likely to descend upon him, and at all costs he must protect himself. He therefore invited the Pope to call another council, and at Lyons in 1274 Eastern ecclesiastics once more met those of the West.   All the Roman demands were granted, and the Greek clergy present, the nominees of Michael, went so far as to chant the Creed *with* the *Filioque*.   But there was not really much more reality about this union than the last, and at Michael's death it was utterly repudiated.

---

[1] It was at this Council that the doctrine of the " Double Procession " of the Holy Spirit was made an article of faith.   But the Easterns were *not* pressed to insert *Filioque* into the creed.

The glories of the mediaeval Papacy barely outlasted the thirteenth century. In the last year of that century Boniface VIII., crowned with the imperial diadem, proclaimed himself as " Caesar " and " Emperor." In the famous bull *Unam Sanctam* he had already claimed that the temporal and ecclesiastical swords were both the property of the Church. Three years later, when on the point of issuing an excommunication against Philip IV. of France, he was seized and his person outraged at Anagni, and a few days later he died of the shock.

In 1305 the Gascon Pope, Clement V., determined to escape the turbulence of Rome by moving the Papal court bodily to Avignon, and there for seventy years it remained, losing prestige, and falling more and more under the influence of the French Kings. During all this time constant overtures were passing between Pope and Eastern Emperor. The Ottoman Turks were becoming formidable, and the Emperor saw no chance of staying their advance except by enlisting Western aid. But the memories of the Fourth Crusade were long-lived, and the Emperor's subjects had good reason to doubt whether they would fare better under the tiara of a French Pope than under the turban of the Sultan. No definite steps were taken.

In 1378 there appeared the scandalous phenomenon of two rival Popes, one at Rome and one at Avignon. This was the beginning of the " Great Schism," which produced a reaction important for our present purposes in more ways than one. The Church was distracted, and as the only way out of the difficulty insistent demands were made for a General Council, which was finally summoned at Pisa in 1409. The Council deposed both Popes, and ordered the Cardinals to elect another, after exacting a promise that whoever should be elected would not permit the Council to be dissolved until a reformation of the universal Church " both in its head and members " had been accomplished.

The authority of the Council was disputed, and neither

of the rival Popes paid any attention to its decrees. It was followed in 1414 by the Council of Constance, which found itself faced with the necessity of choosing between no less than three claimants to the Papal throne. Having selected for recognition as the true Pope John XXIII., whose election was subsequent to the deposition of the other two by the Council of Pisa, the Council exacted a promise from him to resign as soon as the others had done so ; but John had no intention of keeping his word, and fled at the earliest opportunity. The answer of the Council was a solemn assertion of its own oecumenical character in spite of the Pope's withdrawal, and, a few days later, a decree was passed asserting definitely that the authority of the Council was superior to that of the Pope. Finally, the Pope having been cited and having failed to appear, his deposition was decreed. Of the two anti-Popes one resigned voluntarily, the other was deposed or decreed to have been already deposed : and the Cardinals proceeded to make a new election. The importance of all this from the point of view of the Papalist controversy is very obvious. It appears that a General Council claimed the right to depose a Pope, and that this right was acknowledged by the Pope himself in submitting to deposition. A feature of the Council which is remarkable for our present purpose is that the Bishops present voted in national groups.

It is also necessary to notice the infamous treachery of which this Council was guilty in the condemnation of John Huss the Bohemian reformer, who had trusted himself to the honour of its members under a safe-conduct. But Hussism was not so easily got rid of. His followers took up arms, and had to be appeased by some concessions. In particular, the demand for Communion in both kinds was granted. Some of the reforming body were satisfied with this and returned to their allegiance : others took refuge in a remote corner of Bohemia, and there founded a community known as the *Unitas Fratrum*. They obtained Holy

Orders from the Waldenses, and the community grew into three branches, but in face of cruel persecution the movement was driven underground and became a kind of family tradition.

The Council of Constance was followed in 1432 by that of Basel. One great object of this assembly was the reclamation of Bohemia from Hussism. But in the end the chief importance of the Council turned out to be in its conflict with the authority of the Pope. It seems difficult to resist the conclusion that in spite of its outspoken reiteration of the decrees of Constance asserting the supremacy of a General Council even over the Pope, the reigning Pope, Eugenius IV., did accept the Council and confirm its *acta*.

Negotiations with the Easterns were also begun at Basel. All three parties, Pope, Council, and Orientals had the best of reasons for wishing to bring about a reconciliation. The Eastern Empire, and with it the Eastern Patriarchates, had well-nigh disappeared into the jaws of Islam. The situation was politically desperate. On the other hand the prestige of having effected a Reunion with the East would be a very valuable asset either to Pope or Council. So strongly was this felt that both the contending parties fitted out and despatched a fleet with the intention of conveying the Easterns to the *rendez-vous* under proper influence. The two fleets met in the Bosphorus, and it required all the Emperor's efforts to prevent the situation developing into a naval battle.

In the end a huge Eastern deputation set sail for Italy. The Emperor himself was on board, the Oecumenical Patriarch, Isidore, Metropolitan of Russia, and no less than five hundred Greek ecclesiastics. The Council met at Ferrara in 1438, and was continued at Florence in the following year. As might have been expected, many of the Easterns put up a fight ; but Pope and Emperor were determined there should be no mistake this time. With the exception of Mark of Ephesus, representing the Patriarch of Jerusalem, all the Easterns signed the decrees proffered to them. The decisions of the Council on the first three points considered appear to the modern mind to be marked by liberality and commonsense.   The *Filioque* was accepted on a declaration being made by the Latins of the unobjectionable meaning which the word bore as used by them.   The use of leavened or unleavened bread was admitted to be equally valid.   The difficulty about Purgatory was got over exactly as we should get over it to-day, and as the Council of Trent got over it in the next century, by refusing to define anything as to its nature.   On the fourth point the Papal cause won a signal victory.   The primacy and the supremacy of the Pope were for the first time embodied in a conciliar decree, and so what had hitherto been treated as a matter of Canon Law was transformed into a doctrine to be held as part of the faith.   The decree is explicit.   " We define that the Holy Apostolic See and the Roman Pontiff hold the primacy over the whole world, and that the Roman Pontiff himself is the successor of blessed Peter, the Prince of the Apostles, and the true Vicar of Christ and Head of the whole Church, and the Pastor and Teacher of all Christians : and that to him in the person of blessed Peter full authority of feeding, ruling and governing the universal Church was delivered by our Lord Jesus Christ in such manner as is determined in the acts of the Oecumenical Councils and the sacred Canons." [1]

As a Western definition it would be difficult to exaggerate the importance of this definition, but as an act of reconciliation with the East it proved still-born.   The bishops had no sooner returned to their homes than their consciences began to smite them.   " We have become Azymites," they cried.   Their flocks could not conceal their disappointment. Isidore, now a cardinal of the Holy Roman Church, was promptly imprisoned in a monastery.   The holders of the other patriarchal sees, compelled by the invasion of their own territories to reside in Constantinople, put themselves

[1] It was definitely stated, however, that the Papal supremacy was " without prejudice to the rights of the other Patriarchs."

at the head of the opposition, and in spite of the despairing efforts of the Emperor the short-lived union was denounced.

In 1452 a last attempt was made.   Messages of repentance were sent from Constantinople, and the Florentine decrees were again signed in S. Sophia on 12th December.   But all to no purpose; the enthusiasm for the union was confined to court circles, and on May 29th Constantinople fell, its inhabitants still cursing the union and all who upheld it.

VI

RESULTS OF THE FALL OF CONSTANTINOPLE

THE repercussion of the fall of the great imperial city made itself felt all over Christendom, and many of its effects were both surprising and of long continuance.

Towards Reunion with the West it gave no impetus at all. The Turks were prudent enough not to drive their new subjects to desperation, and nothing less than desperation would now have moved the Orthodox mind towards a policy of reconciliation. Indeed, one of the first acts of the " disestablished " Orthodox was a definite repudiation of all that had been done under imperial influence in the direction of the acceptance of the Papacy and its ways. There is for the time a definite cessation of all attempts for Reunion.

The most remarkable immediate effect of the Turkish conquest was a definite and dangerous accession of dignity to the Patriarch himself. Mohammedanism in theory forbad all interference with the religious duties of conquered races. True, they must be *conquered* : one of the first duties of the pious Moslem is to subdue the infidel by the sword. But having been subdued, he must be allowed to exercise his religion, and his religion is to constitute his nationality. This is, and must be, a subject nationality. He has no rights against the Moslem, but the Moslem has duties towards him. If he wishes to obtain the benefits of civic rights he can do so when he will by becoming a Moslem. Thus all Orthodox Christians within the Turkish Empire became automatically members of the same nation, the

Roum Millet : *i.e.* the nation of the ancient " Roman " Empire. As such they were, and are still,[1] under the immediate government of their spiritual head, the Patriarch of Constantinople, who had, moreover, to represent them to their Moslem masters. The Christians of the Turkish Empire thus became an enslaved nationality, but it is an ordered slavery in which the slave nation, the *rayah* or " cattle," have an ordered government of their own, the recognition of which is binding on the Moslem conscience. If that faculty fails to perform its function, there is, of course, no remedy.

The jurisdiction of the Patriarch had for centuries been fading away. On the one hand the Turkish conquests had been cutting him off from the physical possibility of communicating with his Greek-speaking subjects : on the other the constant desire of the Balkan Slavs for Emperors and Patriarchs of their own was continually tending to shear away whole slices of territory from their ancient allegiance, either through temporary reconciliation with Rome or through the setting up of independent Patriarchates in defiance of the authority of Constantinople. Moreover, as long as there remained a Byzantine Emperor the powers of the Patriarch were purely spiritual. The Turkish conquest of Constantinople and the Balkan lands meant the restoration to the Patriarch of effective spiritual sway over the Greeks of Asia Minor, and the Slavs of Bulgaria, Serbia and Rumania, together with the temporal charge of semi-religious matters such as marriage and inheritance, *and* responsibility for the good behaviour of his subjects. When in 1516 Egypt and Syria became parts of the Turkish Khaliphate, the Orthodox remnant of the Patriarchates of Antioch, Alexandria and

---

[1] Or *were*, until the expulsion of the Patriarch in January 1925. At the Lausanne Conference it was conceded to the Turks that the Patriarch should be deprived of his " political powers " : but in fact such powers as he possessed outside the spiritual sphere were not political at all. A Christian educational system, Christian marriage laws and the like can only be administered by a Christian authority, and unless the Patriarch is restored to Constantinople, it seems probable that the Christian remnant there will have to migrate.

Jerusalem were added to the temporal dominions of the Oecumenical Patriarch.

When we add to all this the fact that the Patriarch was now free from the possibility of the interference of the Emperor with his spiritual functions, we can see that the effect of the fall of Constantinople was to enhance enormously the importance of the Patriarchate.[1]

A second result was the emergence of Russia as the chief support of Orthodoxy. For although, as we have just seen, the personal authority of the Patriarch was increased by recent events, the prestige of Orthodoxy itself could not fail to be lowered when it became the creed and badge of a subject nation. Providentially the Russian Church was ready to take the sceptre of external power and influence from the hands of the conquered. Russia herself was just emerging from a period of deep oppression at the hands of the Tartars, a period also when the unique missionary powers which the Slav race at times displays had enjoyed remarkable success. Content for a time to remain technically within the Patriarchate of Constantinople, the Russian Church became practically independent ; and seeing in recent events the judgment of heaven on the treacherous attempts of the imperial city to come to terms with her ancient enemy of the West, she ceased henceforth to look to Constantinople for guidance or direction.

A third result of the new *régime* at Constantinople was an enormous impetus to the study of Greek in the West. All through the Middle Ages Greek had been an almost unknown tongue West of the Adriatic. In the fourteenth century a certain scholastic intercourse began between Italy and Constantinople ; but the fall of the latter brought about a migration of Greek scholars on a large scale into Italy, where there was a ready market for what they had to teach. This was the "New Learning," which gave birth to the Renaissance, and so indirectly to the Reformation. An age

[1] See an article by Dr. J. A. Douglas in *The Christian East*, March 1925.

of culture and magnificence was inaugurated. The Papal
court became political, immoral and enormously wealthy.
But all the time the leaven of the new culture was working
towards religious revolution. While poets and philosophers
were ravished and inspired by the new treasures of the
classical literature of Greece, the men of religion fell to
studying the Greek Testament ; and while conservative
theologians took toll of the Aristotelian philosophy to syste-
matise the doctrines of the Church, there sprang to life also
a humanistic theology which drew its nourishment from the
Greek Fathers.

The stage is set for the Reformation and the Counter-
Reformation. National feeling never ran higher. The
critical spirit had sprung into new and vigorous life.

VII

THE ROOTS OF THE PROTESTANT REFORMATION

THE Reformation was destined to destroy for centuries even the hope of Christian unity. We have seen the soil prepared for the movement; we must now witness its inevitable growth. Hitherto the divisions of Christendom have seemed almost casual. The religious outlook of Western Catholicism has not been fundamentally different from that of Eastern Orthodoxy. No doubt there were differences, and that accounts for the constant divergence of opinion which was always leading to schisms, long before 1054. But always there seemed hope of reconciliation if only Christian principles were allowed to operate.

The Protestant movement was a very different matter. The need for reformation was allowed by all good men. But purely disciplinary reformation had been tried and failed. Catholicism, as centred in Rome, seemed secularised and rotten at the core.

The Papacy had become too firmly rooted in the doctrinal system of the Church for any disciplinary reform to take place except on the initiative of the Pope; and there were too many vested interests concerned to make it possible for the Pope to take any action. Adrian VI. attempted reform and paid for it with his life. Even the leaders of the Conciliar movement could think of no better plan of reform than to entrust the executive powers of the Church to a small bureaucracy of Cardinals and Bishops.

The critical spirit was alive as never before : what wonder if men began to criticise what had seemed the fundamentals of the Faith ?   Hitherto it had proved possible to suppress reforming movements which touched dogma : the new learning and the wide-spread disgust with ecclesiastical corruptions had now made the suppressive policy impossible.

The origin of thorough-going and revolutionary reform is chiefly associated with the two names of Luther and Calvin, who are mainly responsible for the form taken by the Reformation in North Germany and Scandinavia on the one hand, and in Switzerland, France and Scotland on the other.   The English Reformation is *sui generis* and must be dealt with separately.

Martin Luther (1483-1546) was a German monk and priest of humble origin.   A visit to Rome opened his eyes to the appalling extent to which corruption of morals had invaded the very centre of Catholicism.   The process of revulsion was completed by the spectacle of the Dominican friar Tetzel selling indulgences openly for money to be spent on the building of the new basilica of S. Peter's on a scale suitable to the Papal dignity.   The theory of Indulgences is briefly as follows.   Every good work done within the Church has its own peculiar merit.   This merit is not strictly confined to the person who did the work.   The Church is a body, and what one part does may affect other parts.   The merits of our Lord are infinite, and those of the Saints are far in excess of what was actually necessary for them.   Most of us, on the contrary, suffer from a defect of merit, and must expect in consequence to suffer a considerable degree of punishment in this world or the next, even though the eternal penalty which our sins really deserve may have been remitted on account of our sincere repentance.   Though forgiven, we may still have to pay a penalty.   But *if* we are forgiven we may escape this punishment, or part of it, either by works of supererogation of our own or by having applied to us the supererogatory works of others.   Or, if charity so impels us, we may make a present to fellow-sinners of the remission of penalty we have so obtained ; even if they are already suffering the pains of Purgatory. The conditions on which the application of the merits of the Saints to men can take place are determined by the Pope, as the supreme steward of God upon earth. He may appoint a prayer as such a condition, or a pilgrimage, or, if he thinks good, a money payment. Under the conditions prevailing at the Papal court under the cultured scepticism of Leo X. it was a money payment that was chosen every time : and no great stress was laid on what should have been a matter of common knowledge, that only those who by true penitence have been themselves reconciled to God can expect to receive the benefits of the good deeds of others. The impression produced was that delivery from Purgatory was for sale, and Luther expressed his abhorrence of the entire disgusting traffic by writing out ninety-five theses, condemning amongst other things the whole doctrine of Indulgences, and nailing them to the door of Wittenberg parish church. This was in 1517. From this moment his opinions hardened against the Papacy and Catholic doctrine in general. A bull was published against him in Germany, but he proceeded to burn it along with decretals on the Pope's supremacy. The rest of his life was taken up with religious controversy, preaching, and translating the New Testament. The central expression of the Lutheran faith is to be found in the Augsburg Confession, drawn up by Luther and Melancthon, and presented to the Emperor Charles V. in 1530.

Luther's position was nationalist, sectarian and anti-Catholic.[1] The centre of his teaching was the doctrine of justification by faith alone. This was pressed to the point of antinomianism. *Pecca fortiter*, he was not ashamed to teach. Bare faith—*fides informis*—this alone was needed. Human merit simply did not exist. Nor did human free will. On the contrary the human will was a slave will. All

---

[1] In the limited sense of " Catholic " as defined on p. 13.

was foreordained according to the predestination of God. Calvin had no need to advance his teaching on this matter a single point.

This doctrine was not, of course, his own invention. It was a combination of one side of S. Augustine's teaching with what Luther believed himself to have recovered from S. Paul. From Augustine he drew his determinism. Augustine had in words preserved the truth of man's free will ; but by making God responsible for the motives which are in fact presented to the will he brings out in the end a doctrine which it is very difficult to reconcile with freedom. His great work in the controversy which concerned grace and free will was to save the Church from the danger of acquiescing in the Pelagian denial of the necessity of the grace of God ; but so far from his having committed the Church to his peculiar doctrine of irresistible grace, it seems that the famous dictum of S. Vincent about the three tests of Catholic doctrine—*Ubique, Semper, Ab omnibus*—was framed especially to exclude the extreme predestinarianism in which the great Catholic doctor had involved himself.[1] But when Luther added to Augustinianism his characteristic mis-reading of S. Paul he prepared the way for that substitution of bare faith for sacramental grace which has worked so much havoc in later Protestant theory. More of a mystic than a theologian his interest was in experience rather than in dogma : and part of the heritage he left to later generations was the conviction that to have the experience of Paul—and of Luther—was a necessary preliminary to the reception of divine grace.

In theology he tended to Monophysitism, the doctrine that Christ has but one Nature, and that a Divine one. In harmony with this he taught that the Body and Blood of Christ were ubiquitous, and that the Blessed Sacrament was a mingling of the substance of bread and wine with this

---

[1] See Kidd, *History of the Christian Church*, vol. iii. p. 155.

ubiquitous substance of the Body and Blood of Christ.[1] So again, the Body of Christ being ubiquitous, the Church was ubiquitous also: *Ubi Christus, ibi ecclesia.* The Church, therefore, was not limited to those in communion with the Catholic hierarchy, but was constituted by any two or three believers among whom the Gospel was preached. This was the true Church and was invisible.[2] The *visible* church must be in strict subjection to the Christian prince, whose authority is to determine what form of religion shall be professed within his domain. *Cujus regio, ejus religio.* For the first time the teaching appears, now universal among men of all opinions, that Church and State are two societies. All through the struggles between Pope and Emperor in the Middle Ages the contending forces were the *Sacerdotium* and the *Regnum* as attributes of the one world-wide society, co-extensive with civilisation. Now, on the contrary, Church and State are separate, but the ruler of the State is to be governor also of the Church.

John Calvin (1509-1564) was a French subdeacon, who after a very short time gave up his ecclesiastical status and devoted himself to the study of law. Like so many of his contemporaries he imbibed the doctrines of the Reformation along with the study of the new and fascinating Greek language. Persecution forced him to retire to Switzerland, where he published, at the early age of twenty-five, his epoch-making *Institutes of the Christian Religion.* From 1536 to

[1] Pullan, *Bampton Lectures*, p. 72. Similarly Zwingli, Luther's contemporary, whose Christology was of a Nestorian character, denied any kind of presence of our Lord's Flesh and Blood in the Sacrament, or in the reception of it. This again is consistent. It is only because of their association with our Lord's Divinity that we can conceive of the truth of the doctrine that His Flesh and Blood are present simultaneously wherever the Sacrament is duly consecrated.

[2] The idea of the " Invisible Church," though the actual phrase seems to have been invented by Zwingli, had its roots in Augustinianism. To S. Augustine, with his doctrine of indefectible grace, it was obvious that the company of those predestined to life must have a fellowship with each other, a *communio sanctorum* as distinct from the institutional *communio externa*. See a good passage in Carnegie Simpson, *Church Principles* pp. 38 ff.; also Robertson, *Regnum Dei*, Lecture v.

1538, and again from 1541 till his death, he lived at Geneva and ruled with a rod of iron. All laxity of morals or faith was mercilessly suppressed. The Consistory, a court consisting of six ministers and twelve lay elders, met weekly, and ungodly, immoral and heretical offenders were regularly handed over to the civil power for punishment.

As compared with Luther he stands for a position less nationalistic and more Catholic (in the sense of supranational).[1] Though using the conception of an invisible Church, composed of the elect, he taught that this Church could be recognised by the preaching of the pure word of God and the due administration of the Sacraments and of discipline. While pouring contempt on the Catholic ministry for its neglect of the all-important function of preaching, and attaching no weight to the Apostolic succession, he laid immense stress on the functions and organisation of his own hierarchy, the details of which he believed to be a matter of divine appointment. While Luther was willing to retain the Episcopate, Calvin considered that he had reinstated the divinely ordained presbyterian constitution of the ministry. Like Luther he thought of Church and State as two separate societies, but unlike him taught that the civil power must be subject to the spiritual. The Prince's duty is to extirpate heresy, and so far from holding *cujus regio ejus religio* Calvin insisted that obedience to the Prince was only due so long as he held to the true faith. His study of Augustine and S. Paul led him to an extreme view of predestination. It has been said with some truth [2] that if Luther stood for the principle that God is Love, the maxim embodied in the Calvinistic theocracy is rather that God is Power. As regards the Blessed Sacrament Calvin's doctrine was a compromise between that of Luther and that of Zwingli. While denying the Real Presence of Christ's

[1] In religious practice pure Lutheranism is of course far more Catholic than Calvinism.

[2] By Dr. Pullan in his Bampton Lectures on *Religion since the Reformation*.

Body and Blood in or with the Sacrament, he taught that they were none the less actually received by the faithful communicant.

Luther and Calvin, and indeed all thorough-going reformers, were agreed in the all-sufficiency of the Scriptures, and in condemning the doctrine of the sacrifice of the Mass.

VIII

THE REFORMATION IN ENGLAND

THE English Reformation presented more than one peculiar and characteristic feature. In its first phase it was little more than an extreme assertion of nationalism, or patriotic feeling as against a Catholicism which had overreached itself and was attempting to use the supra-national prerogatives of the Apostolic see to buoy up the fortunes of a petty Italian state immersed in the whirlpool of continental politics. The Church in England, in the persons of its officials, seemed to be fast becoming an institution conducted in the interests of an absentee landlord, who was almost always an Italian.

It is true that the Bishops themselves were invariably of English birth, as had always been the case even during the most covetous phases of the Papacy. But this was secured by the fact that the King had insisted on keeping the nominations to Bishoprics in his own hands. The Bishops were the governing body of the English Church, and no self-respecting monarch could tolerate foreigners in such a position. Moreover, it was from the episcopal body that the great officers of state were drawn ; and the ordinary mediaeval Bishop was at least as much a statesman as an ecclesiastic.[1] The King appointed, and the Pope confirmed.

[1] This secularising of the episcopate was responsible for the complete separation between Baptism and Confirmation which grew up in the Middle Ages. The Bishop was too busy to hold Confirmations ; and as a result, instead of infants being brought to him to have their Baptism

Nominally, of course, the chapter elected ; but the mediaeval chapter had not really any more voice in the selection of Bishops than has the modern one.

But if the Bishops were English there remained many other wealthy benefices which, having less political connexion than a Bishopric, might be held by a foreigner with less danger to the independence of the realm.   Deaneries, Archdeaconries and Canonries had since the fourteenth century been freely given to foreigners, especially to the French and Italian Cardinals.   The humbler clergy and laity fumed, but nothing could be done : it was all part of the high political game.   The Pope must be kept in a good temper, and there was no better way of doing this than to let some of the rich ecclesiastical revenues of England flow in his direction.[1]

The clergy as a whole had become profoundly unpopular. Their inveterate habit of treating all criticism of themselves as tantamount to heresy was getting on the nerves of the nation.   When Wolsey bungled Henry VIII.'s nullity suit and had to meet his master's wrath there was no doubt where the sympathies of England lay.   The opportunity

completed by Confirmation, they had to wait upon the convenience of his Lordship, or of his assistant Bishop.

This is a matter which has a direct bearing on Reunion problems. The Puritan party, like their descendants, the modern Nonconformists, found a difficulty in Confirmation as a separate rite, which had come to be associated with a " prelatical " episcopate.   On the other hand the Anglican Church, forsaking its usual appeal to the primitive Church, made the separation more complete still.   Finally, in later times, by throwing all the emphasis on the renewal of Baptismal vows, her Bishops have, until recently, taught the people of the country (only too well) to look on the rite as a kind of ecclesiastical coming of age, admitting to the " status of a communicant."   As long as Confirmation is popularly conceived of in this way it is very difficult to press for it as a condition of Reunion.

Such a conception of Confirmation reduces it to a local ordinance of a purely ecclesiastical character, and Free Churchmen naturally say that they have already been accepted as communicants.   If we could but get back to the Apostolic idea of the laying on of hands as the appointed complement to Baptism, and forming, in theory at least, one rite with Baptism, the difficulty would be far less formidable, and we should have a far better case for insistence.

[1] See G. M. Trevelyan, *England in the Age of Wycliffe*.

had come for getting rid of the Pope's administrative oppression, and the laity jumped at it. There was at first of course no question of denying his spiritual prerogatives. It was simply one case of the ancient struggle for the national rights of the English Church. These had been in abeyance during living memory, but the record of successful protests against Papal exactions remained on the statute book, and it only needed the strong hand of a masterful and typically English King to re-enforce them. Such a King was on the throne, and his passions were engaged. More autocratic than any of his predecessors, he determined to be master in his own house. The political necessities of the Pope foreshadowed defeat for the King at the bar of Peter, and Henry determined to enjoy his revenge. No man in Europe had less love for Lutheranism, but that did not prevent him from stealing a leaf from Luther's book. He would play the " godly prince " to some effect. His plan was simple and ingenious. The clergy had dutifully accepted his recent favourite, the great Cardinal of York, as a Legate of the Pope. In so doing they were subject, one and all, to the ferocious penalties enforceable under the statute of *Praemunire*. They should be pardoned under two conditions : the inevitable cash payment, *and* a declaration that the King was the Head of the Church, " so far as the law of Christ allows."

Henry now had the ball at his feet, and events moved quickly. In 1532 the clergy accepted the King's directions that no further canons were to be passed without his permission, and that the whole Canon Law was to be submitted to him for ratification. He obtained, by a promise which he had no intention of keeping, the Pope's acknowledgment of the already married Thomas Cranmer as Archbishop of Canterbury, and in the next year the said Archbishop obediently decreed the nullity of Henry's marriage, and gave him the temporary desire of his heart. In the same year appeals to Rome on any matter were forbidden on the ground that the King was the Head of the English Church. In 1534

Convocation decreed that " the Bishop of Rome hath not by Scripture any greater authority in England than any other foreign Bishop," and a new Pope, Paul III., answered by preparing a bull of excommunication and deposition. It seems doubtful, however, whether the bull was ever promulgated.

Such was the full extent to which Henry would allow the Reformation to proceed in England.

The Pope was indeed very unwilling to proceed to extremes. Under the influence of Pole, who at this time was on the moderate side, he even negotiated with the followers of Luther in regard to a General Council. Henry exerted his influence to get these negotiations broken off, and made attempts at some sort of political union between the Lutherans and the English Church. Luther's adherents, however, would be content with nothing less than the Confession of Augsburg, and these plans for union also came to nothing. The King had no intention of encouraging or allowing a reformation on the continental model. The whole body of Catholic and mediaeval doctrine and discipline was maintained with the exception of the Papal authority. Nor, indeed, was *this* altogether repudiated : for it must be remembered that the bulk of the Canon Law consisted of Papal decrees of one kind or another, and although Henry claimed the right to revise the Canon Law, no actual steps were taken to relax anything that was not on the face of it inconsistent with the royal prerogative. All that had really been done was to put a practical stop to Papal *interference*. Impugners of the King's authority might be, and were, executed without mercy, but Lutherans and Zwinglians were sent to the stake with equal ferocity.

Henry's reign was but the beginning of a long period of Caesaro-papism, or, to coin a word, Regi-papism. The religious allegiance of England sways back and forth throughout the Reformation period according to the will of the civil power.

In 1547 the boy King Edward VI. came to the throne, and the government at once fell into the hands of the particularly unscrupulous set of scoundrels who formed the Council during his brief reign. Henry's persecuting acts were repealed, with the natural result that the country became a refuge for Protestants of every kind from the Continent. Opinion in England fell into a confusion from which it has never altogether recovered. No one seems to have missed the Pope very seriously, indeed the chief figure on the Catholic side, Bishop Gardiner, had made himself conspicuous twelve years earlier by writing a treatise against Papal authority. But in the practical matter of religious worship and of the doctrines by which it was affected feeling ran high. Gardiner and Bonner upheld the doctrine of Transubstantiation, and desired no revolutionary changes in worship. In consequence they soon found themselves in prison and deprived of their sees. Other Bishops had been deeply influenced by Luther : others again, among whom was Archbishop Cranmer, were beginning to forsake Luther for Calvin. Indeed, Cranmer's object was now to effect a union with the Calvinistic French Protestants, and much of his activity during Edward's reign was bent towards this end.

The 1549 Prayer-book, however, teaches Catholic doctrine, and was meant to keep in being a considerable amount of the traditional ceremonial. It does not seem to have met with much opposition from the Catholic-minded laity. During the remaining years of Edward's reign extreme Protestantism and the rapacity of the nobles had their own way with the English Church, and it seemed as though against its real will it was about to be transformed into a pale copy of Genevan religion, *minus* the Genevan discipline, when the death of the young King reversed the engines of religious government.

The reign of Mary brought England for a time within the sphere of the Counter-Reformation. It is of the greatest importance that we should have a sympathetic understanding of this great movement, which should always be reckoned as the countering of reformation by reformation rather than as a mere reaction against reform.

The Counter-Reformation is the recognition among those who retained their loyalty to the Papacy of the need of disciplinary reform. This need expressed itself in the Council of Trent, invitations to which were issued not only to the Bishops in Communion with the Roman see, but to Easterns and Elizabethan Anglicans as well. Elizabeth, however, refused to allow her Bishops to attend, and the Easterns declined the invitation.

But twenty years before the meeting of the Council the influence of the reforming spirit was making itself felt in Italy, and for a time it seemed as though disciplinary reformation on moderate lines, and even a new theological orientation, might yet do wonders for the healing of the wounds of the Church. The influence of Spain, however, decreed otherwise. The Society of Jesus was sanctioned by the Pope in 1540, and the Inquisition set up in Spain in 1542. Under such influences as these the reforming Council of Trent assembled in 1545, and pursued its troubled but unhurried course for eighteen years.

Doctrinally the Council fell into the fashionable habit of elaborate definition. This was hardly to be wondered at, and in view of the detailed and complex Protestant " Confessions " which were now beginning to abound it may have seemed necessary to be equally explicit in reply. But the complicated doctrinal formulae of the Reformation period have proved a *damnosa hereditas* to the Church of a later age. We are to-day less confident in the powers of the theological mind to provide an answer to every question which may legitimately be asked. Yet the decrees of the Council of Trent are a less awkward heirloom than many of the Protestant Confessions ; what would not the Church of Scotland give to be free of the Westminster Confession ! What stress do Anglicans have to lay on the blessed word " assent " in their dealings with the Thirty-Nine Articles !

The views upheld by the Council on the contemporary controversies as to free will, grace, faith, concupiscence, the Fall, assurance, were at least far more in accordance with commonsense and with the " Modern mind " than the terrible doctrines of the reformers. In the matters of Indulgences, Purgatory, the Invocation of the Saints and Transubstantiation, the Council recollected that its object was reform, and refused to countenance mediaeval corruptions and superstitions. In regard to the relationship of Papal and Episcopal authority somewhat ambiguous decrees were passed. Abuses connected with non-residence and simony were condemned in clear and definite terms.

The whole influence of the Counter-Reformation was thrown into the scales against nationalism in any form. In spiritual matters the Roman Catholic Church has become increasingly centralised, and every generation has seen the authority of the Curia growing, and almost every national peculiarity smoothed out so far as possible. Under the pressure of facts the overt claim to the right of interference with the secular government has been gradually dropped, and even in Elizabethan times we find that the Jesuits in England were ready to accept the Reformation doctrine that Church and State were separate societies ; but too often the discarding of S. Peter's temporal sword has been balanced by the seizing of the dagger of conspiracy and the cloak of intrigue, to say nothing of the stake and faggot of persecution.

The first thing to remember is that the very idea of toleration was unknown : the only people to broach it were heretics so extreme that they could never hope to be on the persecuting side themselves : it was universally acknowledged that the civil power must suppress false religion. Neither side in the struggle of Reformation and Counter-Reformation can afford to be proud of its record in this matter of persecution. It seems to be true to say that the sufferings of Protestants (in the original sense of non-Papalists) were more cruel (except perhaps in Scotland), and on a wider scale.

It is reckoned that a quarter of a million were burnt as heretics in the sixteenth century, of whom three or four hundred suffered in our own country. And of these a very large proportion could not be accounted a political danger in any sense. On the other hand, so far as England is concerned, after the publication of the bull *Regnans in excelsis* in 1570, it could with some justice be maintained that every Papalist was obliged in conscience to be disloyal to the Crown. However, almost everyone was agreed that it was right that heretics should be burnt, if only it could be settled who really were the heretics ; and when Calvin burnt Servetus at Geneva there was nothing but praise for his action from the Reformed.

At Mary's accession in 1553 Cranmer, Ridley and Latimer were imprisoned on political grounds, and the Edwardine ecclesiastical legislation was repealed. Gardiner was forced into the background to make room for Pole, who as Legate absolved the nation from the guilt of schism. Under the joint influence of a Spanish husband, a morbid conscience, a childless marriage and miserable health, the Queen threw to the winds her great opportunity of winning England back to Catholicism, and initiated a policy of terror which has set back for centuries the hope of reconciliation with the Mother Church of Rome. It is hardly possible to exaggerate the influence, conscious and sub-conscious, of what we have learned from our history books as children about the exploits of " Bloody Mary."

The breach with Rome was reopened by the accession of Elizabeth, or rather by the enactment of the Acts of Supremacy and Uniformity. But the position did not seem quite hopeless from the first. The Act of Supremacy itself accepted the first four General Councils, and when we remember the position which those Councils assign to the Pope it will be obvious that there was at least a basis for negotiation. It was stated by English diplomatists that the Pope would offer no objection to the Elizabethan Prayer-Book (practically the same as the one used in the Church of England to-day) if she on her part would acknowledge his supremacy. Some at least of the Pope's adherents for three years attended services of the Anglican rite, until forbidden to do so by the Papal authority : and the Spanish ambassador, himself a bishop, defended them for so doing.

But the change from the Marian position was very drastic from the first. All the English Bishops but one refused to take the oath of supremacy and were forcibly deprived. Of the other clergy all but two hundred accepted it.

Was this the destruction of the Catholic Church in England and the setting up of a new body ? It might almost seem so at first sight, but there is much to urge on the other side. Convocation in the reign of Henry VIII. had as a fact, though under duress, accepted the theory that the King was the " *Head* of the Church of England so far as the law of Christ allows," and Elizabeth was only demanding to be accepted as " *Supreme Governor*." Convocation had also asserted by canon that " the Bishop of Rome hath no more authority than any other foreign Bishop." Thus Elizabeth was technically within her rights in demanding individual acceptance of what was already corporately binding.

The Archbishop of Canterbury had died almost on the same day as the late Queen. Eleven Bishops in all died before any coercive action was taken. This left fifteen Bishops who were deprived by Elizabeth in accordance with the law, and not simply by royal commission as in the case of the Bishops deprived by Mary. Of these, four, or five, had themselves been placed in their sees by Mary without any canonical deprivation of their predecessors, and in regard to four, or five, others, their places were not filled until their death. Therefore, out of twenty-seven sees there were only six the Elizabethan occupants of which can with any justice be considered intruders.

Parker was elected by the chapter of Canterbury in due form to succeed to Pole's office : he was consecrated by

Bishops of the Province : no protest was made from Rome or elsewhere : no attempt was made even formally to fill any of the sees with rival claimants ; and for eleven years there was no actual and formal breach with Rome.[1]

If we are going to question every case of deprivation or appointment in Church history which took place through the action of the civil power we shall find ourselves in serious difficulties.   Again and again the Church all over the world has had to acquiesce in having her machinery manipulated by the secular arm, and in the earthly Jerusalem we mostly live in houses of glass.   Stone-throwing is therefore forbidden.

But was Parker's Consecration valid, or, to ask a broader question, was the Ordinal of 1550 a valid method of Ordination ?   It is well known that both questions are answered in the negative by the authorities of the Roman Church.

There are only two grounds which are now seriously asserted for denying the validity of the Ordinal.   The first is that taken up by Leo XIII. in his bull *Apostolicae Curae*. The Pope considered that the alterations made in 1550 were evidence that it was not the intention of the rite to make Bishops, Priests and Deacons in the Catholic sense.   The omission in particular of any mention of " the power to offer sacrifice " seemed to suggest that the new " Priests " were not sacrificing priests, but merely " priests " in the etymological sense of " elders."   It is not suggested that the form in itself is actually invalid, but that the evidence goes to show that the reformers did not as a fact believe in the Catholic doctrine of the Priesthood, and that as they expressed their disbelief in the official words of the rite, the rite itself must be treated as invalid.   The sufficient answer seems to be that the Preface to the rite does show that the Reformers intended to keep the divinely ordained Order of Priesthood, *whatever that might be*, and that their private opinions as to the nature of priesthood do not appear in the Rite which they drew up.

[1] See Dr. Gore, *Roman Catholic Claims*, pp. 166, 167.

All that they did was to replace the complex and somewhat corrupt Sarum Ordinal by a more straightforward rite, and to safeguard themselves in regard to the doctrine of Holy Order by making the " form " of Ordination consist of the words of our Lord Himself. It was supposed at that date that an *imperative* " form " was essential, and by using Christ's own words to His Apostles they implied that they intended to pass on the *Apostolic* ministry.

We need not be perturbed by the fact that Cranmer omitted all reference to the offering of sacrifice. The Ordinals of the primitive Church were no more explicit on this point than our own, and if the Priesthood does give this power then it is sufficient that the Priesthood should be mentioned, as it is again and again in the course of the service. The same is true, *mutatis mutandis*, of the Episcopate. There can be no doubt that the intention of the words, " Receive the Holy Ghost," is to make a Bishop or a Priest, as the case may be.[1]

It is not always realised how confused and unsatisfactory the Latin Ordinal was and is. The sources of confusion are twofold : an unscientific fusion of two methods of Ordination, the Gallican and the ancient Roman ; and the various theories which have been held at different times both as to the form and as to the matter of Ordination.[2] The first accounts for the fact that there are two impositions of hands, either of which might be supposed to be the " matter " of

---

[1] See Fr. Puller, *The Bull Apostolicae Curae and the Edwardine Ordinal* ; Procter and Frere, *A New History of the Book of Common Prayer*, c. xvi.

[2] The scholastic distinction between the " form " and the " matter " of the Sacraments is a useful one. Both words refer to the outward part of the Sacrament. The " matter " is the outward material or action which is necessary : the " form " is the words which make it clear that there is an intention to make or confer a Sacrament. In Baptism there is one fixed form which alone is certainly valid, consisting of the words which S. Matthew reports our Lord as having used in the institution of the Sacrament. Roman Catholics would say the same about the Sacrament of the Eucharist. As regards the other Sacraments there is no *fixed* formula. All that is necessary for validity is that some words should be used which make it clear with what intention the " matter " is being used.

the Ordination. This did not seem to do any harm in mediaeval times when it was supposed that the matter of Ordination was the "porrection of the instruments," *i.e.* in the case of a priest the giving to him of a paten and a chalice. But now that it is acknowledged that the imposition of hands is the necessary matter, it is certainly very awkward that the ceremony should be repeated. Moreover, the earlier imposition takes place in silence, and is separated from the "form" of Ordination. This would suggest that the second imposition which is actually accompanied by the words, "*Accipe Spiritum Sanctum*," was the actual Ordination. Yet this cannot be the case, for the new priests have already joined with the Bishop in consecrating the Blessed Sacrament. The fact seems to be that the earlier imposition is really the important and essential one, and was originally performed while the consecratory prayer was being said : for in earlier days the "form" of Ordination was always thought to be a *prayer* and not an imperative formula. When the newer view as to the "form" was combined with the newer view as to the "matter," it is not surprising that insufficient care was taken to keep the true form and matter in close connection as the central act of the service. Our own Ordinal, though adopting the newer theory as to the "form," is less unsatisfactory than the Roman service, inasmuch as it is quite clear that the intention of the rite is to convey to the candidate the gift of Holy Order by the apostolic method of imposition of hands, accompanied by words which make clear the character of the act which is being performed.

A difficulty is sometimes raised on the ground that the Edwardine Ordinal did not specify at the moment of Ordination what Order it was which was being conferred ; to which the answer is, " Neither does the Roman Ordinal, in the case of Bishops." But the general tenor of the service in both cases makes clear what is being done.

The other objection made to Parker's Consecration is the idea that there is an uncertainty as to the Consecration

of Barlow, who was the chief Consecrator of Parker.   The
only real evidence alleged for this is that there is no record
of the Consecration in Cranmer's register, and the register
of S. David's having been lost, it is not possible to check the
fact of the Consecration.   But in fact, Cranmer's register
was kept very carelessly.   There are other indubitable
Consecrations of which it contains no record.   And on the
other side there is the fact that Barlow took possession of
his see in 1536, eleven years before the end of Henry VIII.'s
reign, and that no objection was taken to his administration
of the Diocese, or to his taking his seat in the House of
Lords ; and that in spite of the fact that he was constantly
engaged in quarrelling with his Dean, who, if there had been
anything suspicious about his Consecration, would have had
an easy way of victory made ready to his hand.   The vacilla-
tion of Barlow's own opinions has, of course, no bearing on
the matter.

In regard to the omission of the record of Consecration,
Mgr. Barnes has sought to prove [1] that both the Register and
the Patent Rolls preserved at the Record Office have been
deliberately mutilated in order to conceal the fact that
Barlow was never any more than Bishop *Elect* ; and further,
that the account of Parker's Consecration in Cranmer's
register is a forgery.

In the course of an elaborate examination of this theory
Dr. C. Jenkins calls attention to the following facts.[2]   He
points out that Barlow on all important occasions signs the
acts of Convocation *before* Warton of S. Asaph, who was
consecrated in 1536, thus proving that he himself had been
already consecrated.[3]

Again, the complaint made against Barlow's opinions in
that very year accuses him of saying that a bishop-elect was

[1] *Bishop Barlow and Anglican Orders.*

[2] *Journal of Theological Studies*, Oct. 1922.

[3] A bishop *elect* might sit in convocation, but would sign *after* consecrated bishops.

as good a bishop as he was himself : which makes nonsense if Barlow himself was only a bishop-elect.

Thirdly, Dr. Jenkins points out that there is in existence a letter of Barlow's brother stating, apparently without fear of contradiction, that Barlow was *enthroned* at S. David's ; which undoubtedly implies that he had been consecrated as Bishop.

Finally, we are reminded that he took part in a Consecration and himself gave Holy Orders outside his own Diocese, and was therefore clearly presumed to be a Bishop.

Mgr. Barnes does not seem to have won any conviction for his theory of the account of Parker's consecration being a forgery.   Dr. Jenkins shows that as a mere matter of bookbinding there was no need for a forgery on the enormous scale which Mgr. Barnes' conjecture assumes : and that the careless omissions in this part of the register are not such as a forger would have left.

The importance of the genuineness of the account of Parker's Consecration is that it contains the statement that the four consecrating bishops *all* said the words of Consecration.   If this is true it would destroy the force of any doubt that any one might raise about the Consecration of Barlow ; for quite clearly the validity of Parker's Consecration would no longer depend on that at all.

As regards the Patent Rolls it does so happen that there is a gap in one of them for the twenty-eighth year of the reign of Henry VIII. ; but there never was any reason to suppose that the missing record referred to Barlow : and a search enabled Dr. Jenkins to discover in the previous year what was obviously the duplicate of the missing passage.

The inner history of the Church of England through all this time is miserable reading.   By the confession of Latimer and his associates at the end of the reign of Edward VI., the religious and moral state of the country was in a state of unprecedented corruption.   Add to this the horror of the Marian persecutions, and it will be seen that Elizabeth and her ecclesiastical advisers had an impossible task.   Inevitably everyone had become an extremist for one side or the other. With the exception of Parker himself, the new Bishops were to a man fervent Calvinists.   The old policy—Catholicism with a good deal less of the Pope—which might once have been successful, if Englishmen had been left to themselves, was thrown into abeyance for centuries.   This policy probably represented the Queen's own views.   She was by temperament a " ritualist," and as Queen she wished by judicious compromise to weld her subjects into a homogeneous mass.   A daughter of Henry VIII. was not likely to abate a jot of her own prerogatives, real or assumed.   If possible, she would have conciliated the Papalists ; but it was not possible.   The Reformation and the Counter-Reformation had diverged too far, and on both sides exile had made for extreme views.   The Marian exiles had been sitting under John Knox, and the Papalists had been fed on blood.   In 1570 Pius V. with his *Regnans in excelsis* excommunicated the Queen and dispensed her subjects from their allegiance.   In 1571 conversion to Romanism was declared high treason.   The mischief was done.   For the first time there were two rival obediences in the same country, each claiming the name of Catholic, and each looking on the other with fear and loathing.   Missionary priests from the new seminary at Douai began to be smuggled into England, and were soon followed by the Jesuits with their characteristic combination of sincere religion with political intrigue.   Of the Douai priests alone, one hundred and thirty-five were executed.

Was the one body a schism and the other the true Church ? On all the ancient principles of Catholic order no other verdict could be given.   And yet . . . who is going to say which is the Catholic and which the schismatic ?   If we put ourselves in the position of members of either party, can we not find reasons of unblemished character for upholding our position ?   On the one side there was the *de facto* hierarchy claiming canonical possession of their sees, and claiming it as we have seen with some justification, and for the present no opposite numbers making a corresponding claim. It is difficult to accuse the easy-going Englishman who simply stayed, as he thought, in the community in which he was baptized, of being in schism because that community had changed its mind about the Pope, as it had done several times before. And if that Englishman were a priest the same holds good. And if he were Archbishop Parker himself— well, it was unfortunate that there had been a clean sweep of the hierarchy, but after all the late Archbishop was dead, and he, Parker, had been chosen by the canonical electorate, and what was wrong with his position ? But it is equally difficult to justify a charge of schism against a man, layman, priest or bishop, who found himself excluded from his parish church for believing just what he had always believed. Why should he suddenly turn against the Pope, and take an oath which the Pope instructed him not to take, and join in worship which the Pope had forbidden ? Unless, of course, someone could convince him that he had been wrong all this time. It seems that an altogether new position had arisen. Once before, five centuries ago, the Catholic Church had fallen apart. The unthinkable calamity had happened : separation had come about within the fold. Only in that other instance the accursed schism had been mitigated and disguised by the fact that the two parts of the Church—the East and the West—were separated geographically. This time they were neighbours and familiar friends and relatives. Neither party had done anything schismatic, unless, of course, communion with the Holy See is necessary to membership in the Church. If not, each party might deplore the other's error, but could not accuse it of schism. Two Catholic obediences had arisen : that was a familiar fact : what was new was that they were existing side by side, in the same country. Yet even that was not altogether new. There were already in other parts of the Church, in Southern

Italy for example, Catholics of the Latin rite existing side by side with those of Eastern customs and outlook. The novelty was that they were divided on a point which one party made a matter of faith, and that they were mutually excommunicating each other. The application of the strict theory of territorial jurisdiction is henceforth really impossible. A question has arisen *within* the Church as to what constitutes membership in the Church, and this fact throws all previous theories as to the nature of schism into confusion. What is the position of a French Catholic who crosses the Channel : does he straightway become a schismatical *Roman* Catholic ?

Caelum, non animum, mutant, qui trans mare currunt.

Again, what of the new countries ? In America, who are the Catholics, and who the schismatics to-day ? And it is hardly an anachronism to raise this question at this point. For the period of the Reformation is also the period of the discovery of the New World and the first attempts at colonisation. Religious difficulties, the results of Christian disunion, were not slow to follow. It seems that the only statement which corresponds with the facts is that which is not afraid to say that the Catholic Church in England *bifurcated* in the sixteenth century. And the ultimate question is this : Is communion with the Holy See so vital that we must put up with anything rather than run the risk of having it broken ? Or, to put it somewhat differently : Have we an assurance that in any dispute the Pope must be in the right ?

During the earlier period of Elizabeth's reign it seemed only a matter of time for the Church of England to be thoroughly Calvinised. Close relationship was maintained with the Swiss Reformed, and all the leaders of theological thought were deeply influenced by the religious dictatorship of Geneva. In some cases those who had received only the nominal ordination of the foreign protestants were even admitted to English benefices.[1]

[1] There was no pretence that this was in accordance with the law of the English Church, and proceedings were actually pending against

This period also saw the beginning of Nonconformity. In the strict sense the word means the non-observance of the Act of Uniformity, and should be applied to those whose opposition to the Catholic ceremonial was so strong that they could not be induced to observe the very moderate amount of ceremony enjoined by the Elizabethan Prayer-Book. Parker attempted to bring back some order into the Church by the issue of the "Advertisements" of 1566. The "Ornaments Rubric," in its literal interpretation, ordered the use of the ancient vestments of the Mass. The Advertisements, however, did not insist on this, but merely commanded the use of the surplice in parish churches and the cope in Cathedrals. The result was the secession of a small body of extremists, who thus became Nonconformists in the modern sense. But there was no weight behind this movement. John Knox, now in the heyday of his power in Scotland, and the Swiss Calvinists threw all their influence into the policy of remaining in the Church and refusing to conform, while at the same time carrying on a violent propaganda for the removal of Antichrist. The propaganda took the form of "Admonitions" to Parliament, in which the rich stores of Elizabethan English were freely drawn upon to express the abhorrence which all right-minded people must feel for surplices, square caps and anything which seemed "culled out of that popish dunghill, the Mass-book." The avowed objects of the most influential party in the English Church were now the substitution of Presbyterianism for Episcopacy, and the abolition of all non-scriptural adjuncts of worship. A pedantic and fanatical puritanism seemed, at the moment, to be the only contribution which the Anglican Reformation had to offer to a distracted Christendom.

The Papacy had in fact been the keystone of the mediaeval

Whittingham, who had been intruded into the Deanery of Durham without episcopal Ordination, when the case was stopped by the death of the defendant. In 1586 Whitgift was able to state that he knew of no one ministering in England, who had not been episcopally ordained.

system, and an Anglican theology, Catholic but not Papal, was still to seek. The great name of Hooker springs to mind as the first to give a reasoned exposition of the position of the English Church. It could not be expected that his attitude should be at all points unassailable. The traditions of his youth and education had been Calvinistic, and it was difficult to shake off the trammels of the Genevan system. He was to the end a believer in " the Invisible Church " : his Eucharistic theology was receptionist : he was a thorough-going Erastian : but he taught the English Church to maintain against Calvinism what Henry VIII. and Stephen Gardiner and Tunstall had maintained against the Papalists : that " to reform ourselves is not to sever ourselves from the Church we were of before : in the Church we were, and we are so still." Without dissociating himself from the characteristic Reformation doctrines of justification by faith and the all-sufficiency of Holy Scripture he adjusted the balance by showing that after all these were not the only doctrines of the Christian faith, and in particular that the Sacraments are the extension of the Incarnation rather than a mere accompaniment to the preaching of the Word, which to the Reformed was the real business of religion.

We have seen that Calvinism was closely bound up with a theory of Church government. Calvin taught that by divine institution there were four orders in the church : Pastors, or Ministers, Doctors, Elders and Deacons. The Church must be organised as a national establishment. Membership in the Church so organised is a duty from which there can be no excuse. We are not, therefore, surprised to find that Presbyterianism, which *is* Calvinism from the point of view of polity, makes its first appearance in England not as a form of dissent, but as an attempt to change from within the methods of Church government. The possibility of holding Calvinistic doctrine within the Church seemed settled by facts. But under the rule of the Bishops, and indeed of the Crown, it was by no means so easy to " preach the pure word of God." Preaching stirred up enthusiasm, and enthusiasm might lead to schism, or to troublesome attempts to set up a theocratic control of public morals on the model of Geneva. "Prophesying" was, therefore, suppressed on the initiative of the Queen, and Archbishop Grindal was driven into retirement for showing favour to anything so dangerous.

On the suppression of the Prophesyings the Calvinistic party contrived a new scheme, the directing motive of which was the bringing of the polity of the Church into line with the "holy discipline" of Geneva. It was attempted to carry this out by setting up a voluntary Presbyterian system *within* the Church with the idea that later on this might supplant episcopacy. The plan was that all the Puritan clergy in the country should form themselves into *classes*, and proceed to govern themselves according to Presbyterian standards, while accepting Ordination and Institution from the Bishops as a mere formality, so that their position as Ministers and as Incumbents might be unchallenged as a matter of law. But they had no intention of observing the law in regard to the use of the Prayer-Book. On the authority of the *classis*, they would meet the situation by employing someone to read Morning and Evening Prayer, while they themselves arrived in church only in time to preach the all-important sermon.

These irregularities were rigorously suppressed by Whitgift, who succeeded to the Archbishopric of Canterbury in 1583, with the aid of the Court of High Commission.

Presbyterianism from its nature only flourishes when it is in a majority, and we hear little more of it under the strong hand of Elizabeth.[1]

[1] While Anglicans and Calvinists were in relations so close, it is noteworthy that the Eastern Church was also interesting itself in the reforming movements. The Patriarch of Constantinople was actually in communication with Melancthon in 1559, and there was a correspondence between him and the Lutherans from 1573 to 1581. As might have been expected, no progress was made, and the Patriarch finally, in characteristic Orthodox phrase, begged them to write in future of friendship rather than of dogma.

The reign of Elizabeth also saw the beginnings of what is now called Congregationalism. Robert Browne set up an independent congregation at Norwich in 1580. The movement at first was, as is natural, somewhat hesitating, and seems not to have had any clear and definite objective. On the one hand the principle that the Church consists of true and consistent believers only, and that belief is a private and individual affair, would make it impossible for the system to be universally imposed ; but on the other the full implications of these beliefs were not at first recognised, and it seems that during the reign of Elizabeth the object which Browne and his followers consciously set before themselves was rather the reform of the Church of England than the supersession of it. Browne himself was excommunicated, and soon gave up his self-appointed ministry and returned to the Church. His followers, however, fled to Holland in 1595, where, amid much quarrelling, they thought out their principles.

These principles may be defined as follows :

Jesus Christ is the Head of the Church : and ultimately there *is* no other authority.

The Church is a congregation of believers.

Every Church, however small, is independent not only of the state but of all other Christians, and the form of its government should be settled by the majority of its members.

The theological system is that of Calvin.

The Pope is Antichrist.

It will be seen that this system is far more radically anti-Catholic than anything which has hitherto come into being as an organised religious polity. Both the Anglican and the Presbyterian reforms had been reforms of the mediaeval Catholic system : Independency was the reform of a reform. Anglicanism in fact and Presbyterianism in intention had retained some idea of a Catholic Church, with a liberal admixture of the leaven of Nationalism. But Independency

threw over Catholicism and Nationalism alike in the interests
of the purest Sectarianism.   There is no *Catholic* Church.
There is no *National* Church.   A church is a voluntary
group of God's own people who agree to worship together.
God gives them a pastor, and they " recognise " him.

IX

THE REFORMATION IN SCOTLAND

HAVING brought our survey of the English Reformation down to the point at which the two Kingdoms of England and Scotland are on the verge of union, it seems best to go back and pick up the threads of Reformation history in the latter country, so that we may be in a position to deal with them jointly from the moment when they begin to form a civil unity.

The need of Reformation was from all accounts particularly urgent in Scotland. The Church was extremely corrupt, the Bishops and Abbots quite unworthy of their positions, and the wealth of the Church, which was great, was almost entirely in the hands of these same scandalous prelates. The Papal court itself could hardly produce worse instances of murder, lust and simony in high places. A five year old Abbot and an Archbishop of sixteen are only two instances of the shameless and grotesque which so often form an element in tragedy. It is, therefore, only natural that on soil so prepared the reformed teachings took early root.

Isolated burnings for heresy took place in Scotland as in other places during the fourteenth century, and when the Reformation was fairly started each wave of the reforming movement broke on Scottish shores. Lollards, Hussites, Lutherans and Zwinglians all alike suffered in the flames. But the Scottish Reformation in the end, under the influence of Knox, settled down to the purest Calvinism.

John Knox (1513-1572) enters history as a young secular priest who had come under the influence of the Zwinglian George Wishart. This reformer was burnt by order of Cardinal David Beaton in 1546. Soon afterwards the Cardinal was murdered, and his murderers took refuge in the castle of S. Andrews. Here they were joined by Knox, and the whole party were captured by the French fleet, and Knox with others was sent to the galleys. At the intercession of Edward VI. he was released, and for a time it seemed as though he might devote his energies to preaching the word in England, where indeed he was actually offered a Bishopric. He married an English wife, and on Mary's accession escaped to the continent. He visited Geneva, and became a whole-hearted Calvinist. Thence he transferred himself to Frank-fort, where he acted as chaplain to the English refugees, and succeeded in indoctrinating them with the Genevan theology, and a longing for the grim and fierce Genevan discipline.

Meanwhile the Reformation was simmering in Scotland. No very extreme steps had been taken on either side. The reforming nobles were demanding no more than the use of the 1552 English Prayer-Book, which had, of course, been discarded on the accession of Queen Mary, while the Bishops were busy with reforms on more conservative lines. All this was changed by Elizabeth's accession, which brought back Knox's flock to England, but Knox himself to Scotland.

His arrival meant the end of compromise. His first sermons against the Mass at Perth plunged the country into civil war, and the victory of the Reformers was marked by riot and destruction. We observe at once the difference between a Reformation influenced as that in England had been by the teaching of Luther, and one founded on the unadulterated doctrine of Geneva. In England the Refor-mation took place at the dictation of the sovereign : in Scotland in the teeth of her opposition. For Mary of Scotland hated the very name of Protestant, and had Knox been a Lutheran he would have been compelled by his principles to teach the doctrine of obedience to the civil power. Being a Calvinist, he approached the Queen of England, and so worked on her fears of a political combination of France and Scotland to crush the Scottish rebellion, that at last she sent a fleet to the Firth of Forth, and made a treaty with the reforming party which effectually disposed of all hope of help from France. In 1560 Calvinistic Presbyterianism was set up by Parliament in the teeth of the wishes of the Queen, Apostolic succession was flouted, and the doctrine of admission to the ministry by the congregation without imposition of hands was substituted for it. It was further enacted that anyone hearing or saying Mass should suffer death for the third offence.

Queen Mary meanwhile was in France, at the deathbed of her husband who, having succeeded to the throne in 1559, died in 1560 after a reign of eighteen months. She returned to Scotland, a young widow of nineteen, and found herself face to face with the savage and embittered reform party. Six years of unhappiness and sin ended in a general rebellion of her subjects, and a flight to England, and so to imprisonment and death.

An attempt was made to preserve Episcopacy as a matter of Church government, or a convenient means of disposing of the vast incomes attached to the more important sees. The new bishops were not bishops in the Catholic sense at all. The whole theory of Presbyterianism is repugnant to the idea that a bishop is a specially consecrated person with authority to bestow the ministry on others. They were bishops only in the sense that a " lay impropriator " in England is called a " lay Rector." The only connection between the office and the title in both cases is that the holder of the latter receives the emoluments of the former.[1]

Still, the mere existence of " bishops " was inconsistent

---

[1] This abuse was not an invention of the Reformation period. There had been holders of Archbishoprics and Bishoprics in earlier days who were mere receivers of the income of their sees. But side by side with them there existed consecrated bishops who exercised episcopal functions.

with the purity of Calvinism, and in 1592, under the influence of Andrew Melville, Parliament abolished the title of Bishop, and established the Presbyterian discipline on the model of Geneva.

This arrangement of Church government is of great importance, and represents the ideal at which all Calvinists aimed. It is still the polity of the Established Church of Scotland and of the Free Church in the same country, and commanded the enthusiasm of vast numbers of the reforming party for generations.

Of Calvin's four orders, that of " Doctor " ceases to be of importance. " Ministers " alone are ordained.[1] Of the other two orders the Elders are associated with the ordained Ministers in spiritual government, while the Deacons administer temporalities. The Minister and Elders of a congregation form the " Kirk Session," and there are superior bodies, exercising a wider jurisdiction, culminating in the General Assembly, which is the supreme authority of a national Church.

In regard to the claim of this polity to be of scriptural and Divine appointment it is necessary to say (1) that there is absolutely no scriptural basis for the distinction between Ministers and Elders. It seems indeed to be true that the Jewish " Elders " of the Synagogue were secular officers, and so can be thought to correspond with the " Elder " rather than with the " Minister " of Presbyterians, or the " Presbyter " or " Priest " of Catholics. But this only proves, as Dr. Headlam shows,[2] that the name of Elder or Presbyter was merely suggested to the primitive Church by the Synagogue official, and that the office was in no sense the same. It is clear from the Acts and Epistles that the " Elders " of the primitive Church were Ministers, and had been ordained as such by imposition of hands. (2) It must be pointed out

---

[1] This ordination was conferred by laying on of hands in the Church of Scotland from 1581 onwards. But there was an interval of twenty-one years during which there had been no such ceremony.

[2] *Bampton Lectures*, chap. i.

that whatever uncertainty there may be as to the ordaining authority in the primitive Church, there is no particle of evidence of anyone conferring Ordination unless he or they had received authority to ordain. This is the authority which seems lacking in Presbyterian Ordinations.

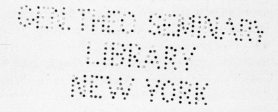

X

RELIGION UNDER THE FIRST STUART KINGS AND THE COMMONWEALTH

THE accession of James VI. of Scotland as James I. of England meant the union of the two Kingdoms, and was fraught with remarkable consequences for the history both of unity and schism in the Church. The new English King had had a bitter experience of Presbyterianism in his own country. He had seen the judgment of God fall on the corruptions of the ancient Church ; but he had also seen how bitter and unchristian a thing the reformed faith could show itself to be. His new Kingdom seemed to show promise of better things, at any rate from the standpoint of the Throne. The tradition of the English Reformation had been intense, indeed servile loyalty. Calvinistic as its theology had been for the most part, there were signs of a reaction. The influence of Andrews was great, and was uniformly bent towards the recovery of that attitude towards the historic Church as a living body which is the true meaning of the expression Anglo-Catholicism. No success had attended the feverish efforts of the extremists to introduce the discipline and ministry of Geneva, and even in externals an Anglican tradition of comparative decency was beginning to assert itself. The Puritans were no longer the dominant faction. James had no inclinations to Romanism, but he was heartily sick of a system under which the King could not call his soul his own, and thought he saw a chance of effecting a union between the Church of England, which was the Church of his ideals, and the Church of Scotland, of the presbyterianising of which he had been so unwilling a spectator.

It is therefore not surprising to us, though it was unpleasantly so to the Puritans, that he threw all his newly acquired royal influence against those who were desirous of completing the Reformation in the anti-Catholic sense. Religious controversy was the breath of his nostrils, and he jumped at the suggestion of a conference ; but the whole result of the meeting at Hampton Court in 1604 was in the opposite direction from what the Puritans had hoped.

His real designs were soon made clear. There had recently been a revival in the North of Scotland of that titular episcopacy which Melville had succeeded in abolishing. James contrived to secure the assent of the General Assembly of the Church of Scotland to the Consecration of three Presbyterian ministers to the Episcopate. Holy Orders were conferred *per saltum*, *i.e.* the new Bishops were not first ordained to the Diaconate and the Priesthood. This was a method of Consecration which did not lack precedent. To mention only one instance, it is possible that S. Ambrose was thus consecrated. But it was at least irregular, and it made it possible to maintain that the Presbyterian Ministry was recognised as a true Priesthood. This impression is confirmed by the fact that the Presbyterian ministers in Scotland were not required to be ordained afresh, but continued to minister in their Presbyterian Orders. Those who were to be made Bishops were duly consecrated ; but no other Orders were conferred. Under this arrangement the Churches of England and Scotland remained in communion with each other from 1610 to 1638. It is one of the curious inconsistencies of the Anglican Divines of this period that while insisting with all their might that Episcopacy was divinely ordained, and that no one should minister in the Church of England without episcopal Ordination, some of them were yet perfectly willing to acknowledge the Orders

and even to accept the ministrations of the irregular ministries inaugurated by Calvin and his followers. It is difficult
to resist the conclusion that they thought of Episcopacy
rather as a necessary method of government than as a *sine
quâ non* for the transmission of Orders. It does not, of
course, follow that they were right.

In 1618 steps were taken with the approval of the Scottish
General Assembly to restore some of what had been lost to
the Scottish Church under the rule of the Presbytery.
Kneeling at Communion was again ordered, together with
the administration of Confirmation and the observance of
the great Christian festivals. But it was not until 1629 that
a Liturgy for the Scottish Church was drawn up, which was
a very curious compound of the English Book of Common
Prayer and Knox's Book of Common Order.

All this is an important precedent. It shows the spectacle
of the Church of England in Communion with a Church
which had Bishops but no Priests, dispensed with Confirmation, and employed a Prayer-Book which contained *no* form
of Consecration for the Eucharist. It is true that the first
was an irregularity which would cure itself by degrees as the
older ministers died out, while the second and third only
existed for eight years; and, of course, some pledge to have
these things put right may have been exacted from Spottis-
woode and his colleagues. But in these three points the
English Bishops did go further than there is any likelihood
of their being followed by the Episcopate of to-day.

The reiteration of Episcopacy, in this modified form, was
productive of a great improvement in the tone and temper
of Scottish religion, which continued until the disastrous
experiments of Charles I. " The substitution of forbearance
and courtesy for fanaticism and violence, and of theological
study and discussion for pamphleteering and the invective
of the pulpit, was the most permanent gift of the First
Episcopate to Scotland." [1]

[1] Rev. E. G. Selwyn in the *Church Quarterly Review*, July 1920.

To this period belongs the emergence of another of the great sectarian communities, the Baptists.

The Baptist sects were offshoots from the Independents who had taken refuge in Holland. They were two in number and had little in common with each other except the refusal of Baptism to children and the stress which both laid on the " inner light," the illumination of the believer's heart by the Holy Spirit. The General Baptists stand for a strong reaction from the dominant Calvinism of the Reforming sects. They went so far in opposition to Calvin as to deny the whole conception of Original Sin, and thus aligned themselves with the earlier heresy of Pelagius. They described themselves as a society of " baptized believers who own universal redemption." The other special tenet now associated with the Baptist community, insistence on immersion at Baptism, has its origin in the other sect, the Particular Baptists, who in splitting off from Independency retained the Calvinistic theology.[1] Both of these bodies continued the Independent church polity. The General Baptists first appear in England in 1611, the Particular in 1616.

As regards the tenets of these two sects it must be observed that the rejection of Calvinism by the one cannot be thought of as a return to Catholic ways of thought : it was rather a loosening of hold on dogmatic Christianity, which in later days went further and tended to lapse into Unitarianism. The insistence on immersion and the denial of Baptism to children were characteristic attempts to reproduce what was believed to be the practice of the primitive Church, and from the Puritan point of view were amply justified. If all Church history from the times of the Apostles is to be thought of as no more than the gradual corruption of primitive simplicity, it is obvious that unless we can find much clearer evidence than exists for the Baptism of infants in the New Testament, we have no right to continue the practice. The whole trend

[1] But Immersion did not become one of their principles until 1642.

of Protestant theology, moreover, especially in its Calvinistic form, seems to make the Baptism of children almost a mockery. As regards immersion it used to be commonly held that this practice was invariable in the primitive Church. But strong evidence has lately been brought forward to prove that this is more than doubtful.[1]

A portion of the distressful history of Ireland falls to be mentioned at this point. It had been a centre of disaffection during the reign of Elizabeth, and with all the Tudor unscrupulousness she had made large parts of the country into a desert. The attempt to settle Munster with English colonists had been a failure, and the whole land was in ruin. James had the happy thought of trying the same experiment with settlers from his own country, and the " Plantation " of Ulster was taken in hand by Scotsmen, who seem to have found the country more acceptable than their English predecessors. The transformation of the little town of Derry into the great port of Londonderry was taken in hand at the same time by English settlers from London. Thus was formed the nucleus of the present rich and powerful community whose occupation of the North of Ireland forms in every possible way, and not least in the religious sphere, so strange a contrast to the Celtic twilight in which their compatriots, if such they can be called, pursue, and are pursued by, their tragic destiny.

Meanwhile continuous but futile efforts were made to suppress Romanism ; but the Reformation had never been anything but an external tyranny in Ireland, and the effect of persecution was only to weld together the hitherto hostile elements of native Irish and the Anglo-Irish nobility of the " Pale." English statute law had no validity in Ireland, and the King's attempts were everywhere defeated.

The same period saw the opening of communications with the Eastern Church. Constantinople had been almost entirely

[1] See a pamphlet by Prof. C. Rogers, " Baptism in the Early Church," *S.P.C.K.*

closed to the West until the conclusion of a commercial treaty with the Sultan in 1579. The reopening of the port aroused mutual interest, and in 1611 George Sandys, son of the Archbishop of York, paid a visit to Cyril Lucar, then Patriarch of Alexandria, and received from him the remarkable statement that " the differences between us are but shells." In the following year Lucar sent a Greek priest to study at Balliol at Archbishop Abbot's expense. In 1621 Lucar became Patriarch of Constantinople, and as such conducted a correspondence with Laud. Unfortunately he conceived a scheme of uniting the Orthodox Church with the Calvinists, having himself imbibed the Calvinistic principles both at Geneva and in Lithuania. In 1629 he astonished the Orthodox world by sending to Geneva a Confession of Faith which embodied the Genevan doctrines. His own people and the Jesuits, who were now becoming very active in the Near East, united to oppose him. His printing press was closed, and he himself thrown into prison. Finally he was put to death by the Sultan on a charge, preferred by the Jesuits, of inciting the Cossacks against the Turks. After Lucar's murder, one of his officials, Conopius, came to Oxford, was befriended by Laud, and became a Chaplain of Christ Church. Returning to the East during the troubles of the Commonwealth he was appointed Bishop of Smyrna.

During the whole of this period the Orthodox Church was passing through many vicissitudes. The position of the Greeks in the Turkish Empire was precarious in the extreme. The Patriarch's position was one of gilded slavery, ended in many cases by the bowstring of the executioner.

Protestants and Jesuits alike were making serious inroads on Orthodox territory. It was the time of the ascendancy of Poland, and the traditions of Poland were Catholic rather than Orthodox. Uniate Churches were founded in Russia and Ruthenia, and it seemed as though the Orthodox themselves were in danger of surrendering to the fascinations of Calvinism, so difficult for the modern mind to appreciate.

Returning to our own country, we must notice the attendance of four English divines at the Calvinistic Synod of Dort. They appear to have gone there with no commission except from the King, but they made a consistent stand for Catholic principles when a statement was put forward denying the rightfulness of Episcopal government, and one of their number made use of the occasion to utter a strong defence of the doctrine of Apostolic Succession.

The accession of Charles I. marks a vital period in the history of schism. We are not here concerned with the wisdom or otherwise of the King's policy, and that of the great Archbishop, William Laud. But we must trace the pitiful course of events with their countless reactions on the subsequent course of Church history.

But before we come to the miseries of the Civil War it is necessary to narrate the astonishing negotiations which took place between the English Court and the Holy See in the earlier and happier days of King Charles's reign. The facts may be found in Canon S. L. Ollard's book, *Reunion*, and in the same writer's article " Reunion " in the *Dictionary of English Church History*, and are briefly as follows.

In 1632 an English Benedictine (a Roman Catholic of course), with the curiously un-English religious style of Dom Leander a Sancto Martino,[1] was sent from Rome to treat with the English government on the matter of the form of the oath of allegiance, which was so unacceptable to the Roman authorities that Roman Catholics were forbidden to take it, and so were exposed to all manner of penalties. The Benedictine is reported to have stated that " Reunion seemeth possible enough, if the point were discussed in an assembly of moderate men, without contention or desire of victory, but out of a sincere desire of Christian union." What could be more admirable ?

[1] His name " in the world " had been John Jones.

In 1634 his place was taken by an Italian, Panzani, who was prepared to carry on the good work. Sir Francis Windebank, one of the Secretaries of State, is reported to have said to him : " If we had neither Jesuits nor Puritans, I am confident a union might easily be effected," and to have received the surprising answer that it was not improbable that His Holiness would sacrifice the interests of the Jesuits on the prospect of so fair an acquisition. Again, on another occasion, Windebank informed the Italian that all the moderate men in Church and State thirsted after a union. Bishop Montague of Chichester, one of the Caroline divines, further informed Panzani, according to the latter's own account, that both the Archbishops, as well as Juxon, Bishop of London, and others of the Episcopal order, were ready to fall in with the Church of Rome as to a supremacy purely spiritual. This is perhaps not altogether inconsistent with the story that Laud was offered a Cardinal's hat, but refused it on the ground that he did not desire reunion until Rome were other than she was.

In 1633 an English Franciscan, Francis a Santa Clara, Queen Henrietta Maria's chaplain, had anticipated Tract XC. by the statement that the Thirty-Nine Articles were " patient, but not ambitious " of a Catholic interpretation. The same learned friar gave his opinion in favour of the validity of Anglican Ordinations.

But the strength of Puritanism was greater than it seemed, and far greater than Charles or Laud realised. It had had some encouragement from Laud's predecessor, Abbot.[1] The clergy had not recovered from the laxity which characterised the Elizabethan period, and while Laud had his own plans for their reform, the Puritan party were convinced that

[1] But Abbot was not such a Puritan as Clarendon painted him. He did much for the seemly appointment of churches, and his last public action was to forbid the Puritan custom of administering Holy Communion to the laity in their pews. (The writer owes this information to the researches of the Master of the Hospital of the Holy Trinity, Abbot's foundation at Guildford).

nothing but the " holy discipline " would be of any use. Thus while Laud and the ecclesiastical party were looking to the authority of an anointed King to remedy the just discontents of the time, the Puritans were beginning to turn their eyes to Parliament as the power most likely to give them what they wanted. And every political blunder of the King and his advisers meant an accession to the strength of Puritanism.

Laud stood for all that was unpopular. He believed, and made no secret of it, that Christ died for all : therefore he was unpopular with the Calvinists. He believed in reverence, and was determined to enforce it : therefore he was unpopular with the negligent clergy. He used his archiepiscopal authority impartially against rich and poor : therefore he was hated by lax and ungodly men in high places.

He carried on and developed the Anglican theology of which Hooker had been the first great exponent. He was quite ready, when pressed, to enter into the Roman controversy, in which he made use of the characteristic Anglican appeal to the undivided Church, and to the witness of the Easterns against the Papal monopoly of doctrinal and disciplinary authority. But his great work was to restore the definite witness of the English Church to essential Catholicism, to bring back outward reverence and seemliness to religion, to assert afresh the truth of sacramental doctrine and to challenge the hardness of Calvinistic bigotry. He was the first great Anglo-Catholic. His services to learning and the faultiness of his statesmanship do not concern us here ; but it is worth pointing out that his much criticised severities were directed rather against civil offenders and moral reprobates than against those who failed to come up to his standards of ecclesiastical observance.[1]

The religious struggles of the time can only be understood when it is realised that we have to deal not only with Presby-

[1] See article on " Laud " by Dr. W. H. Hutton (now Dean of Winchester) in the *Dictionary of English Church History*.

terians who wished to transform the Church of England from within, but also with the new and growing force of Independency, which was now growing bold enough to organise itself sporadically in churches which made no pretence of being in any organic connexion with the ancient Church. Owning no authority but their own, and smarting under rigorous repression, they were being prepared to be the decisive factor in the coming struggle. Many were driven to emigrate, and it must be confessed that in exile they showed no more tolerance than they had themselves experienced. Others worshipped in secret or conformed outwardly and bided their time.

1637 was the first year of the storm which was for a time to overwhelm Church and Monarchy alike. It was in Scotland that it broke. Charles had already earned himself more unpopularity than he knew by his high-handed justice in taking control of all Church property which had been alienated in the recent troubles and handing it back to the Church ; and henceforward the majority of the nobles found themselves to be strongly Presbyterian. The King's French marriage and the reputation of Archbishop Laud brought his loyalty to the Reformation into deep suspicion. The climax was reached when he attempted to restore liturgical worship to the Scottish Church. A fine liturgy was drawn up and was to be used for the first time in S. Giles's, Edinburgh, in July of this year. The Puritan answer was to organise that famous brawl which, with its legendary accompaniments, has been handed down to tradition as a noble assertion of the rights of the laity.

The opposition of the nobles was the beginning of the ruin of the King. It took the traditional Scottish form of a " League." But *this* League was to be on a national scale. It consisted of three parts : the renewal of what was known as " The King's Confession " of 1581, a violent anti-Roman document, which King James had been induced to sign, in condemnation of the " erroneous and bloody " decrees of the Council of Trent : a statement that Charles's action was opposed to the Confession : an oath to defend the Crown and recover the purity and liberty of the Gospel. The nobles led the way, and willingly or unwillingly, intelligently or unintelligently, the Lowlanders affixed their signatures. This was the famous Solemn League and Covenant. The most notable abstentions were the Universities of S. Andrews and Aberdeen.

The Covenanters sent a demand to the King for the abolition of Episcopacy and the Prayer-Book, and the calling of a Parliament and a General Assembly. The Bishops were brought before the Assembly, which seems to have been pre-eminent even among ecclesiastical gatherings for turbulence and disorder : they were charged with every conceivable crime and vice, and " deposed " from their office.

Next year the Scots Parliament voted for the abolition of Episcopacy. The King dissolved it and called another, with the same result. The Privy Council then took steps to see that every Scot should, willy nilly, sign the Covenant. The Bishops had fled for their lives, and Scotland was Presbyterian again.

We pass over the civil history of the next few years. Ecclesiastical divergencies only come to the front of affairs again when in 1643 the English Parliament, desiring to enlist a Scottish army against the King, found that money alone would not secure their services. Parliament must sign the Covenant.

In the same year the Westminster Assembly met and drew up the famous Confession, which is still the nominal standard of Presbyterian doctrine. The Assembly itself was a mixed gathering, but Presbyterian influence predominated. Independency was beginning to make its voice heard, but its representatives were few in number, and had to be content with the abolition of the use of the Book of Common Prayer.

The direct result of the Westminster Assembly was the setting up of Presbyterianism in England. This was hardly the wish of Parliament as a whole, but it was the price of Scottish assistance, and it had to be paid. The Westminster Confession is almost pure Calvinism, but there is one very important point in which it differs from its model. Whereas Calvinism is a supra-national system, depending on a Church which consists of the elect, Presbyterianism makes a distinction, borrowed from Luther, between the Visible and the Invisible Church. The Visible Church is to be organised on a national basis, and it is the duty of the state to protect it and to suppress heresy. Outside it " there is no ordinary possibility of salvation." Yet membership in the Visible Church does not seem to be in any sense the instrument of salvation, which depends entirely on the inscrutable decree of God, by which every soul is either compelled to be saved or allowed to be lost. The Invisible Church is thus an inner select body, known to God alone, and chosen by God alone, *within* the Visible Church. It need hardly be said that the Conference contained the inevitable identification of the Holy Father with Antichrist.

In 1645 the Directory for Public Worship according to Presbyterian forms was put forth, and in the next year it began to be enforced and the Prayer-Book was proscribed. A religious union had once more been achieved between the three kingdoms of the realm, this time on the basis of Presbyterianism.

The establishment of Presbyterianism, however, was by no means complete in practice. There were still some, even on the parliamentary side, who wished for a modified Episcopacy, and Independency with its repudiation of the Presbyterian insistence on a national Church was daily growing in strength. Nor was the Genevan discipline likely to be popular with the laity.

The rise of Cromwell was the downfall of exclusive Presbyterianism in England. His " New Model " army swept all before it, and brought into power the men whose professed desire was freedom for all Christians except the Church, and the deposition of the King and abolition of the monarchy. It must be remembered that those who signed the Covenant had taken an oath to defend the Crown and recover the purity and liberty of the Gospel. Charles therefore had among his opponents a party who were nominally acting only for his good, and when in desperation he took the step of surrendering to the Scottish army it was by no means certain what would be the result of his action. In fact, the army leaders found themselves committed to an oath the two parts of which seemed inconsistent. Charles declined to do anything for " the purity and liberty of the Gospel," in other words he refused to sign the Covenant. Without doing this he could not be allowed a refuge in Scotland, whither the Scottish army was now anxious to return. They therefore set down the King at Newcastle, and washed their hands of the matter. They had done their part and had every reason to be satisfied with it.

The King had one more opportunity to save himself. Had he thrown in his lot with the Presbyterian faction, as against the Independents, the prestige of the Crown might still have won the day. The Scots army were always ready to assist Presbyterians, for a price, and the combination would be too strong even for the generalship of Cromwell. But the conditions were too hard. " There are three things," he said, " I will never give up : the Church, my Crown, my friends." This is Charles at his best, and gives him at least a technical right to the title of the Royal Martyr. The shifts to which he was reduced in the subsequent negotiations between the two parties of his enemies do not concern us here ; but the death of the King was the triumph of Cromwell, and the end of Presbyterian ascendancy. The new " Church " was to consist of Independents, Baptists and Presbyterians with equal rights, and gradually there ensued the complete domination of Independency. From 1644 onwards the process of ejecting the clergy continued : slowly and quietly at first, but with more severity as time

went on. In 1653 Toleration was definitely withheld from
" Popery, Prelacy, and such as hold forth licentiousness,"
while about the same time Cromwell contrived to send
Independent and other ministers to Wales, and gives thereby
a date for the beginning of Welsh nonconformity.[1]

The third class to whom toleration was denied call for
some comment. It is evidence that the antinomian poison
with which Luther had infected the wells of Protestantism
was having its result. Certainly both Presbyterians and
Independents were, as far as personal uprightness goes,
exemplary. They were Calvinists, and Calvinism with all
its faults is a great religion. Without Calvinism Protestantism decays. The Baptists were also for the most part
Calvinistic in England, but " Anabaptism " is associated
with " licentiousness " in the Preface prefixed to the Prayer-
Book in 1662, and it is possible that this may mean more
than the mere neglect of Baptism, which is the point there
insisted on. Anabaptists in earlier days in Germany had
certainly been guilty of the wildest excesses. In addition to
the teaching of almost every possible theological error they
are credited with practising communism in matrimony as
well as in property, and with teaching that " no man's laws
should be obeyed." It is, perhaps, most likely that such
antinomianism as was to be found under the dictatorship of
Cromwell made its appearance in some of the smaller
Baptist sects.

But it is probable that the charge of " licentiousness " was
really aimed against the " Quakers " of all people, and the rise of
this remarkable body calls for some remark. They represent
the extreme and consistent expression of all that is anti-
Catholic and anti-national in religion, the very climax of

---

[1] At first Cromwell found it difficult to supply preachers to take the
place of the ejected clergy. By 1651 fifty-one parishes had been deprived
of their incumbents, and only twenty ministers had been found to occupy
their benefices. But we have evidence that before the Restoration nearly
every parish in the Diocese of S. Asaph had its Puritan Minister. See
Bp. A. G. Edwards, *Landmarks in the History of the Welsh Church.*

sectarianism ; but the purity of their aims, their fortitude and meekness under the cruellest of persecution, their lofty spiritual tone, the truth which underlay so much of their essential Protestantism, make it impossible for any man who can recognise the Spirit of God to write of them with anything but appreciation and reverence. One might almost say that Quakerism represents the essential truth of Protestantism. This, or something very like it, was what the earlier Protestants were groping after, and in the main the Quakers are gloriously right *in what they affirm*. Here we have in essence that critical spirit, an infusion of which is the very thing most needed to keep Catholicism true to the Holy Ghost. For the critical spirit is not, or need not be, a spirit of negation. Faced with corruption it will of necessity be driven to deny, but its function is equally to appraise. At its best Quakerism is the quintessence of that mysticism which all along has represented the best thing in the Protestant movement. Held in isolation it never has been, never can be, and has hardly tried to be, a world-religion [1] ; but the true world-religion knows that a touch of it is the very thing it needs if it is not to harden into an institution and a creed ; and the Catholic mystical Saint is precisely the Catholic who has a dash of the Quaker in his composition.

George Fox, the founder of the Quakers, first became prominent in the time of the Great Rebellion, and he and his followers were the victims of relentless persecution under the spiritual tyranny of the Protectorate and the unspiritual Anglican domination of the Restoration. They were accused of blasphemy, of infidelity, even of Popery. They suffered in an extreme form the characteristic fate of those who " go too far " for their own side. With hearty good will Presbyterian and Independent alike threw them to the

---

[1] " George Fox did not reform the Church nor preach a doctrine which *could* be of world-wide acceptance, but what he did was to found a new Protestant and spiritual quasi-monastic community which has been on the whole of great benefit to the Church and to the world." George Hodgkin (himself a Quaker).

wolves : while to Restoration Anglicans Quaker principles were abhorrent because they seemed to be the very antithesis of that type of Churchmanship which had gained an artificial prominence in that reactionary period. To refuse to take an oath of allegiance to the King, to have scruples about the use of any liturgy, to insist on a separate and peculiar worship, these were to deny the first principles of the doctrine of triumphant Anglicanism.

But it must always be remembered that George Fox's protest was not in the first instance against the Catholic Church, but against an unspiritual Protestantism. The enemy was the New Scholasticism, in which the text of Scripture had taken the place of the traditional doctrine, and all religion was held to be contained in the " Notions," as Fox called them, of Justification by faith only, and absolute Predestinarianism. To Fox and his followers the official hierarchy, Presbyterian and Independent as it was, was an interference with the believer's access to Christ ; the identification of the Bible with the Word of God was a worship of the letter as against the spirit ; and the use of the Sacraments was the sheerest formalism.

Yet in some ways Fox's protest was that of the Catholic mind. If there is one thing which more than another distinguishes the ultimate basis of the Catholic idea (at any rate in the mind of a theologian) from that of the older Protestant orthodoxy, it is the doctrine of grace.[1] To the Catholic grace is something which makes a difference to the character of the soul which receives it ; to the Protestant it merely signifies the disposition of God towards that soul. To the Catholic every actual grace is God's offered help ; while habitual grace is the actual permanent indwelling of Christ Himself in the soul, whereby the whole personality is gradually changed and sanctified. The Catholic idea of grace is a consequence of Christology. But to the Protestant, more especially to the Lutheran, but also to the Calvinist,

[1] See Möhler, *Symbolism, passim.*

grace is a soteriological expression, having to do with for-
giveness rather than amendment, with justification rather
than union with God.

Fox based his whole position on a mystical foundation ;
but the mystical experience conceived as necessary was not,
as with Luther, conversion, but the abiding inner Light of
Christ by the Holy Spirit. To enable this Light to shine,
Atonement and Redemption must be an inward work, not
an external transaction. Sin must be *removed*, really, not
only in a forensic sense. A seed of life must be implanted,
more powerful than the seed of death. This is Catholic
mysticism.

But, as every Catholic knows, there are pitfalls for the
mystic, and the very ingenuous mysticism of the Quakers
did not escape them. Mystics are commonly tempted to
undervalue the Sacraments, and the nearer Sacraments are
thought to approximate to mere ceremonies, the less important will they appear to be to men to whom the spiritual
is everything. The *tendency* of Protestantism has always
been to get rid of the idea that God really does something to
us by means of the Sacraments ; but unless this is a true
idea it is difficult to blame the Quakers too seriously for
doubting whether Christ could really have instituted them
at all. It would indeed be surprising to find a mere " form
and ceremony " among " the first principles of the doctrine
of Christ."

So the Quakers declined the Sacraments, and went very
near to abolishing the Ministry. Their foundation principle
was to trust in the Inner Light, and their foundation doctrine
that this Light was available for all. Against the exaggerated
Protestant belief in words as the only vehicle of spiritual
power they set the value of silent waiting upon God till He
should be pleased to give a revelation. Against all static
conceptions of Christianity they maintained the doctrine of
the continuous guiding light. The emphasis was shifted
from theology to experience. It was all perhaps very crude,

but the childlike simplicity of the Society of Friends is an element in the history of Christianity which we could ill afford to lose. Their honesty and philanthropy, their hatred of slavery and of war, their candour and consistency, make us love them, even if in our sophisticated world we are acutely conscious that there are many other truths beside those which they grasp so firmly.

Meanwhile some of the " prelatical " clergy had been so fortunate as to escape to the Continent. The question inevitably arose as to their relation to the Reformed Churches there, and it appears that for the most part they joined in their worship and that some at any rate communicated with them. So deeply had anti-Romanism penetrated into the minds of English churchmen that at the very moment when they were suffering for Episcopacy they seem to have been Protestants (*i.e.* non-Papalists) first and Episcopalians afterwards. Some did decline to communicate with the foreign Protestants, but the general view seems to have been that the Protestants were the Reformed Church abroad, and must be recognised as such. Even Cosin, though himself using the English Prayer-Book throughout his residence in Paris, was apparently ready to acknowledge the " Reformed " as brethren, who through no fault of their own were deprived of Episcopacy. The logical corollary of this view would have been for the refugee English Bishops to offer to consecrate Bishops for the Calvinists. The offer would, of course, have been refused, but we hear of no such suggestion.

Meanwhile religious chaos reigned in England. Unitarianism and every kind of strange belief and practice were gaining ground, and the Presbyterian party, now thoroughly alarmed, began to work for the restoration of the monarchy.

XI

THE RESTORATION PERIOD

THE most striking development in the philosophy of Anglicanism during the period of the Restoration is undoubtedly the new stress which was laid on the doctrine of the Divine Right of Kings and the duty of passive obedience on the part of their subjects, in religion as in all other matters. It was the natural reaction against that regicide which had so deeply seared the conscience of the nation. Historically it was not a Catholic conception at all. It was rooted in Luther's principle of the " godly prince," and had been developed by the German Swiss Erastus in the preceding century. He had maintained that the clergy were ministers of the state, which was bound to provide sound religion as well as other necessaries of a good life. To this must be added the view of the English free-thinking philosopher, Hobbes, who had developed the idea that the sovereign was the supreme pastor, who had a right to compel the consciences of his subjects in externals.

The nation was therefore prepared to make amends for the judicial murder of the Martyr King by making the royalist religion a matter of compulsion. In this direction Parliament went far beyond the wishes of either the King himself or even the Bishops. The King had promised complete liberty to all, and there is no reason to doubt that he sincerely wished for it. It is true that his special tolerance was directed to Roman Catholics, whose religion had so much commended itself to him during his " travels," but the easy-going monarch was not of the stuff which goes to make a persecutor. So long as no one interfered with his pleasures he had no wish to interfere with theirs. Indeed, he seems to have thought that some accommodation could be come to between the Church and the Presbyterians. No doubt the Presbyterians thought so too, and were bitterly disappointed at the unbending attitude of Bishops and Parliament alike.

The nation was at cross purposes. The King was frankly delighted at the prospect of enjoying his own again, and desired nothing so much as to be let alone. The Bishops were determined to restore the Church to its former position, and were in no mood to make concessions. The Parliament wanted revenge. The Presbyterians, with their strong belief in the national establishment of religion, were looking for some compromise which should make it possible for Puritans to continue in the Church of England. Independents, Baptists and Quakers thought that all was lost, and steeled themselves for opposition and its consequences. The multitude of the irreligious simply let themselves go.

It is difficult to blame the Bishops for their course of action. The requests for the alteration of the Prayer-Book preferred by the Puritans at the Savoy Conference were for the most part captious, and few indeed would recommend themselves to modern ideas. They were partly concerned with the ancient grievances about the Sign of the Cross in Baptism, the ring in marriage, the use of the surplice : partly with a wish for increased power on the part of the minister to repel unworthy communicants : partly with desire for such liberty in the conduct of service as would have made every minister a law to himself. But the point which more than any other aroused the resentment of the Puritans was the rubric asserting the undoubted salvation of baptised children. This was sheer anti-Calvinism, and as such intolerable. Certainly the Bishops might have been more conciliatory, and probably they did take too prelatical a view of their office. Some of Baxter's requests at the Conference remind us of the modern demand for a " constitutional " Episcopacy and synodical government. But to the Royalist Bishops any idea of the rights of an inferior as against his superior smacked of the Rebellion and the Presbyterian discipline : their idea of Episcopacy was government by Bishops in accordance with the will of the King : their position was that they knew of nothing wrong with the Prayer-Book, but were willing to listen to any objections that might be made.

The result of the Savoy Conference was to make it clear that there was no room for the Puritans within the Church. It may be thought that some concessions might have been made with advantage and generosity ; but it is very doubtful if the Puritans would have accepted anything less than the destruction of the liturgical form of the Prayer-Book, and there does not seem any reason why the Bishops should have assented to that. The inevitable consequence followed. Incumbents of parishes had to accept the Prayer-Book, and consent to be ordained by a bishop, if they were not already so ordained, or else vacate their cures.

It is difficult to see what else could have been done. The Church had decided not to abandon Episcopacy and the Liturgy ; those who wished them to be abandoned had failed to win their case, and, like many others, had to suffer for their convictions. That they were willing so to suffer is honourable to them ; but our sympathy cannot but be modified by the consideration that many of them had been quite recently intruded into benefices which were already occupied by their lawful owners.

But little excuse can be offered for the vindictive persecution to which innocent and godly Nonconformists were subjected. The only thing to be said is that the idea of toleration was almost unknown. The Puritans themselves were horrified at the wording of the King's first Declaration of Indulgence. It actually seemed to include Roman

Catholics : surely the King could not be serious ! Nor was
the persecution of Nonconformists any more severe than that
to which Episcopalians had been subjected during the latter
years of the Commonwealth. Baxter's attempts at the
Savoy Conference were not directed towards toleration,
which was the very opposite of a Puritan principle, but
towards comprehension, a very different matter.   It was only
when this attempt had failed that Baxter, who, though it is
doubtful whether he was himself a Presbyterian,[1] represented the Presbyterian interest at the Conference, began to
appeal for toleration.   He failed to get it, but the mere appeal
marked the beginning of the end of English Presbyterianism.
It seems impossible for the Calvinistic polity to flourish in
a minority.   The appeal for liberty to worship according to
conscience, even if in isolation, is the watchword of the
Independents, the Baptists, the Quakers, and these took to
the suffering of persecution as a natural fate.   " When I am
weak, then am I strong " is a maxim which corresponds with
their whole outlook on life.   But not so with the Presbyterians.   The subsequent history of the sect in England has
been the story of a gradual lapse into Unitarianism.   What
is called the English Presbyterian Church to-day is trans-
planted from Scotland, and possibly depends for its vitality
on the immense vigour of the Presbyterian Churches there.

Baxter seceded from the Church in 1662, before he was
actually obliged to do so, but continued his efforts to induce
the authorities not to press for Episcopal Ordination and the
use of the Prayer-Book.   Tillotson and others were working
in the same direction, but the feeling of the nation was
against them, and the long series of persecuting Acts were
passed through Parliament with little opposition, and have
left behind them a heritage of bitterness which even now
has hardly passed away.   In 1664 the Conventicle Act for-

---

[1] He was ordained to the Diaconate by the Bishop of Worcester in
1638 ; but it seems impossible to discover whether he was ever made a
priest.

bade meetings for worship which included more than four persons not one family. This was followed in 1665 by the Five Mile Act. An oath was offered to all Nonconformist ministers pledging them to attempt no alteration of the established forms of government in Church and State : those who refused it were forbidden to stay within five miles of any corporate town, or of the parish in which they had exercised their ministry. The heroic devotion of many of the ministers during the Plague of London availed them nothing, and the persecution proceeded relentlessly.

In 1672 the King made another attempt to secure toleration by the issue of a Declaration of Indulgence, but all to no purpose : Parliament suspected, not without good reason, that Charles's real sympathies were with the Papists, and indulgence to them was not to be thought of. Nor were the Commons any longer in a mood to sanction the regal claim to dispense with the observance of the law. They retorted in the following year with the most iniquitous and sacrilegious of all devices for securing the *status quo*. By the Test Act it was provided that no one should in future be admitted to any public office until he had received the Holy Sacrament according to the Anglican rite.

In Scotland there is the same story to tell. It would be a great mistake to suppose that that country was uniformly Presbyterian in sympathy. Indeed the opposite seems to have been the case. It was only in the South-West that covenanting principles were predominant. But the reinstatement of Episcopacy was brutally carried through, and the seeds of religious hatred were sown and watered only too effectually. But, as before, no attempt was made to insist on the Ordination of those who had not already received Holy Orders from a Bishop. Nor, indeed, was liturgical worship imposed. All that was pressed for was Episcopal government, Episcopal institution to the cure of souls, and the recognition of the rights of patrons. Four Bishops were consecrated, and on this occasion the irregularity of consecration *per saltum* was not committed. But it was all a miserable business, and as unlike normal Catholic Episcopacy as anything that could be imagined. The opposition to this tyrannical and Erastian method of enforcing government by Bishops culminated in the murder of Archbishop Sharpe in 1680.

The course of Irish history during the period of the Rebellion and the Restoration is of great importance as having left its permanent traces on the alignment of religious parties in that country down to the present day.

The combination of the firmness and consistency of Strafford with the comparatively tortuous, though excusable, policy of Charles I., had prepared all the materials for an explosion. Strafford's religious policy had been simple : the strengthening of Anglicanism, the suppression of Presbyterianism within the Church, and the drawing of the teeth of Romanism. On the news of his execution all parties were seized with panic. Self-interest drew the Romanists to the side of the King. He was their only hope of toleration. Presbyterianism made the Ulstermen natural members of the Parliamentary party. National antipathy decided that the long naturalised Anglo-Irish gentry should be against the new and prosperous settlers from Scotland. The country was in a blaze, and there was a massacre of Ulstermen. Scottish soldiers came to the rescue, and in gratitude all Ulster flocked to sign the Covenant. Cromwell's revenge was delayed, but when it came it was of unexampled ferocity. The royalist army was either butchered or sent into slavery. The native Irish were despatched " to Hell or Connaught," and it is said that a third of them died. All the land worth having in the South of Ireland was divided up between Cromwell's soldiers or sold to speculators. The howling of wolves was heard in the suburbs of Dublin.

But the North had never been touched by the regicide fever. The Covenant included an oath to protect the Crown, and to Presbyterian Ulster January 30th, 1649, was the Accession Day of Charles II. No part of the three kingdoms was more zealous for the Restoration. But they had given no trouble to the Cromwellian government, who in turn had had no leisure to take any steps against them. The only Republicans in Ireland therefore at the Restoration were Cromwell's soldiers, and a just policy of restoration of land to its proper owners might have brought peace to the troubled country. Such a course, however, seemed too difficult and dangerous, and little was done.

For a time there was friction between Episcopalians and Presbyterians. Episcopal Ordination was insisted on as it had been in England. It seems, however, that the Irish Bishops were content to give *conditional* Ordination to those who had received Presbyterian Orders. This was a compromise between the definite Ordination which English Presbyterian ministers were required to submit to as a condition of holding a benefice, and the Scottish plan by which the ministerial position of those in Presbyterian Orders was fully acknowledged, in spite of the fact that Episcopal government had been introduced. Many of the Irish ministers, however, were unwilling to submit even to this modified admission of the possible necessity of Episcopal Ordination, were ejected from their benefices, and in many cases went to swell the number of those who sought to set up the Church of their ideals in the New World.

As time went on, however, the course of events divided the sympathies of the country between Papalists and anti-Papalists, and the divisions between Anglican and Presbyterian became less bitter.

There was too much truth in the suspicion that the King was trying to foment a Romanist rising, and the atmosphere of plots and rumours of plots in which men lived made the idea of tolerance impossible. All the best of the land and all commercial undertakings were in Protestant hands, and while Protestants lived in daily dread of a massacre Romanists

found that they had been reduced to penury. The line
between the Haves and the Have-nots coincided with that
between the nervous and the desperate, and also with that
between the haters and the adherents of the Pope. The
miseries of Ireland and her disastrous religious differences
were attaining their zenith as the time of the Revolution
drew near.

During the reign of Charles II. there was a good deal of
discussion as to the possibility of Reunion with Rome. It
must be remembered that the Roman Church was now at
one of the brightest of her periods. The reforms of the
Counter-Reformation had done their work, and Roman
Catholicism was beginning to wear that air of learned and
devout efficiency which we associate with it to-day, without
the more recent developments which are now the chief hind-
rances to Reunion. An enlightened Pope, opposed alike to
coups de main and to persecution, sat on the Apostolic throne.

The interest of the terms which were actually discussed
lies in the light they throw on the attitude of the Papacy of
that day towards national Churches in general and the Church
of England in particular. Naturally the basis of Reunion
was to be the decrees of the Council of Trent. If these were
once accepted the only further difficulty was the question
of Anglican Orders. The Pope, it seems, was not willing
to accept Sancta Clara's views of their validity.[1] But he
was prepared to sanction the re-consecration of all the
existing Bishops, and to give the King the right of nominating
in future. The Archbishop of Canterbury was to enjoy a
patriarchal position : the national peculiarities of the English
Church were to be recognised : the spoils of the Reformation
were not to be disgorged : Communion in both kinds was
to be allowed, if desired : Mass must be said in Latin, but
the addition of English hymns was permissible : married
clergy were not to be required to put away their wives,
though in future celibacy must be observed : there was to

[1] See p. 109.

be no persecution of Protestants. It will be seen that this was a scheme for the formation of a Uniate Church, in accordance with the policy which was at the moment proving so successful in the East. The Roman attitude was that where there was unity of faith, diversity of custom could be tolerated : and although in the West the Roman Court itself has never [1] done more than tolerate such diversity, there still existed in many places in the seventeenth century strong nationalist feelings and customs in conjunction with unhesitating loyalty to the Apostolic see.

On this side of the Channel, however, it was all a matter of backstair negotiation. The Bishops had no cognisance of it. It is doubtful if even the King took part in it at first, though he was, of course, deeply implicated later on, after he had, in the secret Treaty of Dover in 1670, agreed to declare himself a Roman Catholic. The anti-Roman feeling of the English Church and nation as a whole was too strong to bring the matter within the range of practical politics, and most of the statements in favour of it seem to emanate from court circles ; but it is said that Archbishop Sheldon actually assented to the opinion expressed by one of the Royal chaplains, that the differences between the separated Churches were easily to be reconciled, and that there was no dispute about fundamental points of faith.[2]

An important event in connection with the possibility of Reunion with the Orthodox East occurred in 1672. In that year the Council of Jerusalem met under the presidency of the great Orthodox theologian, Dositheos, and promulgated a statement of the faith which ranks in Orthodox eyes only second to the Oecumenical Councils themselves. The Council accepted and promulgated two important documents, which are henceforth to be accepted substantially as the official doctrine of the Orthodox Church, the Catechism

[1] Since the ninth century.

[2] S. Carisbrook, *The Life of the Lady Warner*. Quoted by Canon Ollard in *Reunion*, p. 31. Of course this *may* be only a bit of Court gossip.

of Peter Mogila, and the Confession of Dositheos himself.
It is a curious fact that, although the object of these documents was, in part, to produce a counter-statement to the
definitions of the Council of Trent, both of them exhibit
strong traces of the influence of Western scholastic theology.
In spite of the proselytising activities of the Jesuits it is
evident that the Easterns still looked on Latin theology with
very great respect.   In order to exclude Calvinism they use
language which appears to correspond exactly with the
official Roman definitions of Transubstantiation.   But it is
important to notice that when the decrees of the Council of
Jerusalem were translated into Russian for acceptance by
the Russian Church in the nineteenth century, alterations
were made in the text which very considerably changed its
meaning.   The Russians belonged to a different civilisation
from that of the Mediterranean ; and, moreover, the passing
of two centuries had stiffened the opposition between the
two branches of the Church.   The Russian Church then
has not committed itself to the " substance and accident "
explanation of the Real Presence, nor to those Scriptures
which we in England call the " Apocrypha," nor to any
subtle distinction between the " Dulia " paid to the Saints
and the " Hyperdulia " due to the Holy Virgin, nor to the
idea of penalty as attaching to the suffering of the souls of
the faithful in the next world.   The importance of all this
in connection with Reunion is not that these doctrines are
necessarily to be refused, but that they will not be demanded
by the Easterns as conditions of Reunion.   There remain,
as we shall see, great difficulties in the way of full dogmatic
Reunion between ourselves and the East, for there are large
sections of the English Church which would be by no means
ready to accept all that the Easterns would feel it necessary to
demand ; but the points here mentioned need not divide us,
for they are no part of the essential doctrine of the Eastern
Church.[1]

See Pullan, *Bampton Lectures*, p. 306.

XII

THE DAWN OF TOLERATION

THERE can have been few periods or countries in which a greater revulsion of feeling took place than that which showed itself in England between 1660 and 1689. Charles II.'s natural indolence and shrewdness kept him safe on his throne in spite of the disgust caused by his known foreign alliances and his suspected change of faith. For the last twelve years of his reign he left Romanists and Nonconformists alike to their fate.

But the accession of his brother brought matters to a climax in a surprisingly short space of time. It is an irony of fate that the exploit which cost him his throne and changed the whole character of religious and political life for many generations was an act of toleration. He claimed by virtue of the royal prerogative to override the law and grant toleration to all men to worship according to their conscience. Yet the reception which his action received is easy to understand, and perhaps to justify. His French ally had just embarked on a policy of persecution, and, to men who knew James and the past history of the methods by which Romanism had been propagated, it was natural enough to fear that there was a plot to set up the Roman Terror once more. Dreadful things had happened already in Ireland, and there was good reason to believe that worse was to follow. So James's plan, which was to make Anglicanism hoist itself with its own petard of Passive Obedience, overreached itself, and the refusal of the Seven Bishops to read the Declaration of Indulgence or cause it to be read was not only the signal for an extraordinary outburst of affection for the Church of England, but also the immediate precursor of the King's own flight.

The succession of William of Orange brought no peace to the Church. The bishops who had refused to read the late King's Declaration were the fine flower of the Anglican revival, and with much searching of heart and after long debate had come to the conclusion that there were limits to what could be required of a churchman under the constraint of Passive Obedience. But Passive Obedience and the Divine Right of Kings were doctrines interwoven with the whole Stuart conception of churchmanship. The last thing they had thought of was the possibility of driving out the King. It was but a generation since the Church had herself been driven into the wilderness on this identical issue. The very men therefore who had taken the lead in resistance to the royal will found themselves in the position of being unable in conscience to take an oath of allegiance to his *de facto* successor. So strong was their conviction that the oath must be resisted that conscience forbade them even to resign their sees. Thus it was possible to assert that their successors were uncanonical, and that by holding communion with them the rest of the Church of England had fallen into schism, they themselves and those who held with them alone constituting the legitimate Church of the country. On the death of Sancroft they actually consecrated new Bishops to continue the succession in the minute body to which, in their view, the Church of England had now dwindled. It is impossible not to sympathise with their scruples, and equally impossible not to regret that the Church of England should have lost at one blow her noblest, ablest and most pious sons.

A Dutch Calvinist was now on the throne, and it might seem as though Puritanism were likely to be once more in the ascendant. But though the High Church party was out in the cold, the Low Church, or Latitudinarian, party was no better disposed to the Puritans. For the Low Church-man of the seventeenth century was as far as possible removed from the Evangelical of the present day. He hated fanati-cism, enthusiasm and mysticism quite as much as he disliked dogmatic religion and Tory politics ; his tendency was to reduce Christianity to an ethical theory. The last thing he desired was to have an army of hot Gospel preachers let loose upon the Church. William's first scheme of amending the constitution of the Church in such a way that the Puritans, and particularly the Presbyterians, could find a home in a national religious body had to be dropped in a hurry. Parlia-ment referred it to Convocation, and the Lower House without hesitation threw it out. It is interesting to observe that they refused to accept the phrase " the Protestant religion in general," " lest it should own the Presbyterian Churches of the Continent."

England as a whole accepted its new master. Her Celtic neighbours, touched by emotional loyalties unknown to a harder race, looked coldly on the foreigner. Irish Roman Catholics, Scottish Highlanders and many Lowlanders too, and, though less conspicuously, the Welsh, were Jacobite. The Irish, as the most dangerous, were attacked at once. Scotland was struck at through the Church. Episcopalian-ism was put down and Presbyterianism established. The active persecution of Episcopalians as such did not begin until the time of the Jacobite risings ; but with no considera-tion for the wishes of the people the miserable process of ejecting one minister to make room for another began all over again. In Wales no active measures were taken. But the authorities continued the bad custom of appointing no Bishops who could speak Welsh, and a hundred and forty more years of that treatment was enough to kill all power that the Church might have had for good or evil in the Principality.[1]

---

[1] Since the twelfth century the custom had existed of treating the Welsh sees as mere pieces of preferment. But Welsh names are fairly

Still, until the time of the Methodist revival the bulk of the Welsh remained faithful to the ancient Church.

The one gain to religion that can be assigned to this depressing period is the recognition of the necessity of a certain measure of toleration. Clearly the King's religion must be permitted, so long only as it was not the hated Popery. An Act was therefore passed permitting the exercise of any religion except Roman Catholicism, Judaism and Unitarianism. But the civil disabilities of Nonconformists continued, unless indeed their consciences permitted them to make use of the device of " occasional conformity."

The Non-juring schism—a schism *within* not *from* the Church—was instrumental in reviving interest in plans for intercourse, or even Reunion, with the Eastern Church. In 1716 a bishop of the Scottish Church proposed to the Non-jurors that they attempt a union with the Easterns. Arsenius, Archbishop of the Thebaid, was then in England on a begging mission, and offered to convey their proposals to Peter the Great, who had assumed a more than imperial position over the Russian Church, having suppressed the Patriarchate and taken personal control of the Holy Synod. Peter was interested in the suggestion and submitted the matter to the Patriarch of Alexandria, who in turn consulted the other Eastern Patriarchates. The suggestions of the Non-jurors exhibit a certain simplicity, and a complete failure to appreciate the unbending conservatism of Oriental Christianity.[1] Their scruples were as follows :

1. They could not follow the Easterns in giving equal authority to Oecumenical canons and to Scripture. (The Easterns would probably reply that they honoured these canons with the general tradition of the Fathers *next to* holy Scripture.)

frequent in the registers until the end of the seventeenth century, and the chief honour for the revival of the Welsh tongue is due to a sixteenth century bishop, William Morgan, of Llandaff and (afterwards) of S. Asaph.

[1] See Ollard, *Reunion*, p. 60.

2. They feared too much honour being paid to the Blessed Virgin.

3. They could not employ the invocation of Saints or Angels.

4. While adoring our Lord as truly present in the Eucharist they could not adore the sacred symbols. (Of course neither the Easterns nor anyone else have ever thought of doing this.)

5. They found a difficulty in the Eastern use of Icons.

Still they approached the matter very hopefully, and were prepared to enter into negotiations for the building of a church in London for the Orthodox, and proposed that the Church of England service should be celebrated there sometimes, while in return the Easterns might have the occasional use of S. Paul's. But the strangest of their suggestions was for a re-arrangement of the Patriarchal sees, transferring the primacy from Constantinople to Jerusalem. Who had put this into their heads ? It almost seems as though they had heard complaints of the yoke which the Constantinopolitan Greeks—the " Phanariotes "—were beginning to lay upon the Orthodox throughout the Turkish Empire, and made this ingenuous suggestion for their relief. Had Arsenius given them a hint ? We have seen that all Christians within the Turkish Empire were officially " Romans," *i.e.* members of the extinct Eastern Roman Empire, and as such were under the authority of the Oecumenical Patriarch. Under the influence of nationalist Greek feeling attempts were being made throughout the seventeenth century and afterwards to Hellenise all the Eastern Church, with the exception of Russia and parts of Hungary, which were never included in the Sultan's temporal, or the Patriarch's spiritual, dominion. Arabs and Slavs alike suffered in this way, and the Sultan found it expedient to encourage the Phanariote policy. Wherever possible a Patriarchate was suppressed, as happened in Serbia and Bulgaria, and the higher places in the Church handed over to Greeks from Constantinople.

But, of course, a rearrangement of the Patriarchates was not to be thought of. The primacy of Constantinople dated from the second Oecumenical Council, and moreover the Sultan would not have allowed it even if the Church had been willing. The four Patriarchs entered willingly into a polite and protracted correspondence with the Non-jurors, but conceded nothing whatever. Proposals were also made for a meeting between the Non-jurors and the Russian Synod, but the death of the Tsar put an end to the arrangement.

At this point Lambeth intervened. Archbishop Wake, better known for his negotiations with the French Church, which we shall come to immediately, discovered what was going on. Indeed it is quite possible that the Patriarchs had only just become aware that it was not the *de facto* Church of England with which they were negotiating, and they may have written to the Archbishop to ask for an elucidation of the matter. In any case his action consisted of a single dignified letter in which he informed the Patriarch of Jerusalem that the Non-jurors were schismatics, and had no right to the titles they assumed. He claimed that the true Church of England was already in union with that of the East in spirit and effect, and professed the same faith in every fundamental article. Distance prevented anything further. The Patriarchs, probably somewhat puzzled, allowed the correspondence to lapse.

More important was Wake's correspondence with the Gallican ecclesiastics. It might have been supposed, in view of the attitude taken by almost all Englishmen to the possibility of Romanism being tolerated in England, that any sort of negotiation with Roman Catholics was out of the question for an Archbishop of Canterbury. But so far from that being the case we have evidence from the year 1699 that it could be asserted even at that date that the true difference between the High and Low Church parties was that the former " were for finding means of reconciliation with Rome and bringing the Pope to terms ; while the other party were for accommodating matters and forming a union between the English Church and foreign Protestant Churchmen." [1] Whether this statement would have been accepted by a High Churchman is another matter ; but it is sufficiently surprising that it should have been possible even to make it. It is true that there was very little love for Rome among the French clergy who were in touch with the Archbishop, but at least there was nothing in their views which suggested Protestantism in the remotest degree. Moreover Wake was emphatically a " Central Churchman." In earlier life he had been associated with the court and with diplomacy, and had been commonly reckoned rather " Low," or, as we should now say, " Broad Church." After his elevation to the throne of Canterbury the necessities of his office seemed to bring him insensibly round to the position of a defender of the faith and a supporter of Church authority. It is worthy of note that such a man should have welcomed a *rapprochement*, but it is only one of many indications that there is no truth in the popular view that the Catholic idea was dead in the Church of England until the revival of the nineteenth century.

The Archbishop's French correspondents were " Gallicans." That is to say they represented a definite attempt to combine a certain tincture of nationalism with the full acceptance of the Catholic faith. In other words reaction against the growing force of Ultramontanism had brought them to very much the same position as reaction against an over-emphasised nationalism has brought the Anglo-Catholics of the present day. The principles of Gallicanism were very moderately expressed by the great Bossuet in the famous " Four Propositions " of 1682.

They were as follows :

I. In secular matters the Pope and the hierarchy have no authority.

II. The Papal power is subject to a General Council.

[1] Quoted by Canon Ollard in *A Dictionary of English Church History*.

III. This power is also limited by the canons of the Church, and Gallican usages should not be condemned.

IV. Papal decrees are *only* irreformable *by consent of the Church*.

A Gallican theological treatise had been condemned in 1713, by the bull *Unigenitus*, and the Gallican party in the French Church, including as many as thirty Bishops, brought matters to a crisis by appealing to a Council. The Doctors of the Sorbonne, looking round for support, bethought them of the Church of England, which had revolted against the Papacy without apparently having thrown off all semblance of Catholicism as foreign Protestants had done. The English chaplain in Paris was sounded and wrote to his own Archbishop. Wake's reply was so favourable that Du Pin, the leading Gallican theologian, wrote to him, with the concurrence of Cardinal de Noailles, the Archbishop of Paris, proposing a Reunion between the Church of France and that of England. Apparently the Gallicans were prepared, if necessary, for a complete breach with Rome.

The correspondence continued for two years, when it was brought to an end by the intervention of the French government and the death of Du Pin. Notable statements were made in the course of it. Du Pin professed himself satisfied of the validity of Anglican Ordinations, and concluded that the Thirty-Nine Articles were capable of satisfactory explanation. Wake on the other hand stated that the difficulty of accepting Transubstantiation was not insuperable. Regarding the position of the Pope as " first among bishops," he wrote, " The honour which you give to the Roman Pontiff differs so little, I deem, from that which our sounder theologians readily give him, that on this point, I think, it will not be difficult, on either side, either to agree altogether in the same opinion, or mutually to bear with a dissent of no moment."

Finally he summed up the correspondence in these remarkable words : " In dogmas, as you have candidly proposed them, we do not much differ : in Church government, less : in fundamentals, whether regarding doctrine or discipline, hardly at all."

In the end, however, Du Pin was less compliant, and seemed to demand such changes in the Church of England as to put the Archbishop on his dignity. He very properly declined to negotiate about such matters with anyone less than de Noailles himself. The Cardinal had not really made up his own mind how far he was prepared to go, and in 1720, after the death of Du Pin, he signed a qualified acceptance of the *Unigenitus*, and the incident was closed. The Jesuits had succeeded in dividing Gallicanism, and it fell. The moderates submitted, the more extreme spirits maintained themselves as a small body, which, persecuted out of existence in France, has continued in Holland to the present day, and may yet be influential in witnessing to the principle that an alloy of nationalism does not necessarily destroy the Catholic religion.

Further attempts to limit the power of the Pope without separating from the Catholic Church were made later in the eighteenth century in Germany and Austria, but they were ill-directed and short-lived.

Various schemes were propounded in the earlier part of the century for some measure of Reunion with the Protestants of the Continent. But the Anglican Church, in spite of her absorption of so much of Protestantism, remained too Catholic for coalescence with the definitely Lutheran or Calvinist churches of Europe. Frederick I. of Prussia, having obtained the Emperor's permission to assume a crown, desired to add to the prestige of the ceremony by having it performed by Bishops. He therefore gave the episcopal title to two of his chaplains, one a Lutheran and the other a Calvinist, hoping in this way to unite his subjects into one Protestant national Church. Subsequently he decided that it would be better if they received regular Consecration, and entered into negotiations with the English court and hierarchy for the purpose. But his death and that of the Archbishop of York brought the scheme to nothing.

In 1718 a Swedish statesman appealed to the Bishops of the Swedish Lutheran Church for closer union with the Church of England, and his appeals were seconded by Robinson, the Bishop of London. Most of them, however, refused to consider such a thing. In their eyes the English Church was merely Calvinist! Only one of the Swedish Bishops could be found to countenance the idea, on the ground that Episcopal Protestants ought to hold together against Presbyterianism.

That untiring apostle of Reunion, Archbishop Wake, was also in touch with the Calvinists of France and Switzerland at the very time when he was carrying on negotiations with the Gallican Catholics. He was also in communication with the Moravians of Bohemia, whom he was prepared to recognise as a true " Protestant Episcopal Church." The English dissenters alone seem to have been excluded from his schemes for unity.

But indeed English dissent was going through a bad time. Independents and Particular Baptists alone maintained the strictness of their Calvinism. Presbyterians and General Baptists were already exhibiting that gradual slide into Unitarianism which has been the bane of creedless religion. Those who wished to remain orthodox had to join or form other bodies. Orthodox Presbyterians took the former course and abandoned the Presbyterian polity altogether by joining the Independents. The orthodox General Baptists on the other hand were driven at last to form a " New Connexion " as the only means of combining non-Calvinistic orthodoxy with Antipaedobaptism.

The last attempt to comprehend the English Presbyterians within the Anglican Church has a special interest in view of recent proposals. Dr. Chandler, a London minister, is reported to have said in conversation with two Anglican Bishops that no Presbyterian minister would be willing to renounce his present Ordination. " But if their Lordships meant only to impose their hands upon us and by that rite recommend us to public service in their society or constitution, that perhaps might be submitted to." [1] We seem to hear the tones of the Lambeth Appeal, with its words about a " commission through Episcopal ordination, as obtaining . . . a ministry throughout the whole fellowship," and its rejection of the idea that anyone " could possibly be taken to repudiate his past ministry."

The present negotiations for Church Reunion in India lend a special interest to the first emergence of the problems occasioned by Christian disunion in that great dependency.

The first freehold settlement of the English in India was at Fort S. George (Madras), and dates from 1640. No English chaplain was provided, and religious difficulties at once arose. The only female society consisted of Portuguese Eurasians, and marriages naturally took place between them and the young English factors. Equally naturally the local Roman clergy exerted their influence to get hold of the husbands of their flock, and to give Baptism by any means to their children. A remarkable exception was a certain Capuchin friar who somehow so adapted his ministry as to make it acceptable to the English of the settlement. We should like to know more of this ecclesiastic beyond the unfortunate fact that he received a sentence of five years' imprisonment from the Inquisition. An English chaplain was appointed in 1647, but continual strife went on between the Roman Catholics and the East India Company.

On the other hand very friendly relations were maintained with the Lutheran missions. The Danish mission to Tranquebar was given financial support both by the S.P.G. and the S.P.C.K., and the strength of South Indian Christianity to this day is very largely due to the labours of Schwartz and other Lutheran missionaries. At a later date, however, we

[1] Canon Ollard, *Reunion*, p. 119.

see the beginnings of a different policy.   In the early days of the nineteenth century we find Bishop Heber ordaining to the Diaconate Lutheran missionaries who had been working for the C.M.S.

XIII

THE CENTRIFUGAL PERIOD

THERE has probably never been a period of Church history which has seen the beginning of so many schisms as that which in our own country began with the preaching of the Wesleys and Whitefield, and ended with the first Lambeth Conference. In every part of the world the tendency seemed to be for the separated portions of the Church to fly into fragments. The series of Lambeth Conferences which began in 1868 have had as their most conspicuous effect the growth of a desire to end our schisms, and it is not without significance that 1870 is the date of the Vatican Council, the decisions of which were probably influenced very deeply by the determination so to tighten the adhesion of Roman Catholics to the Papal throne as to weld them into a mass compact enough to resist all influences which threaten to impair the unity of the Church.

We must begin with Methodism ; and first with that side of it which owes its foundation to the brothers John and Charles Wesley.

John Wesley, unlike many reformers, lived a life of piety and simplicity from his earliest days. A communicant at eight years of age, at seventeen he began as an undergraduate to " set in earnest upon a new life." Returning to Oxford as a Fellow of Lincoln (and therefore in those days necessarily in Holy Orders of the Church of England), he became the leader of a little group of younger men, among whom was his own brother Charles, already known as " Methodists," from their strict adherence to the ways and methods of the spiritual life enjoined by the English Church. In this little group we find the beginnings of a veritable Oxford Movement. The " Holy Club," as they were called, were not only zealous for prayer and good works, but regular weekly communicants, and upholders of fasting and sacramental confession.

In 1735 the Wesleys sailed for America for pastoral work in the new colony of Georgia. They proved, however, too " High Church," as we should now say, for the colonists, and their work was not a success. But the voyage marked the beginning of the Wesleys' intercourse with the Moravian Brethren,[1] which no doubt accounts for the characteristic Lutheran stress on Justification by Faith only which always marked their teaching. Under this same quasi-Lutheran influence they both experienced within a few days of each other that experience of conversion which was also to play so leading a part in their future Evangelistic work. Convinced that their own experience must be repeated by all, they consistently preached the necessity of a conversion which should be both sensible and instantaneous : and this sudden coming to feel that all our hope of salvation is in Christ, and that Christ has then and there saved *us* individually is the very heart of Methodism. Methodism is essentially a particular doctrine of salvation, or rather perhaps a stress on a particular point in the doctrine of salvation coupled with the teaching of the necessity of a special spiritual experience. There was nothing in all this to cause a separation, and, as we shall see, it is only incidentally that Methodism has become schismatic.

[1] We have already come across the *Unitas Fratrum*. See p. 60. This society was marvellously resuscitated in 1722, and ten years later began to develop a very remarkable missionary organisation. Their missionary activities were not confined to heathen countries, and the year 1735 found a body of them in England, where for some years they conducted evangelistic missions parallel to the efforts of the Wesleys. They have left some traces, and there are still as many as forty-five of their congregations in this country, as well as in Germany and America. The official name of the society is still *Unitas Fratrum*. " Moravians " is in origin a kind of nickname.

Next year, after another visit to the Moravians at Herrnhut, John Wesley for a time crossed the path of a younger product of Oxford Methodism, George Whitefield, also an Anglican clergyman. Whitefield persuaded him to preach in the open air in Bristol, since no incumbent would give them hospitality. This outdoor preaching in defiance of the timid and conventional Church authority of the period was the beginning of the characteristic Methodist revolt against eighteenth century churchmanship, and has everything to excuse the technical irregularity of the act.

But soon a deep-seated theological difference began to make itself felt between the Wesleys and Whitefield. Whitefield was deeply imbued with the Protestant orthodoxy, which is Calvinism : Wesley, inheriting the traditions of Caroline and Non-juring churchmanship from his mother, was in the language of the time an Arminian. Arminianism had come to be a purely negative word, meaning simply one who refused the doctrine of irresistible grace. It was as a rule associated with rather lax principles ; but where, as in Wesley's case, it was combined with a strong churchmanship, it was simply equivalent to the sober Catholic view of the relationship of Divine grace to human freedom. In 1740 John Wesley preached a sermon on Free Grace, and after this a split was inevitable. The leaders made up their personal quarrel, but their followers were hopelessly at variance, as indeed were Wesley and Whitefield themselves so far as their theology was concerned. The two movements developed henceforward on totally separate lines. Whitefield, whose churchmanship was always of the most nebulous description, gathered together his own followers, and had himself elected " Moderator." But he soon resigned the leadership into the hands of two Welsh leaders, Jones and Charles, and Calvinistic Methodism, for which there seemed to be no permanent demand in England, proved extraordinarily successful in Wales.

Frowned on by the Anglicised hierarchy it was accepted

with enthusiasm by the genuinely Welsh element among the clergy, and for a long time no separation took place. There were ordained priests ready to minister the Sacraments, and Methodist principles required that Holy Communion should if possible be received in the parish church. But circumstances forced on a schism. The Methodists had been forced to register their meeting-houses as dissenting chapels. They had organised themselves into " Societies " altogether apart from the organisation of the Church. They had no Church traditions, and their sympathies were at least as much with the Presbyterian as with the Episcopal form of Church government. Their founder had discarded the surplice, which had come to be thought of as symbolic of Anglican churchmanship, and had exchanged pulpits freely with dissenting ministers. All that was needed for the formation of a new sect was a private ministry of their own, distinct from that of the Church. It was not, however, until 1811 that Charles took the final step of laying hands on some of the lay preachers of the Society, and so initiating the Calvinistic Methodist Church which is the most important of the Welsh sects. All that gave it any particular right to the name of " Methodist " had by this time been dropped, and Welsh " Calvinism " is really simply a form of Presbyterianism, as is shown by the fact that it is in full communion with the English Presbyterians and the Free Church of Scotland. In England, on the other hand, the movement developed into the Countess of Huntingdon's Connection, an organisation which began as a society of preachers in Anglican Orders, who were usually the Countess's chaplains, and ended as a highly Calvinistic form of Congregationalism.

Wesleyan Methodism is enormously more important, and it is necessary to trace the stages by which it emerged as a separate religious body.

John Wesley's society was at first interdenominational. His own wish was that all his adherents should receive the Holy Communion in their own churches. This proved

impossible from the fact that in some places the nonconformist ministers excommunicated a Wesleyan at sight.
They would have no Arminianism corrupting the pure
Calvinism of their flocks. It was easier in the case of those
who had been Anglicans. In spite of the infrequency with
which Holy Communion was celebrated, it was generally
possible to bring all the Wesleyans in a town together on a
Sacrament Sunday, and so give them something in the nature
of a corporate Communion, supposing of course that they
were confirmed members of the Church of England. Meanwhile Wesley's preachers continued their work. Some
devoted their whole time to preaching; these were the
" Travelling Preachers "; others, called " Local Preachers,"
continued their secular callings, and only preached occasionally in the neighbourhood of their homes. Some of the
former class were actually priests of the Church of England,
but in the nature of things this was a dwindling number:
no Bishop would have considered that a vocation as a Travelling Preacher constituted a title for Holy Orders.[1] Yet in
practice this whole body of Travelling Preachers came more
and more to occupy a ministerial position towards the
Methodist people. And the people began to demand that
they should be ministers of Sacrament as well as Word.
Sporadically cases began to occur of their celebrating Holy
Communion. The thought of an unordained man doing
this was as hateful to Wesley as it could be to anyone; but
then slowly the question formulated itself in Wesley's mind,
Why should they be unordained any longer? Was not a
Presbyter in primitive times the same as a Bishop? and if so,
why had not the Presbyter as good a right to confer Holy
Orders to-day as any Bishop? It was long before he took
action. And even when he did he had no intention of
causing a schism. Believing as he did that he had the *power*
of Ordination, he yet recognised that to *exercise* this power

[1] He could not well have done so ; for the theory of a " Title " is that
it is a security for maintenance.

in such a way as to set up a rival ministry of the Sacraments was to create a formal schism. From this responsibility he always shrank, and it does not seem to have occurred to him that the setting up of an order of preachers, licensed by himself, was just as *schismatic* an act as the appointment of a minister to celebrate the Sacraments. But Wesley's own " Ordinations," as he fully believed them to be, were not for this country at all, but for America or Scotland, where the ground was not covered already by a properly organised Church.

At this time he also took a step far less justifiable, even on his own principles. He laid hands on his assistant, Thomas Coke, who was already a priest, to give him the office of " Superintendent " over the other ministers ordained for America. Coke promptly changed the title for that of Bishop, which has been borne ever since by the chief Ministers of the important Episcopal Methodist Churches in the United States.

Wesley began to ordain in 1784, and he seems to have realised to some extent the possible implications of his action. He saw that in any case he had founded a permanent society, and that it needed a constitution. He therefore executed a Deed of Declaration defining the character of the Society with some minuteness, and spent the remaining years of his life in minute and detailed organisation. But no schism was yet in existence. On the contrary Wesley was at last *persona grata* with the Anglican clergy as a whole, and frequently preached in Anglican churches all over the country. In 1789 he declared afresh his determination to live and die a member of the Church of England.

But it was only Wesley's personal influence which acted as a restraining force. Immediately after his death in 1791 the agitation for treating the Travelling Preachers as full ministers began afresh, and in 1795, as was inevitable, separation was accomplished, and the Wesleyan Methodist

Church took its place among the religious bodies of the world.[1]

Nor had Wesley succeeded in imbuing his followers with his own ideas as to the importance of Ordination by imposition of hands, and of maintaining a presbyteral succession. There were no further Ordinations of this kind until 1836 : and although the imposition of hands is now practised, the modern Wesleyan theory of Ordination is that it consists in the conviction of a call from God on the part of the candidate, and the recognition of that call on the part of the Church.

If it is right that every divergent religious view should be represented by a different religious organisation, which is the logical outcome of the sectarian spirit, there was some justification for the establishment of Wesleyan Methodism as an independent Church. The Wesleyans were utterly out of sympathy with the Church of England of the period. It was the time of the last flicker of pure Calvinism, and all the most serious-minded representatives of the Church of England were deeply committed to the strict Gospel of the Wrath of God. So also were the Congregationalists and the Particular Baptists. Theologically it is the great merit of the Wesleys to have refused to subscribe to this perversion of the balance of the Christian faith, and their followers have been true to their standards at least in this respect. The Non-juring schism had depleted the Church of England of those who might have welcomed and stabilised the Methodist movement : and the only non-Calvinists left to Anglicanism were unsuited both spiritually and theologically to work in harmony with the Methodists. There remained the General Baptists : but they by this time had become deeply infected with Unitarianism, and so unfitted for an alliance with the strictly orthodox John Wesley. The Wesleyan movement had indeed a reflex effect on the General Baptist community, and so revived the force of orthodoxy as to

[1] In Ireland no separation took place until the Disestablishment of the Irish Church. For eighty years after Wesley's death the Irish Wesleyans continued to communicate in their parish churches.

cause a further schism. The orthodox party in 1770 formed themselves into the New Connection of General Baptists, and remained in separation until the formation of the Baptist Union in 1813.

Nor were Wesley's own followers exempt from the centrifugal tendencies of the time. His own views, not only orthodox but strongly authoritarian, were deeply embedded in the constitution which he had given to his society. The autocratic power which he himself had wielded was put into commission and held by a hierarchy of one hundred senior ministers, whose numbers were to be maintained by the oligarchical method of co-option. At the same time the Wesleyan standard of orthodoxy was to be maintained by perpetual reference to a particular volume of his own sermons !

It was sufficiently obvious that the Wesleyan secession contained the seeds of further separation. In 1796 an agitation for a more popular form of government resulted in the expulsion of a considerable number from the society, and in the consequent formation of the Methodist New Connection. In 1812 the Primitive Methodists (nicknamed Ranters) came into existence. They had come into conflict with the authorities of the Society over the question of the revivalistic method of the Camp Meeting, recently imported from America. This was altogether too much for the staid and respectable organisation which Methodism had now become, and the " Camp-Meeting " Methodists were duly expelled. So in 1818 the Bible Christians were the result of a similar expulsion. In 1857, the growing desire for an educated ministry led to a further schism, and those who preferred the apostolic simplicity of the older form of Methodism found themselves compelled to form yet another society under the name of the United Methodist Free Church. Indeed this was only one of several such divisions which took place about the same date. Finally, in 1861, William Booth left the New Connection to found the Salvation Army.

The troubled history of France during this period has a contribution to make to the history of schism. Napoleon Buonaparte, surveying the ruin of all law and all morality in the France he had begun to dominate, conceived the idea of a servile Church in a servile State as an element in his programme of dictatorship. The only possible Church for France must be Roman Catholic, and therefore no action could be taken without the co-operation of the Pope. But Napoleon was master of the situation, and had no idea of establishing a Church which would be a thorn in his own side. The existing Bishops were not to his mind. They were cemented to the old *régime* by the strongest tie—that of having suffered for it. But he who can dictate to a sovereign Pontiff need not fear a shortage of thunderbolts. Let the old Bishops be annihilated : let there be a new hierarchy. When the " First Consul " has nominated, let His Holiness speak the creative word. Such was the agreement made in 1801 under the title of the *Concordat*.

There were eighty-one Bishops still living, in hiding or in exile. Every one was called on by the Pope to resign ; and all but thirteen obeyed. The Pope then proceeded to suppress all the French Dioceses, and to inaugurate an entirely new French Church. But Napoleon did not find it as easy as he had expected to control the new appointments. The Pope had his opportunity to kill Gallicanism, and he made the most of it. The new bishops were for the most part his own nominees. Napoleon retaliated by publishing the *Concordat* in an amended form with new Gallican, or indeed Erastian, clauses to which the Pope had never consented. The diplomatic struggle went on for ten years. On the fall of Napoleon the Pope on the whole had triumphed. Gallicanism at least was dead. The thirteen Bishops continued their ineffectual protest, and for a century there remained in some parts of France a *Petite Eglise*, like the Non-juring Church in England ; but its extinction was inevitable : and although French Catholics have always been characterised by a certain liberalism of thought, the French Church as a whole has been very largely denationalised.

The year 1832 marks the beginning of an important new development in Englishmen's attitude to the thought of Reunion. Hitherto there had seemed to be only two possible ways of reuniting Christians. Either the malcontents must be suppressed or else their grievances must be met. Both methods had been tried, and failed. Now Dr. Arnold suggested for the first time a scheme of federation. Let Parliament intervene and create a new national Established Church to include the present Church of England and all the orthodox Protestant Churches. None of the bodies concerned need alter anything in their constitution or doctrine, but all would become component parts of the Church of England. The scheme enlisted no support. The time was not ripe for plans of unity. It was the age of unrestricted competition, and the proposals would have been unworkable. But the principle is the same as that of the modern plans (Kikuyu and the like), which can be grouped under the common designation of " Pan-Protestant." Nor is it altogether unlike the suggestions of the Lambeth Conference of 1920, as developed by the Bishops of Peterborough, Hereford and Zanzibar, which we must discuss at greater length in a later chapter. The Oxford Movement has enormously altered the situation, and has made impossible any schemes which are content to be merely Pan-Protestant, but the general idea that coercion and compromise are insufficient as bases for corporate Reunion is beginning to hold the field.

Another abortive attempt in the direction of unity must be noticed at this point. Like Arnold's plan, it was crude and unpractical, and yet in more ways than one foreshadowed the movements of to-day. The idea of a Protestant Bishop in Jerusalem originated in the mind of the King of Prussia, Frederick William IV. His motives seem to have been twofold : to provide a representative of Protestant principles in the Holy City, and to introduce Episcopacy into Prussia by a side wind. A special envoy was sent to London to arrange matters with the ecclesiastical and civil authorities in England, and the Bishops, the Government and the Evangelical party all supported the scheme. On the English side a third motive now appeared. It was not only to be a step towards unity of discipline and doctrine between the English Church and " the less perfectly constituted of the Protestant Churches of Europe," but also to establish " relations of amity with the ancient Churches of the East." The new Bishop was to have jurisdiction over Anglicans throughout the Near East, and also over any other Protestants who desired to submit themselves to him. He was also to ordain clergy both for Anglican and German congregations, exacting subscription from the former to the Prayer-Book and Articles, from the latter to the Augsburg Confession. Nomination to the Bishopric was to be made alternately by the Crowns of England and Prussia. Michael Alexander, a converted Jewish Rabbi, was duly consecrated in 1841, and commended to the Eastern Patriarchs by Archbishop Howley, who stated that the Bishop was forbidden to intermeddle with the Prelates of the East. The plan was violently opposed by the High Church party of the time, and was declared by Newman to be one of the blows which finally shattered his faith in the English Church.

Alexander's episcopate was short and ineffective, and the ministers ordained by him failed to secure recognition in Germany. His successor, duly nominated by the King of Prussia, was a Swiss Calvinist, Samuel Gobat. He received the three Holy Orders within the space of one year, and was despatched to the East to do the work of a Catholic Bishop. It is not surprising that his rule was disastrous. He proselytised the Eastern Orthodox, quarrelled with the English, both clerical and lay, and even attempted to exercise his Episcopal office without permission in Scotland, to the great indignation of the Scottish Bishops.

On his death a third Bishop was appointed from the English side, but the King of Prussia, now German Emperor, failed to nominate a fourth, and the arrangement came to an end in 1881.

Something must be said about the domestic affairs of the Eastern Orthodox during this period. Again we shall find it a time of strife and disunion in which centrifugal forces get the upper hand.

We have seen how in the eighteenth century Constantinople had lorded it ecclesiastically over the Balkan lands. The nineteenth century saw these countries everywhere rebelling both against the civil and the ecclesiastical oppression of Constantinople. (Of course the two forms of oppression cannot be compared. The Patriarch and his Greek entourage were ruling the Christians of the Balkans for their own good by means of cultured and able Greek prelates, while the Sultan and the Turkish government had no ideas beyond keeping the infidels in subjection and making use of them. Moreover, as long as the Balkans remained within the Turkish Empire, the Patriarch was responsible to the Sultan for their good behaviour.)

Thus in Serbia the national Patriarchate granted by Constantinople in the middle of the sixteenth century had been suppressed : all Serbian Bishops and many of the clergy were driven out, and Greeks from the Phanar (the Christian quarter of Constantinople) introduced in their place. But in 1804, as soon as the Serbs had asserted their civil independence, the Greeks were driven out, with the inevitable result of an ecclesiastical quarrel between Constantinople and the Serbian Church, which has only just been composed.

In 1821 the War of Greek Independence broke out. The immediate result was the hanging of the Patriarch in full pontifical vestments outside his own Cathedral in Constantinople as a reprisal for the revolt of a part of his *millet*. But when as a result of the war the Greeks attained their

independence, their first anxiety was to cut themselves free
also from the ecclesiastical supremacy of Constantinople.
As Greeks they had always been subject to the direct rule of
the Patriarchate, but national feeling was stronger even than
racial affinity. It was not, however, till 1850 that the
Patriarch recognised the autonomy of the Hellenic Church.

The same story repeats itself in Rumania, and even in
the ancient Patriarchates of Antioch and Jerusalem.

So it was also in Bulgaria. In the eighteenth century the
Bulgarian Archbishopric had been suppressed, and the
native prelates expelled. Now Bulgaria demanded from the
Patriarch first national Bishops, and then an independent
national Church. Both demands were granted, but disputes
arose as to the extent of the latter. The Turkish government intervened and settled the matter in favour of the
Bulgarians. The Oecumenical Patriarch replied with an
excommunication : the other Patriarchs and the national
Greek Church supported him ; but not so the Slavs. It
became a racial question, and the Orthodox Church, with its
strong national and racial character, failed to come to one
mind. The curious situation arose that while the rest of
the Orthodox Churches maintained their mutual intercommunion, the Bulgarian Church was in communion with
some of them but not with others. This is a matter which
perhaps has some bearing on some of the present day suggestions for Reunion. Is it possible for the Church of England,
e.g., to unite with the Wesleyans but not with the Congregationalists, without insisting that the Wesleyans shall break
off communion with the Congregationalists ? The situation in Bulgaria might possibly be pointed to as a precedent.
But it is *not* a true precedent : there is perfect unity of faith
between Bulgaria and the rest of the Orthodox Church, and
in the case supposed it would be a matter of faith, not a *mere*
matter of jurisdiction, which prevented the union between
Anglicans and Congregationalists.

There is another important schism which took place

during this period—that between the Established Church of Scotland and the Free Church. Presbyterianism, as we have seen, holds strongly to two principles : first, that it is the duty of the state to acknowledge and protect the true Church : this is the " Establishment principle " ; secondly, that the civil power must be subject to the spiritual. In accordance with these principles an Act of Parliament was passed after the Revolution of 1688 incorporating all the statements of the Westminster Confession concerning the bounds of the respective powers of the Church authorities and of the civil magistrate. In the reign of Queen Anne, however, another Act was passed, restoring the system of *patronage* in Scotland. The Act caused great discontent, and more than one schism from the Established Church ; but the General Assembly, as long as it was dominated by the " Moderate " party, acquiesced in the action of the state. In 1834, however, the " Evangelical " party gained a majority, and at once passed through the Assembly the " Veto Law," which declared it to be " a fundamental law of this church, that no pastor shall be intruded on any congregation contrary to the will of the people."

This at once brought the Church into conflict with the civil Court of Session, which decided a long series of judgments on the principle (upheld also by the House of Lords) that " Parliament is the temporal head of the Church." The result was to split the Presbyterian Church of Scotland. No less than 474 Ministers out of a total of 1203 resigned their charges rather than acquiesce. Thus amidst extraordinary scenes of emotion the Free Church of Scotland was founded, and Dr. Chalmers was elected its first Moderator.

It is impossible not to feel the most profound admiration for the courageous protest of the seceding ministers, and the greatest satisfaction at the recent healing of the breach. A noteworthy point in the schism was that both sides were in perfect agreement as to their ideals : division only came about over the question which was the lesser of two evils, the forsaking of the Establishment principle, or the loss of religious liberty.

In 1874 Patronage was abolished, and so the actual occasion of the dispute disappeared ; but no change was made in the general conditions attaching to union with the state, and the Free Church saw no reason to rescind its action.

XIV

THE VATICAN COUNCIL AND THE OLD
CATHOLIC MOVEMENT

THE Vatican Council of 1870 forms the climax of the Centrifugal period : and it is probable that in the minds of those who promoted it it was meant to be the final security of the unity of the Roman Church. Gallicanism, it is true, had ceased to be a serious menace, but even the reconstituted French Church was not Papal enough for the Jesuit and Ultramontane party. In Germany too a spirit of independence was beginning to show itself. And, most alarming of all, a strong Catholic reforming party was springing up in Italy itself, connected with the name of Rosmini and Italian nationalism. The connection between nationalism and reform in this case seems to be almost accidental; but the Pope's secular policy was directed towards an ideal of a federated Italy, presided over by the Papal States, and, as usual, nationalism and religious reform were found to be in concert. The reformers' programme was a sweeping one. The Pope was to be declared Primate of the Church, but the supreme authority in matters of faith was to be a Council with the Pope as President. Full Episcopal jurisdiction was to be restored. The Pope, the Bishops and Parish Priests were to be elected by the clergy and laity. Services in the vernacular were to be allowed, and the Bible was to be freely circulated. Confession and clerical celibacy were to be voluntary. Synodical government was to be restored. The movement won widespread support, especially in Milan and Turin. Three Bishops were associated with it, and the great Cardinal d'Andrea was known to be in sympathy. It was put down by a high-handed exercise of Papal authority, and action was determined on which should make such disturbance of the minds of the faithful impossible for the future. Had the reformers appealed to a Council ? To a Council they should go. But the Council should be compelled to sterilise itself. There must be no mistake this time : if the Council could be made to decree Supremacy and Infallibility in sweeping terms it need have no successors. It must be confessed that the arrangements for the Council do not reflect credit on its promoters. All known opponents of Infallibility were excluded from the preliminary meetings, and when the Council actually met, free discussion was suppressed by the Papal legates who presided. The closure was applied and the main substance of the decrees passed almost before the opponents of them knew what was being done. At the decisive meeting 451 votes were cast for Infallibility without limitation : 62 for Infallibility *juxta modum* : 88 voted *non placet*.[1] Of those who had voted *non placet* fifty-five received permission to leave Rome, so that at the final public meeting the voting was almost unanimous.[2] These figures are, of course, far from representing the real state of opinion in the Roman Church. The immense overweighting of the ship of the Church with Italian prelates was never more conspicuous. The Papal States alone with less than a million inhabitants provided the majority with no less than 65 votes, and the Italian Bishops altogether numbered 276.[3] Still, as Fr. Thurston points

[1] Granderath, *Geschichte des Vatikanischen Kanzils* : iii. p. 479.

[2] The final voting on July 18 was : Placet, 533 : *Non placet*, 2. Granderath, *op. cit.* iii. p. 499.

[3] The fifty-five who left Rome numbered amongst them some of the greatest names in the hierarchy, and if, as Döllinger averred, the function of Bishops in council is to bear witness to the faith of their Dioceses the victory of the Infallibilists was a very hollow one. At the preliminary meetings, however, the composition of the Council had been arranged on a very different principle from Döllinger's. All Bishops, diocesan or not, were summoned. If they were unable to attend they might not be represented, and their votes were lost.

out,[1] as far as the subsequent consent of the Roman Church is concerned, the decree has been abundantly ratified.

By what means that consent was obtained is another matter. Resistance to it began in Germany, but spread to Poland, Austria and Switzerland : and very soon the air was thick with excommunications. The German Bishops had been among the foremost of the opponents of the decree until it was actually passed. Then they submitted and called on their flocks to do the same. Certainly it was difficult for them to do anything else. One and all they had sworn allegiance to the Pope in the most stringent terms. And, moreover, they depended on Papal faculties for many of their Episcopal rights, and were even subject to deposition without any chance of appeal. It was not difficult to apply the screw. The famous historian Hefele was the last to give way, and his case is a good example of the way in which the Papal supremacy may work at its worst. His quinquennial faculties had just expired when the Council was prorogued, and he found himself in the undignified position of being unable to give those dispensations which are part of the ordinary working of a Roman Bishop's Diocese. There was no need to proceed to extremes. His position became impossible : he must submit, or resign, or find himself automatically deprived of power to administer his Diocese.

The leader of opposition was not a bishop but a priest, Dr. Döllinger, Professor of Theology at the University of Munich. But though the cyclone whirled round him as its centre, he himself preserved an extraordinary passivity. Having made his protest, and averred that he could not reconcile the demand for submission with his oath never to interpret Scripture in a sense other than that of the ancient Fathers, he acquiesced in the excommunication which was promptly issued against him, and never again performed any priestly functions. When delegates from all over Germany met at Munich to consider their course of action,

[1] *Catholic Encyclopedia.*

he alone advised that nothing should be done to create a schism. On the other side it was urged with much force that there was nothing else to be done. Schism is evil, but it is not the worst of evils. This is a position with which Anglicans should sympathise. If union with Rome is, or used to be, the ordinary rough and ready token of unity with the Church, it does not follow that there are no circumstances in which it is a duty to organise a Church apart from Rome. And if Rome casts out her children unjustly, who can show that they are not justified in continuing in the Catholic faith and practice outside her jurisdiction ? Providentially the very help that was needed was at hand. The little remnant of the ancient Church of Holland, nicknamed " Jansenist," had suffered similar things at the hand of Rome and the Jesuits in earlier days. A quarrel which seems almost absurd, considered as the foundation of a schism,[1] had resulted in the excommunication of the chapter of Utrecht Cathedral and all who held with them for refusing to accept a Bishop from Rome when the see was not vacant. This was at the beginning of the eighteenth century. On the death of the true Archbishop, the Church of Utrecht remained without a bishop for fourteen years, when the Bishop of Babylon, *in partibus*, of all places in the world, took pity on her and having applied in vain for a bull to authorise his action at last took the matter into his own hands and consecrated a Bishop. It was as irregular as anything could be ; but necessity seemed to know no law, and the action

---

[1] It must not be supposed that Jansenism is a heresy. Cornelius Jansen was Bishop of Ypres in the seventeenth century, and wrote a treatise on freewill and grace, in which he showed himself a more whole-hearted supporter of Augustinianism than was popular with the moral theologians of the time. The Jesuits obtained from the Pope the condemnation of five propositions which were said to be contained in Jansen's teaching. These propositions certainly bore a very Calvinist appearance : but Jansen's followers always denied that they represented his teaching. But the form in which the condemnation was proposed for the signature of suspected Jansenists implied not only that the propositions were untrue, but also that Jansen had taught them. Thus it became easy to accuse those who were merely loyal to the memory of Jansen of favouring a heresy which they continued to assert that he had never taught.

of Rome had been so unjust that it is difficult not to sympathise with his action. It was to this Church of Utrecht, as representing the ancient Church of Holland, that the Old Catholics, as they were now beginning to call themselves, decided to appeal. It had become a very small body indeed, with but three Dioceses, and about thirty priests. One of the Dioceses was vacant, and the Old Catholic Bishop for Germany had no sooner been elected than news came of the death of the " Jansenist " Archbishop of Utrecht, who had promised to perform the Consecration. The first Old Catholic Bishop for Germany was therefore, like the first " Jansenist " Archbishop of Utrecht, consecrated by a single prelate, who, of course, was also acting irregularly in consecrating a Bishop to inaugurate a schism. It is one of the cases where nobody can be blamed for the final act of schism, however much we may feel that the whole policy of making Infallibility a matter of faith was a disastrous mistake. When the decree had been passed it was quite right for any who could bring themselves to believe it to do so. But it is also quite impossible to blame the minority for refusing to acquiesce in excommunication as heretics when they knew quite well that they were nothing of the sort. Certainly they committed an act of schism : it was not only the Pope from whose communion they seceded, but their own Bishops as well. Clearly they were founding a new church. The only question is, What else were they to do ?

The Bishop of Deventer, the sole remaining " Jansenist " Bishop, therefore consecrated Joseph Reinkens at Rotterdam as first Old Catholic missionary Bishop of Germany. From Germany the movement spread through Bohemia and Switzerland. From the beginning the movement has shown far more anxiety for reform than the Dutch had ever done.[1] Catholics in Holland, whether Roman or Jansenist, are a

---

[1] In 1908 the Church of Holland published a vernacular service, and made some other less happy liturgical changes ; but her body of doctrine is precisely that of the Roman Church before 1854 ; all that has been changed is the *emphasis*.

small minority, and in such cases it always happens that the religious minority is determined to keep itself absolutely distinct from its surroundings. Partly this is caused by the instinct of self-preservation, but partly also by the fact that in such circumstances it is only men of very clear and definite views who have individuality enough to belong to the minority Church at all: and men of clear and definite views tend to be extremists. On the other hand, in Germany, Switzerland and Bohemia, there was far more equality of numbers between Catholics and Protestants, and these par-ticular psychological forces did not come into play.

In any case among the first actions of the Old Catholics are to be numbered such arresting changes as the following. Confession and clerical celibacy are voluntary. Transub-stantiation is no longer insisted on as the official term to express the nature of the Eucharistic Presence. Vernacular services are employed. The benefits of a particular Mass can no longer be applied at the will of the Celebrant to some special purpose. (Obviously this is not an attempt to limit the scope of the Celebrant's intercessions, but merely a denial of the somewhat over-businesslike view of the effect of the Mass which seems to be current in some Romanist circles.) An indication of the extent to which Protestant influence had affected the Old Catholics may be found in the fact that when the Old Catholic Church was founded in Switzerland some of its supporters wished to dispense with Bishops altogether.

The most important influence on Reunion which has hitherto been exercised by the Old Catholics is to be found in the convening of the two Conferences of non-Papal Episcopal churches at Bonn, under the presidency of Dr. Döllinger in 1874, 1875. The influence of these conferences cannot be calculated by their *acta*, which indeed amounted to very little. The idea of a common Catholicism uniting all Churches which had retained the ancient ministry would have been a commonplace in the seventeenth century, but was a novelty for the nineteenth. The Oxford Movement had had its natural effect in stimulating desire for Reunion, but Pusey's efforts in that direction in France and elsewhere had been brought to an abrupt close by the Vatican Council and the Franco-Prussian War, and nothing had been done except by individuals. The Bonn Conferences were on a large scale and represented the sowing of seed over a very wide area. The only important result, however, which can be set down in black and white, is the acceptance of a formula of concord in the matter of that ancient difficulty, the *Filioque* clause in the Nicene Creed. With the help of the writings of S. John of Damascus it was shown that there was no difference between Eastern and Western belief on this point, so that the only cause of dispute was one on which the Westerns were very ready to own themselves in the wrong, the insertion of the clause in the Creed without proper authority.[1] The immediate effect of the Conferences seems, however, to have been thought disappointing, and it must be acknowledged that there is no step towards Reunion which can be directly traced to their influence.

A similar movement took place a few years later in Spain. A small body, about two thousand in number, under the leadership of a priest named Cabrera, seceded from the Church of the Roman obedience and organised themselves as an episcopal national Church. Cabrera was consecrated by the Archbishop of Dublin and two other Irish Bishops, and took charge of the new body. It is difficult to feel much sympathy with the indignation so freely expressed in England at the mere fact that the Irish Bishops gave Consecration. What was right in Germany, if it was right, cannot have been so very wrong in Spain. It is no doubt undesirable and unfriendly to proselytise directly, and does more harm than good. But if a body of Catholic Christians are *unjustly* ejected from their own national Church, what are they to do ? We cannot assert surely that they *ought* to believe

[1] It is said that the Dutch Old Catholics have recently taken to reciting the Creed in the Oriental manner without the *Filioque*.

what we ourselves think untrue, yet it is only if they do believe it that they can remain members of the Spanish Church. It seems then that we must recognise that if we are right in our contentions as to the Papacy, and right in the action which we took as a majority of the national English Church, it is very difficult to say that the Spanish schism was wrong because it was the schism of a minority. The truth seems to be that the attitude of the Papacy has destroyed, for good or for evil, the ancient theory of territorial jurisdiction. It might then be argued that if the Archbishop of Dublin as head of an autonomous national Church was satisfied as to the orthodoxy of the Spanish seceders, he was not blame-worthy. It would have been a different matter if he himself had fished in Spanish waters (it might indeed be possible to construct a theoretical defence even for this ; but in practice it would probably be indefensible). But in this case he was himself approached and asked to consecrate. If the Episcopate is necessary to the Sacraments, how could he have refused ?

Still there was much in the transaction as actually carried out which was open to serious criticism. The Bishops at the Lambeth Conference had washed their hands of the matter. The Archbishop of Dublin then called an informal meeting of the Irish Bishops and announced that he and two of his Comprovincials proposed to proceed with the Conse-cration, unless the other Bishops made a formal protest. Then the Bishops passed a resolution that " they would not regard such an action as an indefensible exercise of the powers entrusted to the Episcopate." This was all the authori-sation which the Archbishop and his two colleagues had for so grave a step. It cannot be said that they really repre-sented any one but themselves. No very serious inquiry seems to have been made into the doctrines of the Reformed Spanish Church, and in sacramental teaching their formu-laries certainly fell short of Anglican standards. Nor indeed does Señor Cabrera appear to have been a very suitable person for the office of a Bishop.

XV

LAMBETH AND AFTER LAMBETH [1]

THERE is no doubt that the Lambeth Conference of 1920 marks a crisis in the history of efforts for Reunion : but indeed the tide had begun to turn in that direction long before that date. Even during what we have called the " Centrifugal period " there are sporadic efforts after unity. In 1811 Dr. Shute Barrington, the Bishop of Durham, speaks in glowing words of the possibility of union between England and Rome. In 1824 Dr. Doyle, an Irish Roman Catholic Bishop, wrote to the Chancellor of the Exchequer suggesting a conference between Protestant and Catholic divines, and later in the same century, Dr. Murray, Roman Catholic Archbishop of Dublin, actually wrote these words : " Were the Church of England people true to the principles laid down in their Prayer-Book, the doctrinal differences, which appear considerable, but are not, would soon be removed." [2]

Meanwhile the Oxford Movement, with its stress on Catholic doctrine, naturally turned men's eyes in the direction of the unity of the Church as a fundamental principle of her being. At first, it is true, the movement was very strongly anti-Roman and anti-dissent : indeed, the " Tracts

[1] The present chapter is based on the following books : *Reunion*, by Canon Ollard ; *Lambeth and Reunion*, by the Bishops of Peterborough, Zanzibar and Hereford ; *Documents bearing on the Problem of Christian Unity and Fellowship*, 1916-1920, S.P.C.K. ; *Documents relating to Christian Unity*, by Dr. Bell, the Dean of Canterbury.

[2] H. N. Oxenham, *An Eirenicon of the Eighteenth Century*, p. 69. Quoted by Canon Ollard.

for the Times " were first published under the title of
Tracts against Popery and Dissent. And further, the Rome-
ward drift of a section of the Tractarian party, culminating
in the secession of Newman in 1845, as well as that of other
less distinguished converts, meant that there was a period in
which the movement was anything but a mediating force
between the English and Roman Churches.

In 1857, however, there was formed the Association for
promoting the unity of Christendom, composed of members
of the Roman, Eastern Orthodox and Anglican Churches.
The Association was condemned in Rome, but for the next
ten years there were many interviews, and much correspondence, both public and private, on the subject, including
the three famous *eirenica* of Dr. Pusey.

The Vatican Council was so obviously a defeat of the
moderate and conciliatory party that its decisions put an end
to all hopes in that direction for the time being, and the
subject of Anglo-Roman Reunion was not reopened until
1894. Then, as so often before, it was *French* Catholicism
which showed itself most friendly, and the chief opposition
came from the side of English Roman Catholics. The chief
subject in debate was the validity of Anglican Ordinations
from the Roman point of view ; but the discussion was
brought to an end by the Papal decision, embodied in the
Bull *Apostolicae Curae*, which pronounced them null and
void. For the moment there was no more to be said. The
Pope had spoken : and though he had uttered no anathemas
and had left the conscience of his subjects free, yet as a
matter of discipline the mouths of Roman Catholics were
sealed ; and even as a matter of personal opinion it had
become " temerarious " to believe in Anglican Orders.
The English Archbishops returned a reply which besides
being a model of Latinity vindicated the Eucharistic teaching
of the English Church, and the matter dropped until it was
raised in a new and perhaps more hopeful form by the
Lambeth Conference of 1920.

But the Conference in its discussions on unity and
Reunion was not dealing only, perhaps not even chiefly,
with the subject of Anglo-Roman unity. That subject was
deliberately and pointedly brought forward, but the Reunion
problems which were crying out for immediate attention
were rather those concerned with the agreement which
seemed so urgently needed between Anglicans and Nonconformists, especially in the foreign mission field.

The rest of the chapter will be devoted to considering the
events which produced the immediate situation which that
Conference had to face, the Conference itself, its recom-
mendations, and its subsequent action.

The three Bishops (see footnote, p. 165) point out that
there were three principal factors which accounted for the
advance of the idea of Reunion from the stage of pious
aspiration to that of practical politics, between the last
meeting of the Conference in 1908 and the momentous
gathering of 1920.

The first was the great interdenominational missionary
Conference in Edinburgh, with its sense of shame at disunion
in the face of the heathen and the new Christians in heathen
lands.

The second was the appointment by the American Episcopal Church of a Commission to establish a World Conference on Faith and Order.

The third fact was the growth and influence of the Student
Christian Movement.

Of these the first and third are of course connected. This
is a young man's century, and the young are becoming
increasingly impatient of the religious divisions of their
elders ; and when youth and missionary enterprise are
pulling in the same direction some result must surely be
attained.

The second factor needs more detailed attention. It is
an effort on the part of the American Episcopal Church on

a characteristically grandiose scale to get representatives of *all* Christian bodies together for discussion as to the measure of our differences, and with the ultimate object of transcending them.   With the exception of the Roman Catholic Church every other community to which an invitation was sent has appointed a committee to further the scheme.

One of these committees, appointed by the English Archbishops met a similar " commission " selected by the Free Churches of England and Wales for a preliminary discussion. Two reports were issued, one in 1916, the other in 1918. They put the general situation so clearly that it is worth while to give their conclusions in some detail.

On the broad basis of faith there was found to be agreement up to a point.   They agree that the Christian religion is a real revelation, beginning with the prophets and culminating " in One who is more than a prophet, who is the Incarnate Son of God, our Saviour and our Lord."   This revelation is the basis of the life of the Christian Church, and constitutes the permanent spiritual value of the Bible.   The miracles recited in the creeds are not contrary to the principle of order in nature, and their acceptance is not forbidden by historical evidence.

In the matter of Order it was agreed that the purpose of our Lord was that there should be one visible society of believers, that He appointed two Sacraments as effective channels of grace, and that He conferred a Ministry on the Church.

Disagreement showed itself as to the nature of the Church, and the degree of uniformity required in polity, creed and worship : as to the conditions of the validity of the Sacraments, and as to the source of the authority of the ministry.

In the second report it was agreed that visible unity was inadequately expressed by co-operation in good works, but was only fully realised through community in worship, faith, order and Communion.   Further, that Episcopal Churches *ought* not to abandon Episcopacy as the recognised organ of unity and of continuity. But there are non-Episcopal churches in existence, which have been used by the Holy Ghost and came into existence through reaction from grave abuses. What was desired was not grudging concession, but a willing acceptance of the wealth of each body.

The necessary conditions of such unity were agreed to be :

Continuity with the historic Episcopate.

Episcopal election and government should be " constitutional."

Only the fact, not any theory or doctrine as to the Episcopate, should be insisted on.

Further it was agreed that there should be freedom for the exercise of a prophetic ministry. (It will be remembered that at that date the theory of a twofold primitive ministry, the ordained and the " charismatic," was still in favour.)

The measure of agreement and disagreement could hardly be better put, with one important exception. What we all want to know is whether we can rely on those Nonconformists who wish to come into union with us accepting the doctrines of the Holy Trinity and the Deity of our Lord in the sense of the Creeds and Councils.

In 1919 a deputation representing the Conference was sent to Europe and the Eastern Churches, and was cordially received by the Pope.

A preliminary general meeting was held in Geneva, in August 1920 (it will be noticed that we have now passed the date of the Lambeth Conference : it is better, however, to deal with our present subject continuously). At this meeting the general scope of the Conference was determined on, and a Subjects Committee appointed. The central subjects for discussion were defined as (1) The Church and the nature of the reunited Church : (2) The place of the Bible and a Creed in relation to Reunion.

The Subjects Committee met in 1923 at Oxford and produced a statement of which the following are the principal points, as to what is necessary, on the human side, to the unity and life of the Church :

Belief in God as revealed in Christ, this revelation being brought home to the individual by the Holy Ghost.

This belief is trust in a Person, but the trust has intellectual implications.

The substance of one of the creeds is the minimum possible for the Baptismal profession of faith.

The teaching of a reunited Church must include the Apostles' and Nicene Creeds.

The use of Creeds in worship is optional.

The Committee also foreshadowed the likelihood of the World Conference making a declaration of faith.

This document is evidently meant as a basis of discussion at the Conference itself.

In 1925 a further series of questions on the Sacraments was issued, to be discussed by the Churches as a preliminary to the Conference.

They deal with disciplinary questions which would have to be settled before Reunion : *e.g.* Is Baptism necessary to membership in the Church ? Can differences of opinion as to Infant Baptism be tolerated ? Is the Lord's Supper of obligation ? What is necessary for that Sacrament as to form, minister and matter ? Is any particular doctrine of the Eucharist necessary ? Is Confirmation obligatory ? What is necessary, or permissible, in regard to Penance ? What is the Christian marriage law, and should the Church enforce it under pain of excommunication ? What is to be done about the Unction of the sick ? These questions have only to be read in order to realise the enormous amount of work that still has to be done before we are ripe for Reunion on a large scale. A little thought will show that a united Church must have one law about all these controverted matters, if the union is to be more than nominal.

Returning to the period before the Lambeth Conference we have next to notice the Kikuyu proposals, and the alliance between the C.M.S. Missionaries and the Presbyterians and United Methodists which bulked so large before the eyes of the Bishops. The greatest evils of disunion are to be seen in the mission field, and there too is the greatest danger of an impatient solution.

In 1913 the three missionary bodies just mentioned met at Kikuyu in East Africa, and held a joint Communion service. At the same time they entered into a federation of which the following are the chief points :

All recognised as ministers in their own Churches should be welcomed to preach in any of the federated Churches.

The Sacraments should be administered by the recognised Minister of the district.

Full members of any of the federated Churches should be admissible in any of the other Churches.

It is clear that these proposals represent one answer to an urgent question : what is to be done when a native Christian, converted, let us suppose, by the C.M.S., goes to live in a place where the only Christian minister is a Presbyterian. It is obvious that on C.M.S. principles he ought to go to Communion in the Presbyterian Church. But it is equally obvious that on Catholic principles, if the word may be allowed, he cannot do so. It is not a mere question of schism : in the abnormal state of Christendom we cannot always press the proprieties of Catholic life into the very highest notch : it is, to speak frankly, a question as to the validity of the Sacrament. The position of the native Christian just sketched is a most horrible illustration of the evils of disunion ; but " hard cases make bad law," and— there is another way out.

The Bishop of Zanzibar [1] complained to the Archbishop of Canterbury, who sent a cautious reply, deprecating the general United Communion, and disallowing the reception of Holy Communion by Anglicans at Free Church services.

Another conference was held at Kikuyu, and the Bishop

[1] The late Dr. Frank Weston.

of Zanzibar brought forward his own proposals for the way out of the difficulty. They are so important as to what a typical Anglo-Catholic leader actually thought the true solution that they must be quoted almost in full.

He proposed the mutual acceptance of four principles :

There is one Church, and it is entered by Baptism.

The Bible is the Word of God.

The Creeds are the expression of the universal faith.

Episcopacy has always existed and is now in possession of the greater part of Christendom.

But Episcopacy need not necessarily be monarchical. There may even be many Bishops in one local Church. (This is a considerable concession, and goes beyond what was suggested at Lambeth, and beyond anything for which there is any precedent but a very doubtful one. Dr. Weston apparently meant that *all* the Presbyters might be Bishops, so long as they really *were* Bishops. This is exactly the Presbyterian position apart from the question of validity.)[1] The Bishops should be freely elected, and should rule in concert with the clergy and laity. Non-Episcopal bodies accepting Episcopacy should retain in all respects their own constitutions. But the Church cannot compromise on the main outline of the doctrine of sacramental grace. Baptism and Holy Communion are of universal obligation. (The Report does not make quite clear the Bishop's attitude as to the necessity of Confirmation.) The principle of Absolution must be admitted. (This sounds a hard saying : but it only means, in this connection, what any missionary and any Presbyterian would be keenly anxious for, namely the maintenance of spiritual discipline, and the insistence on some token of repentance when there has been a grievous fall. It is quite clear that this is what the Bishop meant.) Further it would be necessary for both parties to the union

---

[1] Perhaps the Bishop only meant one bishop for each group in each place. But the official report of the C.M.S. says, " *Many* Bishops may serve one local church."

to be satisfied that the form and matter of the Sacraments were such as to ensure validity. No other liturgical rules need be asked for.

So far it is almost impossible to conceive that the Bishop's views could have failed to find acceptance. It must be supposed that agreement ended on the point of validity of Orders. The Bishop's proposal in this respect was precisely the same as that afterwards recommended by the Lambeth Conference : that each party should give the other that which he had not got. The Bishop should give the Free Church Minister Episcopal Ordination or Consecration : the Free Church should give the Bishop popular recognition. It is difficult to see why this last condition should seem so much greater a difficulty to the Nonconformist than it does to us. The positions are more or less parallel. We are each satisfied about our own commission to minister, and dissatisfied with that of the other. Each of us in submitting to what the other thinks we lack would *in practice* only be acquiring a wider right to minister, for our own people are satisfied with us as we are. If Anglicans are willing to submit to a public approbation (or disapprobation) as a condition of being allowed to minister to Nonconformists, why will not Nonconformists submit to that acceptance and commission by the Bishop which we believe to be necessary, as the Nonconformists believe popular approbation to be ? For we understand that Nonconformists believe the unrecognised minister to be, strictly speaking, as destitute of authority as we believe the unordained [1] one to be.

As a matter of fact the Nonconformist ministers were deeply impressed by the stress which the Bishop laid on the grace bestowed in Ordination. However, the plan was refused, and an alliance was entered into between the C.M.S. Bishops and the other two Churches. It was recognised that intercommunion was impossible. Non-Episcopalians would be welcome at the Anglican Holy Communion, but Anglicans

---

[1] *I.e.* not ordained by a Bishop.

could not be allowed to receive at Nonconformist services. This is so far of course not Reunion at all, but merely a close federation, with occasional " economic " Communion, as an Eastern would say, on one side only.

As the time for the Lambeth Conference drew near every other imaginable group got together and passed resolutions. There is no denying that everywhere men were nervously trying to prepare Episcopal minds in view of the declaration of policy which would have to be made at Lambeth. Notable Conferences were held at Mansfield College, in which the proposal was made that, " *as parts of one scheme* " (these are the key-words of the proposal), there should come about interchange of pulpits, intercommunion, and a mutual " authorisation " which was *not* to be taken as Ordination. This, of course, was only to be regarded as the roughest outline of a possible scheme, but on the face of it seemed somewhat careless of the special value which the Church of England sets on the appeal to the undivided Church, and to the necessity for orthodoxy in faith. We may be sure that these facts were duly pointed out.

Finally, there came on the very eve of the Conference the first Anglo-Catholic Congress. The idea that this should be taken as a " demonstration in force " was very properly and very truly deprecated ; but it certainly *was* a striking demonstration of the grip which Catholic principles had acquired over a large portion of the Church of England, and an indication, if such were needed, that it was not possible to forget Anglo-Catholicism.

The Conference met in fear of deadlock, if not of schism. In the event their resolutions on the most difficult problem that a Lambeth Conference ever had to face were passed with something like unanimity. People sometimes talk as though the fact that no Reunion has come about as the result of the Conference means that we must consider that part of their work a failure. This is entirely to misapprehend the situation. The Lambeth Fathers seem hardly to have thought of their work as a scheme of Reunion ; rather it was the plan of a reunited Church, and a vision of what God was calling us to in the end rather than in the immediate future.

Lambeth is the heir to Dr. Arnold rather than to the controversialists of Hampton Court and the Savoy. The plan for Reunion is one of inclusion, not of either Compromise or No compromise. Not that anyone supposes that we can enter into corporate union while we are all exactly what we are at present ; but the changes must come from within ; they must come because we have recognized the Face of Christ in our brethren, not because we wish to be dovetailed into a foreign body.

" It is not," say the Bishops, " by reducing the different groups of Christians to uniformity, but by rightly using their diversity that the Church can become all things to all men. So long as there is vital union with the Head, there is positive value in the differentiation of the members. But we are convinced that this ideal cannot be fulfilled if the groups are content to remain in separation from one another or to be joined together only in some vague federation. . . . It is towards the ideal of a united and truly Catholic Church that we must all set our minds." [1]

With the Encyclical the Bishops issued their actual resolutions, in which was incorporated an " Appeal to all Christian people," a document of lofty tone which created a profound impression.

It is in this Appeal that we must look for the actual plan which the Bishops set forth. The famous " Lambeth Quadrilateral " of 1888 is set forth anew with significant modifications. The Creed, the Scriptures, the two great Sacraments are set forth as before as holding the primary place in what is involved in the acceptance of the ideal of the visible unity of the Church, but the Historic Episcopate is advanced in a more conciliatory way in this form : " A ministry acknowledged by every part of the Church as

[1] *Encyclical Letter*, p. 12.

possessing not only the inward call of the Spirit, but also the commission of Christ and the authority of the whole body." " May we not claim," the Appeal proceeds, " that the Episcopate is the one means of providing such a ministry ? " " We believe that for all the truly equitable approach to union is by the way of mutual deference to one another's consciences. To this end . . . Bishops and clergy of our Communion would willingly accept from " . . . the authorities of other Communions " a form of commission or recognition which would commend our ministry to their congregations. It is our hope that the same motive would lead ministers who have not received it to accept a commission through Episcopal ordination, as obtaining for them a ministry throughout the whole fellowship."

It is practically Bishop Weston's plan !

A commentary on the plan which might almost be called semi-official is provided by the three Bishops in *Lambeth and Reunion*.[1]

The two chapters entitled " The Realisation of the Ideal " are worthy of careful study. Beginning with the historic Episcopal Churches they point out that it is inconceivable that Rome should delete the Vatican decrees from her definitions of faith. But, they say, " it is not inconceivable that she should explain them, and while adopting a purified Papacy as the centre of ecclesiastical unity, admit to fellowship with herself communions of Christians who do not now see eye to eye with her. Let Rome modify her statement of her claims for the Papacy ; let the other communions allow more generously the ecclesiastical position already granted to the Pope by Oecumenical decree ; and Reunion of the three communions is at once made possible." As a result they point out it would become possible, *in case of need*, for communicants of one " group " to communicate

---

[1] The three Bishops make it plain that they do not speak with authority in this book ; but if it misrepresents the mind of the Conference it is inconceivable that no one should have repudiated it.

at the Altars of the other groups, and priests likewise to interchange their Altars. And here follow these striking sentences, the contents of which could hardly have been gathered from the Lambeth Appeal itself with the help of any commentary less authoritative. " To meet . . . objections " to their ministry in Eastern or Roman congregations, " they (the Bishops) declare themselves ready to accept such a form of commission or recognition as would make their ministry acceptable within these other groups. They do not refuse ordination, provided they be not asked to deny their present Orders. They say frankly, in effect, that (were all other terms of union satisfactorily settled) they would humble themselves, out of deference to Eastern and Roman consciences, to receive what the East and Rome might wish to give them."

The Bishops go on to give an account of how the plan might be expected to work out in detail. Each " Group," *i.e.* each *Church* as things are at present, would have its own local synod. " These local synods would occasionally be merged in larger councils. And always there would remain a general council with the Bishop of Rome in the chair." " Generally speaking, jurisdiction would be over persons rather than over places," and the old system of strict territorial jurisdiction would have come to an end. In fact, the same system would obtain as is now to be found among the Uniate Christians in the East, where the ancient local Patriarchates have practically been superseded by Patriarchates of groups, as the Melkite Patriarchate, etc.

The next chapter deals with the case of Churches which are at present non-Episcopal. They too, accepting Episcopacy and having come to an understanding on matters of the faith, might form groups in the reunited Church. It would be for them to settle how many groups they would continue to be divided into.

We must remember that *ex hypothesi* we are all agreed in the essential faith, and it is only considerations of ritual and secondary matters that will keep us still divided into groups :

it is therefore to be expected that the groups will be fewer in number than the present separated Churches. It might even be that all the Churches which are at present non-Episcopal, or rather those of them which at any time were able to come into the reunited Church, would form one group. Thus the whole Catholic Church might be subdivided into four groups, Latin, Oriental, Anglican, Nonconformist. The last group would obviously not be *called* " Nonconformist," but the word is chosen here to express the fact that the main lines of division will be those of liturgical custom ; and the distinguishing mark of the fourth group will be that they are permitted by the rest of the Church to sit loose to formal liturgy, except in so far as it is required in order to ensure universally acknowledged validity.

" Each group then would elect some of its ministers to be its own Bishops. . . . They would sit in their own group-synod, to deal with its own internal affairs. They would also sit in the local synod of the fellowship," *i.e.* of the united Church, with the Bishops of the other groups locally represented. It is assumed that Confirmation will be satisfactorily arranged for ; and Absolution is dealt with on the same lines as those of Bishop Weston's proposals at Kikuyu. In both these cases all that will be necessary in the way of liturgy will be that the form of service or its central formula shall be acceptable to and recognised by all groups within the Church. But in the case of the Ordinal the three Bishops consider that all groups must use more or less the same form.

Such was the Lambeth proposal.[1] General intercommunion and general interchange of pulpits were definitely ruled out. But a recommendation was inserted among the Resolutions to the effect that when a minister is thought by the Bishop to be working in favour of such an ideal as Lambeth has put forward he may give permission for occasional interchange of pulpits with that minister.

[1] According to the interpretation of the three Bishops.

We have now to consider the reception accorded to the Appeal, and one or two subsequent movements towards Reunion which cannot but have been influenced by it.

In regard to Rome all that we know is that informal but recognised " conversations " are being carried on between Anglican and Roman scholars under the presidency of the great and noble Cardinal Mercier, the Archbishop of Malines.

There is more to be said in regard to the Eastern Orthodox. An important delegation had been sent to England at the time of the Conference with the express purpose of being able to confer with the Bishops on matters connected with Reunion. They had many such conversations, and presented an elaborate report on their return. As is natural the report begins by raising difficulties as to dogmatic agreement, and explains very courteously that while on Anglican principles it is obvious that we should wish for sacramental intercourse with the Orthodox, it is far from easy for the Orthodox to reciprocate our desire. The Report goes over the familiar differences between ourselves and the East in a very sympathetic manner, but its attitude to the Appeal seems to be a regretful *non possumus* for the present, on the ground, chiefly, that the measures proposed in relation to the Non-episcopal churches conflict with venerated principles and systems.

But the whole outlook as to the East has been changed in a marvellous manner by the formal recognition that Anglican Orders have all the outward conditions of validity. In July 1922, the Oecumenical Patriarch informed the Archbishop of Canterbury that the Synod of his Patriarchate had concluded that Anglican Ordinations had the same historic validity as those of the Roman, Old Catholic, and Armenian Churches possess. The Synods of Jerusalem and of Cyprus discussed the matter at the Patriarch's invitation in 1923, and came to the same conclusion. It will be seen in the next chapter that this is a very different matter from the absolute acceptance of Anglican Sacraments. The Eastern Church holds a theory of Orders and of the Church which would

make that impossible : but it is a great and natural satisfaction to us to know that an impartial judge has come to
the same conclusion as ourselves on the matter of the outward evidence ; and at the same time the recognition that
Anglican Orders have outwardly a Catholic character makes
it far easier for the Orthodox to accept them for special purposes by " economy," than if we appeared to them to be
simply a non-Episcopal body.[1]

The Lambeth Appeal has given rise to much more formal
deliberations between ourselves and a committee appointed
for the purpose by the Federal Council of the Evangelical
Free Churches.   Some account of these must be given.

The Committee just mentioned issued a report in May
1921, of which the following is a brief summary.

The Bishops have now abandoned their old attitude of
asking other churches to join the Church of England.   It
is now co-operation that they invite.

The Committee proceed to state that any movement to
union must have three stages, of which the first is the will
to union, and practical proposals are the *third*.   But the
second is real agreement on vital principles.   All this part of
the Report is, it must be confessed, rather rhetorical.   If
pressed, it would seem to assign to *preaching* the effects
which Catholics attribute to *Baptism*.[2]

But the Committee say very properly that they must
examine practical proposals in the light of vital principles,
and make sure that they do not conflict.   From this point of
view they state that it is essential that there should be cordial
recognition of the Church status which the Free Churches

---

[1] See next chapter.   The other Eastern Orthodox churches have not
yet made any corresponding statement ; but the Metropolitan of Athens
stated publicly on the occasion of the Anglo-Catholic Pilgrimage (1925)
that Reunion was coming near, and the Metropolitan Antony of Kiev
has given equal publicity to the statement that the Anglican Bishops are
Bishops of *the* Church.

[2] " Through this Gospel the Holy Spirit is shed abroad in the hearts of
those that believe."   The words have a Biblical ring, suggesting Rom. v.
6 and Tit. iii. 6, but they do not represent S. Paul's teaching.

already hold, in other words that they are already parts of the Visible Church : and that it should make unambiguous that imposition of hands is *not* Ordination.   Finally, they appeal for immediate interchange of pulpits and intercommunion, stating that their own experience in the Free Churches proves that along this way lies the path to real union.

A Joint Committee of Anglican and Free Churchmen was now appointed and arrived at a considerable measure of agreement.

The Federal Council at their meeting in September 1922 noted certain practical difficulties which would have to be considered.   In particular they would need to know the meaning of the phrase " constitutional Episcopate," and to be assured of the recognition of the status of the present ministry of the Free Churches, the relation of the Free Churches to communions with which they are in fellowship in other parts of the world, and the safeguarding of the evangelical principles of the Reformation.

The Joint Committee had now divided into sub-committees for the consideration of various subjects, and among them was naturally that of the status of the Free Church Ministries. The Anglican representatives on the sub-committee were asked to put forward a statement, which was found to contain the acknowledgment that " Ministries which rest upon a long-established order, which have been conferred by some solemn and authoritative act implying Ordination to the Ministry of the Universal Church and not merely commission to the ministry of a particular denomination, and which are regarded as involving a life-long vocation, which imply a sincere intention to preach Christ's Word and administer the Sacraments as Christ has ordained, and to which authority so to do has been solemnly given by the Church concerned, are real ministries of Christ's Word and Sacraments in the Universal Church."   But such ministries may be defective, and the Anglicans consider that for their own congregations, and in view of relations with other parts of the Catholic

Church and the danger of giving pain and even causing schism, the Anglican Church must " secure the authorisation of its ministers, and no one could be authorised . . . who had not been episcopally ordained." Yet they continue that they regard the rule as much more than one of internal discipline.

The statement is a surprising one. The ecclesiastical and intellectual eminence of its authors makes the critic hesitate, but the Nonconformists' comment was that though a concession had been made, worded in the most satisfactory language, it was not to be given effect to in practice !

There the matter rests for the time being. The Free Churches are a little inclined to say that enough time has now been spent in conference, and that unless we have something more satisfactory to offer we had better break off the debate.

But it is necessary to record such progress as has been made towards Reunion in other parts of the world.

Definite steps have been taken by the American Episcopal Church. In 1919 a scheme for a " Concordat " was drawn up by some members of that Church and of the Congregational Churches. This included a plan, embodied in a proposed canon, by which a minister might receive Episcopal Ordination, without giving up his ministry or membership in his own Church. There is here, it will be observed, no scheme of corporate Reunion ; but of course on Congregational principles the congregation is an independent unity. Therefore by accepting Ordination a Congregationalist minister brings his whole flock into the unity of the Catholic Church. He must, however, presumably as a matter of comity, receive the consent of " his own authorities." He must accept the Nicene Creed, and be confirmed before Ordination ; further he must undertake to baptize validly, and at every celebration of Holy Communion to use the words and acts of Our Lord, and the Lord's Prayer, and (a most curious requirement) the Creed ; and he must then hold himself amenable to the Bishop's authority. If he further engages to conform to a stricter rule of doctrine, discipline and worship he will receive the status of a Minister of the Episcopal Church. It is a very interesting proposal—and not the least remarkable thing about it is the ready acceptance which it has received from the Congregationalists, who go so far as to say that it is a recognition of the Congregationalist ministry. If this were all that was meant by " recognition " our difficulties would be much less. The weakness of the scheme from the Catholic point of view is that it seems to reduce all doctrine which goes beyond the Nicene Creed to the level of approved opinion, and that there is no security for the orthodoxy of the congregation which seeks union with the Church.

The canon was stiffened before it received the approval of the Bishops of the General Convention of the Episcopal Church in 1922. It was then enacted that the congregation to which the minister belongs must afterwards decline the ministrations of any minister not episcopally ordained : that the Minister after Ordination must use an approved form of Liturgical Canon, including an act of oblation and an invocation of the Holy Ghost, and must undertake not to give Holy Communion to the unbaptized.

The Congregationalists evidently thought that the Concordat, and all its implications, had been agreed to. A distinguished minister went so far as to ask for Ordination on these terms. Then, however, it was discovered that the House of Deputies (consisting of elected clergy and laity) had refused concurrence. This was in 1923.

Strong opposition has now developed against the scheme on the grounds of orthodoxy. It is pointed out that while steps have been taken to ensure that the Minister is sound in the faith, no questions have been asked or answered as to the doctrinal standpoint of the laity. On this ground negotiations have for the time being come to an end.

Something must be said about the Reunion of Scottish Presbyterians, though of course that is in no way connected with the Lambeth Appeal.

In 1900 a union was brought about after many years of negotiation between the Free Church and the United Presbyterians, the latter society representing a combination of several of those bodies which had seceded from the Established Church during the period of " Moderate " ascendancy. Here a matter of principle was involved. The United Presbyterians had definitely given up the principle that the Church *ought* to be established : the Free Church had maintained it. Further the Free Church as a whole had come to the conclusion that the time had come when its confessional statements should be revised. It was perhaps too much to expect that no voices should be raised against the proposal to unite with those who had forsaken a central principle of Presbyterianism, when coupled with an alteration in the actual standards of faith. There were 27 such voices against 643, and by an irony of law the House of Lords decided that the 27 were the Free Church of Scotland, and the rightful possessors not only of the name, but of all the property. A special Act of Parliament had to be passed to enable a proportion of the property to be restored to the 643. So difficult is it for the ecclesiastical *imperium* to contract out of its relation to the civil one. The new united body took the name of the United Free Church of Scotland.

In 1921 the way for a greater act of union was made ready. The Established Church of Scotland and the United Free Church are to become one church again, and the only Presbyterians in Scotland who will not belong to the Established Church are the remnants of the old Free Church—the " Wee Frees," as they are called.

But the principle for which the Free Church contended has been won. Establishment need not mean accepting the dictation of the State. The Church's independence of the State is recognised by Parliament in the most explicit manner. " This Church," says the Church of Scotland Act,[1] " receives from the Lord Jesus Christ alone the right and

[1] 11 and 12 Geo. V. 1921.

power, subject to no civil authority, to legislate and adjudicate finally in all matters of doctrine, worship, government and discipline in the Church, including the right to determine all questions concerning membership and office in the Church, the constitution and membership of its courts, and the mode of election of its office-bearers, and to define the boundaries of the spheres of labour of its ministers and other office-bearers." " Establishment," in other words, means recognition by the civil authority, but gives that authority no right of interference. The Free Church has won the day on its famous watchword of the " Crown rights of the Redeemer," without surrendering that " Establishment principle " so dear to the hearts of all good Presbyterians.

Among the most important proposals for Reunion which are at this moment being considered are those which concern South India. The negotiations during the past five years have been long and complicated and can only be summarised here.

Until recently the South of India contained a most extraordinary confusion of religious bodies. In addition to the usual and expected denominations there was a body of Dutch Reformed, and also, along the Malabar coast, a little group of pre-European native Christians, divided into no less than four separate churches. There were and still are the so-called Orthodox Syrians, not really " Orthodox " in the strict sense at all, but owning allegiance to the Jacobite Patriarch of Antioch, and therefore out of communion with the Orthodox Church. This is the body which claims to derive from S. Thomas the Apostle. It is in any case of great antiquity, and numbers about 250,000. In ancient times it obtained recognition from the Hindu government as a *caste*, a fact which is said to account for its non-missionary character. During one period of its history it was governed by Nestorian Bishops from Mesopotamia. It is in touch with the Oxford Mission to Calcutta, whose ideal it is that this body may some day turn out to have been the nucleus of a true native Indian Church.

Secondly, there are those Jacobites who have accepted the Papacy and been received into communion with Rome. Of these, 250,000 are Latins, while the remaining 450,000 form the Uniate Church of Malabar. The story of their " conversion " belongs to the worst period of Jesuit domination and is unpleasant reading.

Thirdly, there are the Mar-Thomas Syrians, a body of reformed Jacobites, numbering 100,000 and claiming to be the original Syrian Church purged of all Jacobite, Nestorian and Roman accretions.

Fourthly, we notice the Syro-Chaldeans, a secession from the Roman obedience, who obtained a Bishop from the Nestorians in 1880. These amount to 40,000.

Of the numerous religious organisations in this part of India the Presbyterians, Congregationalists and Dutch Reformed have united into the " South India United Church."

In 1919 the United Church met a committee of Anglicans with a view to discussing Reunion. It was agreed that the Church needed elements from the three polities : Episcopal, Presbyteral, Congregational. The Anglicans pressed, as was natural, for the *historic* Episcopate, *i.e.* for Episcopal Consecration, the United Church stood out for constitutional Episcopacy, and for spiritual equality (which seems to mean the recognition of Ministers not episcopally ordained, and admission of the unconfirmed to Holy Communion), and stated that they could not disown their Orders.

The Mar-Thomas Church was invited to join in the discussion, but contented themselves with making an unofficial declaration of their own position, while welcoming the idea of union.

It is difficult for Catholic-minded people to feel very much enthusiasm for the scheme, as far as it has been made known to us. We have seen that there is reason to look at Reunion with Congregationalists with some fear. Of course, it is possible that all *these* Congregationalists are orthodox in theology ; and possibly their acceptance of Episcopacy may be taken as a token that they are doubtful of the adequacy of the interpretation of " The Holy Catholic Church " which has hitherto satisfied them. Indeed we must notice this great difference between the South Indian proposals and the reception given to the Lambeth proposals by the English Congregational Union. The United Church is willing to accept the Apostles' Creed and the Nicene Creed. It is true that some church councils did raise objections, but it seems to have been made clear that the matter can only go forward on this basis. Further, it seems that the United Church does restrict the right of celebrating Holy Communion to Ministers. Also it is to the good that the latest plan for the " commissioning " of ministers implies that all, or practically all, of the ministers of both parts shall enter on the ministry of the greater Church at the same time. This would obviate the almost intolerable situation of the *interim* period during which some ministers of each body would be also recognised as ministers of the other, while as yet there was no corporate union between the two. It is a real *corporate* Reunion which is being proposed, of the type contemplated by the three Bishops in *Lambeth and Reunion*.

But it cannot be denied that some of the suggestions seem difficult of acceptance. The most serious difficulty is the form of the " commission " proposed to be given to Ministers on either side to enable them to minister in churches to which at present they have no access. It is hardly possible, with the best will in the world, to accept this as a valid Ordination. The actual form of commission is ingeniously equivocal, and *might*, as it stands, be interpreted as an Ordination. But the Ministers to be commissioned are to make a declaration, apparently during the course of the service of Commission, that " Nothing which we now do or say is to be interpreted as throwing doubt upon our previous ordination." Now it is essential for the satisfaction of those who believe that episcopal Ordination is necessary, that it should be *possible* at least to consider that this service of commission is an effective Ordination. And it is one thing to allow the Ministers who are coming into communion with the Anglican Church to hold and make public the opinion that they have been ordained already and that to them the service is a mere commissioning ; but it is quite another matter if the service itself makes it clear that their view is officially accepted. It would be far better if the declaration of their own belief in the validity of their Orders were to be made as an act of the present South India United Church in one of their own gatherings, rather than in the presence of the ordaining Bishop. For in the latter case it would come very near indeed to an expressed and official avowal of the Bishop that he did not intend to confer Holy Orders. From the Catholic point of view this would invalidate his action.

Further, it seems impossible to *approve*, even though it might be tolerated for the sake of unity, the plan whereby those who have already received Episcopal Ordination should accept a commission for a " wider ministry " by means of imposition of hands. *That* is the token of Ordination, and it seems merely confusing to use it when both sides are agreed that Ordination has already been received. It would be better to reserve that for cases where one party is not satisfied as to the validity of the Orders already conferred.

Another rather important matter which is still under discussion between the two Churches is a suggestion made by Dr. Bartlet of Mansfield College, Oxford, that in all future Consecrations of Bishops, Presbyters as well as Bishops should lay their hands on the head of the new Bishop, to signify the acceptance in the united church of the Presbyterian principle as well as the Episcopal. For this there is the possible precedent of 1 Tim. iv. 14. On the other hand the carrying out of this suggestion would seem to imply that the Bishop's Episcopal character is partly delegated to him by his subordinates. The usual Catholic method by which a Bishop is consecrated by Bishops alone (whereas a Priest

is ordained by a Bishop with the co-operation of the presbytery), implies that the Bishop has at least one essential
power which is withheld from the Presbyter, namely, that of
ordaining. The jurisdiction of a Bishop may be, perhaps ought
to be, assigned to him by his subordinates ; but this fact is
most naturally implied in the election of the Bishop rather than
in Consecration. There does seem something very unnatural
in the idea of Presbyters giving to the new Bishop something
which they do not themselves possess. But if all else were
satisfactorily arranged it is hardly likely that anyone on the
Anglican side would wish to hold out on this point alone.

Something must also be said on the proposals recently
made and accepted at a series of Conferences between
Anglicans and Presbyterians at Montreal. Again we are
faced with very serious difficulties in the method of " commissioning." The form of declaration which is to be read
by the Bishop himself is much more satisfactory than the
South Indian proposed form. It states quite clearly that
the candidates are to receive by the laying on of hands " a
commission to the office of the priesthood, it being clearly
understood that there is no repudiation of . . . their past
ministry." No exception need be taken to this on the
Anglican side. But having accepted so much it seems
strange that the Presbyterians were not willing to accept a
form of Ordination less equivocal than the vague formula
actually set forth : " Take thou authority to execute this
office.". . . It seems that the one thing needful has been
omitted : namely, certainty that now at any rate the minister is
really a Catholic priest. There is no need to raise the question
whether he was one before or not : but why go to all this
trouble to secure the imposition of episcopal hands if the
position afterwards is just as uncertain as it was before ?

In Australia negotiations are also proceeding, but have not
reached so advanced a stage. The non-Episcopal Churches
have accepted the principle of Episcopacy as the means of
government of the reunited church, but have stated that they

cannot accept any form of commission which could be interpreted as an Ordination.

A more hopeful precedent is furnished by a proposed Concordat drawn up by a Commission of the Episcopal Church in America as a basis for negotiations with the Orthodox and the Old Catholics. It is important enough to be quoted almost in full.

" We accept with common mind the traditional and Oecumenically received Faith, Ministry and Sacramental Order of the historic Catholic Church ; acknowledging, however, that . . . each particular autonomous part of the Catholic Church has authority to regulate its own internal government, ritual and spiritual discipline in adjustment to its peculiar racial, national and modern conditions and circumstances.

" In particular :

" (a) We accept the authority of the Catholic Church over all the faithful to teach what is necessary to be believed and practised for salvation, and to enforce by spiritual means such holy discipline as may be required for the protection of the Church's Faith and Order, and for the guidance of souls in the way of eternal life.

" (b) We accept the canonical Scriptures as the veritable Word of God, as given for the upbuilding of believers in the Faith which they have received from Christ through His Church, and as confirming and illustrating all doctrine and practice which is generally to be believed and fulfilled for salvation. In controversies as to the meaning of Holy Scripture we accept the Catholic Faith as affording a true summary . . . .

" (c) We accept the Nicene Creed, the decrees of faith put forth by the Oecumenically accepted General Councils, and the Sacraments as means of grace."

" In accordance with the preceding agreements we do solemnly declare our acceptance of the sacramental acts each of the other, and that they are true and valid. And, holding fast the truth once delivered to the Saints, we pronounce that intercommunion is desirable and authorised for all our members wherever and whenever it is deemed convenient and practicable by the proper local ecclesiastical authorities." [1]

This document was presented by a deputation of the Commission which visited Europe in the summer of 1920 to the Old Catholic Bishop of Switzerland (Bishop Herzog), who with the approval of his National Council endorsed and signed it ; to the Metropolitan (Mgr. Meletios) and Governing Synod of Greece, who endorsed the proposal as " very satisfactory " ; to the Locum Tenens of the Patriarchal Throne (Mgr. Dorotheos) and the Holy Governing Synod of Constantinople, who approved and unreservedly accepted the proposed Concordat, sealing it with the Great Seal of the Patriarchate ; and to the Armenian Patriarch of Constantinople (Mgr. Zaven).

This document is of the happiest augury for the future relations of the Churches concerned, and is the high water mark of negotiations for intercommunion. It does not of course amount to Reunion ; but, if put into force, it constitutes the fullest economic recognition of the Anglican and Old Catholic position on the part of the Orthodox, which is the best that can be looked for at present, and provides all that is urgently needed. Nor is it so unpractical as it may seem at first sight. An Eastern Orthodox is somewhat of a rarity in our own country, but in America there is a considerable number of such immigrants, and the problem of providing them with the Sacraments is a real one.[2]

An arrangement has also been entered into between the American Episcopal Church and the Hungarian Reformed Church in New York on the basis of the Ministers of the

[1] Bell, *Documents on Christian Unity*, p. 49.

[2] A similar agreement between Anglican and Orthodox Bishops has been made in South Africa ; and in many parts of the world Orthodox Bishops are bidding members of their flocks, when isolated, to resort to Anglican ministrations for the Sacraments.

latter receiving " additional Ordination," using the American Episcopal Consecration Prayer, and accepting the Nicene Creed and the two great Sacraments. Presbyteral Confirmation received in the past is not to be repeated, but in future Confirmation is to be administered by Bishops.

NOTE. Since this chapter was written the Joint Committee of Anglican and Free Churchmen (see p. 181) has issued a further statement (dated June 1925).

It contains the following documents :

1. A second Memorandum from the Anglican members of the sub-committee on the status of the Free Church Ministries. Two alternative suggestions are made for the regularising of such ministries : firstly, that ministers who so desire shall receive a " commission," similar to that already suggested in the South Indian negotiations (see pp. 187, 188), which might or might not be interpreted as an Ordination : secondly, that such ministers shall be ordained *sub conditione*. The memorandum points out that the Free Churches have agreed to the principle that in a reunited Church the Episcopate ought to be accepted as the ordaining authority, and that therefore the difficulty only arises during the period between Reunion and the dying out of the pre-Reunion ministers. To this document is appended a note from the Free Church members of the sub-committee, which amounts to a courteous but candid rejection of the Anglican proposals.

2. A Memorandum on the meaning of a constitutional Episcopate, by the Bishop of Truro and Dr. Garvie, to which the Joint Committee gave general approval. This agrees very closely with the plan outlined by the three Bishops (see pp. 177, 178), except that the authors seem to hope that the concurrent jurisdictions of Group-Bishops will ultimately coalesce into the normal Diocesan arrangement. They adduce the interesting parallel of the healing of the Donatist schism by the temporary toleration of two episcopal jurisdictions in one area.

3. Three short Memoranda on the relation of the Free Churches to Communions with which they are in fellowship in other parts of the world ; on the problems of Establishment ; and on the safeguarding of the principles of the Reformation.

XVI

THE PRESENT POSITION

A SHORT conspectus of the state of the Christian world to-day will give us our problem in detail. Statistics of this kind can never be pressed : some religious bodies are naturally far stricter than others in their methods of reckoning membership ; but it is useful when considering the possibilities of Reunion to have a rough idea how the religions of the world are actually grouped.

At least half the Christians in the world are included in the Roman Catholic Church, and we are safe in estimating the numbers of this vast Communion at between 250,000,000 and 300,000,000.

To these must be added the members of the various Uniate Churches, to the number of 6,500,000. The present distress of the Orthodox Church will probably lead to an increase in the numbers of Uniates in Syria.

It is impossible to do more than guess the present strength of Eastern Orthodoxy. Before the War the Greek Orthodox (*i.e.* the Patriarchate of Constantinople with the autonomous Churches of Greece and Cyprus) were estimated at 15,000,000, the Slavs at 100,000,000. The Patriarchates of Alexandria, Antioch and Jerusalem would not, taken together, have amounted to more than 400,000.

The numbers are now of course tragically reduced. Christianity in Asia Minor has been wiped out. In Russia also, under the Bolshevist Terror, the Church has been decimated. A rich harvest of martyrs has been garnered in Heaven ; but the ground where it grew lies bare, desolate and trodden under foot.   We hear of a spiritual revival among the faithful remnant of the Russian Church ; but an un-scrupulous government has done its worst to destroy the ancient faith of that vast country.   The schismatical " Living Church " set up by the Bolshevists has come to grief ; but no one can tell us even approximately the number of Russian Orthodox to-day.

Next to Russia there are more Orthodox to be found in Rumania than in any other country.   They number about twelve million.   Rumania, however, contains large minorities professing a different obedience.   There are about 3,000,000 Roman Catholics, a large proportion of whom are to be found among the Magyar population of Transylvania, and perhaps 1,000,000 Protestants.   Com-plaints are made of serious persecution directed by the government against both Catholics and Protestants.   This persecution is of course political in character, and aims at supporting the national Orthodox Church, and discouraging the religion of the Magyars.   There are also a considerable number—over 1,000,000—of Uniates.   It is said that the currents of conversion are inclined to set from Pro-testantism to the Latin Church, and from Uniatism to Orthodoxy.

In Jugo-Slavia, the new Serbia, no less than five inde-pendent Orthodox Churches have now coalesced under the government of a Patriarch, appointed in 1921 with the full consent of Constantinople.   The Orthodox are said to number 7,000,000 ; but there is much religious unsettle-ment, and a tendency to lapse into Protestantism in some cases, and in others into infidelity.   The Croats and Slovenes are chiefly Roman Catholic, and in Croatia there is much politico-religious discontent.

In Bulgaria the strange ecclesiastical position continues unchanged : the Bulgarian national Church is in communion with the Slav Orthodox, though officially excommunicated by the Greeks on the question of the jurisdiction of the Patriarch.

Poland is predominantly Roman Catholic, with an admixture of Ruthenian Uniates. There are also a considerable number of members of the Mariaviten Church, which is an attempt to combine Catholicism and Nationalism. This body originated with a monastic order which made an attempt to revive the rule of S. Francis in its original form. Its earlier development was marred by a certain amount of wild talk on the part of its visionary leaders, male and female. It is, of course, out of communion with Rome.

Religious affairs in Czecho-Slovakia are in a very unstable condition. Until 1920 the country was mostly Roman Catholic, with the exception of a certain number of Moravians of German race, and, among the Slovaks, a few Protestants of the Calvinist persuasion. In 1919 a hundred and seventy Czech priests appealed to Rome for a married clergy, Communion in both kinds and a vernacular liturgy. Unfortunately the reforms were not granted. Great feeling was aroused and a new national Church was founded amid much enthusiasm. At first as many as 800,000 joined the new body, which was fostered for political reasons by President Masaryk and Edouard Benes, the founders of Czecho-Slovak independence. It can hardly be maintained that the alleged reasons were sufficient to justify the extremely serious step of creating a schism ; but the affair was rushed through, and less than two months after the decision had been taken the new Church was recognised by the State. The authorities at Rome arranged for the resignation of some of the Bishops, who were considered to be hostile to Czecho-Slovakian nationalism, and a large proportion of the more conservative-minded seceders returned to their Roman allegiance. The new Church now began to develop two opposite tendencies. One party, under the leadership of Mgr. Gorazd Pavlik, represented the conservative current, and were strongly drawn in the direction of Orthodoxy.   This party naturally enjoyed the support of their Slav neighbours, the Jugo-Slavs, both for religious and political reasons.   At first this policy won the day. The Czecho-Slovak Church formally accepted the whole body of Orthodox doctrine, but apparently with some hesitation and without complete unanimity.   The question of liturgy was also left unsettled.   Gorazd was consecrated as Bishop of Olmütz by the Patriarch of Jugo-Slavia, other Serbian Bishops and the Metropolitan Antony of Kiev.   Serbian and Russian Orthodox priests came and worked in Czecho-Slovakia at the Bishop's invitation.

But there have been other tendencies at work also.   A strong party among the Czechs resented the apparent Orientalising of the Church.   Others were drawn to a Liberalising policy.   Others again were influenced by the Hussite traditions of Bohemia.   Finally Gorazd resigned his see, and retired to Ruthenia in the extreme East of Czecho-Slovakia, where he has since governed a small flock of Orthodox.

A young priest named Farsky was now elected " Patriarch " of the National Church, and it seemed to have broken with Orthodoxy altogether, even to the extent of dispensing with Consecration for its Bishops.   But it is impossible to say which turning will ultimately be taken. Patriotic and racial feelings are deeply engaged.   There is some possibility of an ecclesiastical alliance with Rumania. Others are looking to the American Church.   Others again to the Church of England.

Externally there has been no abandonment of Catholic practice.   A Czech translation of the Roman Missal is in use, and Communion is given in both kinds.[1]

Gorazd's troubles were not at an end.   There were at Prague some Czechs who had always been Orthodox, and until the emerging of the short-lived Orthodox Church of

[1] Gorazd and his followers had naturally used the Orthodox Byzantine liturgy.

Czecho-Slovakia had been under Russian jurisdiction. Their numbers were enlarged by the addition of Czechs who had wandered as far as Kiev, and had now returned as refugees. Together they chose yet another Bishop, one Savati. He was consecrated by the Russian Church, and claimed jurisdiction over all the Orthodox in Czecho-Slovakia, including 10,000 Russian refugees. This brought him into conflict with Gorazd, who was recognised by the Serbs as having Orthodox jurisdiction in Ruthenia. The Russians, on the other hand, were inclined to support Savati's claim. The dispute seems likely to be settled by the reconciliation of Savati and Gorazd, and the recognition of the former as having general jurisdiction over the whole country.

Hungary is divided between Roman Catholicism and a strict Calvinism : naturally there is no intercourse between the two, and no desire for Reunion.

Austria is Roman Catholic ; but there is a small colony of Old Catholics, numbering about 29,000.

Germany is partly Roman Catholic, and partly Protestant, the division between Catholic and Protestant states being rather sharply outlined. The Protestantism, nominally Lutheran, is of a very much " reduced " character, and hardly any definition of faith is to be looked for. A purely humanitarian view of Christ is almost universal, at any rate in circles which are in any way academic. But in 1912 some stir was caused by the deposition of a minister who had taught that there were no firmly grounded, eternally valid truths whatever !

There has been an enormous output of laborious and valuable work in the department of higher criticism, nor can German *historical* criticism be ignored, deeply though we may distrust its rationalistic assumptions. And among the religious philosophers of Germany there are also very great names indeed.

In recent years, however, the " High Church " Lutheran movement has been gaining ground. In October 1918—

the date is indeed remarkable—the inaugural meeting of the High Church Union was held at Berlin, and an exposition of its principles was put out. In one phrase their object is " the re-organisation of the churches of the Reformation." In more detail they stand for independence of the State, the restoration of the Episcopal Order, more stress on the Sacraments, more ceremonial, less preaching, private confession (voluntary), community life, a reformed breviary and the recovery of the consciousness of belonging to the Catholic Church. In fact this consciousness of Catholicism (as opposed to the mere sense of belonging to a particular church) is by this school made the test of belonging to the true Church. But there is no sign of a desire to accept the Papacy, except as a primacy which might be given to a particular Bishop, if the Church so thought good. Finally, there is a strong sense of the work which lies before Germany in the matter of Reunion. " From them issued the separation of the Church, and in them alone lie the seeds of Reunion."

It is clear that some at any rate of this school would welcome the restoration of the Episcopal succession [1]; and it might be supposed that their principles would naturally lead them to look to the Old Catholics as a link between themselves and a more Catholic polity. Old Catholicism has not made much progress in Germany, and a combination between the two non-Papal Catholic-minded movements might give them both new force and compel an attention which neither seems able to gain by itself. But it is perhaps hardly likely that the party has moved far enough in a Catholic direction to amalgamate naturally at present with Old Catholicism. As a fact it shows a tendency to seek alliances in two different directions. The Bavarians are looking towards the English Church, the Prussians towards Swedish Lutheranism.[2]

---

[1] In the sense of a succession of consecrators, not merely of office.

[2] See an article by Rev. L. Patterson, in *Theology*, December 1921.

Switzerland is divided in much the same way as Germany except that the Protestant cantons profess Calvinism instead of the so-called Lutheranism of Germany. The Old Catholics have a Bishop at Bern. They number about 30,000 with 57 priests and 46 parishes.

In Norway the State Church (Episcopal Lutheran) is said to comprise 98 per cent. of the population. There is no episcopal succession, nor at present much wish for it ; but a claim is made to a presbyteral succession derived from Luther.

In Denmark there is also an Episcopal Lutheran State Church.

The same is true of Sweden ; but in that country it seems almost certain that the Episcopal succession has been preserved. For this reason Reunion between ourselves and the Swedish Church is a living issue. The Archbishop of Upsala is a very prominent figure in the Reunion movement, and is credited with a desire to set up a strong and united international Evangelical Episcopal Church. With this view he has already consecrated Bishops for Hungary and Latvia.

Coming to our own country, it is well known that the inveterate habit of all Englishmen is to call themselves " Church of England " if they bear no other allegiance. This makes statistics difficult.

Nominal Church of England membership is about 20,000,000 for England and Wales combined. Easter Communions actually made in 1923 were slightly under 2,500,000 in England and slightly over 170,000 in Wales. The number on the electoral rolls is only about 1,000,000.

The Scottish Episcopal Church numbers about 60,000 communicant members, the Church of Ireland rather more than 575,000. Roman Catholics number about 2,000,000 in England and Wales, about 500,000 in Scotland and about 3,375,000 in Ireland.

Of other churches we naturally begin with the Church of Scotland, as the oldest fully organised non-Episcopal foundation, and the Established Church. Presbyterian reunion is, as we have seen, practically an accomplished fact. Only the " Free Church," the body commonly known as the " Wee Frees," remains outside. Projects for Reunion with the Episcopal Church have naturally been in abeyance during the negotiations for Presbyterian Reunion. It seems clear that Reunion between the Church of England and the Church of Scotland is only possible by means of the Scottish Episcopal Church.

The communicants of the Church of Scotland number over 700,000 : those of the United Free Church over 500,000.

In England the Congregationalist Churches, as on their own principles they should surely be called, have come very near to uniting into a single church. They maintain the principle of Independency as the *right* of each local congregation in the last resort ; but in practice a list of recognised ministers is kept, and a congregation whose minister was not recognised by the Congregational Union would find itself excluded from fellowship. Creeds are objected to on principle, but a minister is required to state before recognition what " message " he has to give. The condition of membership is a personal faith in Christ as Saviour and Lord. Theologically English Congregationalism is inclined to a rather extreme Liberalism. Its members number almost 500,000.

The Baptists are less numerous in this country. In theory they are differentiated from the Congregationalists only by their well-known practice in regard to Baptism, but they are more closely federated and hence have tended to be more orthodox.

The Methodists number more than 850,000, of whom the Wesleyans—the original stock—are much the largest body. It seems probable that the three bodies, Wesleyan, United and Primitive, will shortly reunite. The difference between them as representing different strata of society, and thus

favouring different evangelistic methods, has almost disappeared. But there is one very serious difference remaining. Alone among British non-Episcopalians the
Wesleyans reserve to a Minister the right of presiding at
the Communion : Reunion would probably mean sooner or
later that this restriction would come to an end. Like other
Nonconformists they have been a good deal influenced by
Liberalism.

The Society of Friends numbers 20,000 in England, and
2000 in Ireland. It is remarkable that out of this small
number over a hundred are engaged in mission work abroad.
The modern Quakers have been deeply influenced by the
Evangelical revival, and by the modern zeal for social service.
Thus has come more contact with men of other views, which
has rubbed off the sharp edge of their peculiarities. They
still have no formal ministers ; but the " monthly meeting "
of contiguous congregations appoints overseers and elders,
the latter of whom have some pastoral responsibilities. They
have no Sacraments, but are admitted to the Society by the
consent of the monthly meeting.

In North Wales Calvinistic Methodism is the predominant
religion, and the Calvinism is still really Calvinistic. The
actual communicant members of this body amount to 187,000
and their adherents to about an equal number. There are
also all over the country very many Independents (still
retaining the Cromwellian name) and Baptists. The
ancient Welsh Church has come to life wonderfully during
the past fifty years, and Disestablishment seems to have
increased her energies and powers. The clergy are for the
most part bilingual, and in many places ungrudgingly double
their Sunday duties in order that both Welsh and English
may have their services in the language most familiar to
them. But the memories of political antagonism are yet too
recent for any desire or serious thought of Reunion to have
emerged.

In Ireland also politics have left their trail, and religious hatred, shameful to say, is still a potent force. The Roman-ism of the South and the Protestantism of the North are in vehement opposition. The Church of Ireland, representing originally English or Scottish Elizabethan and Jacobean settlers, is for the most part strongly Protestant, and under the domination of the wealthy laity ; but in some places the influence of the Catholic revival is making itself felt.

In the United States of America the most striking religious phenomenon at the moment is the great growth of Roman Catholicism : a growth which is helped by the fact that Catholic insistence on the purity of marriage makes for family life and the domestic virtues. It remains to be seen what effect if any the American character will have on Roman Catholicism itself. " Americanism " has made itself felt as a force to be reckoned with and suppressed before now. It may be more difficult to suppress it when it comes to the front again. American Romanism also contains a strong and apparently rather fanatical Irish element.

The other churches which have most religious influence in the United States are in order of numbers the Methodists, the Baptists and the Congregationalists. Of the total number of Methodists in the world (10,000,000 members and pro-bationers, and at least another 22,000,000 adherents) by far the largest number are to be found in the United States. The Congregationalists are even less orthodox than their English brethren, and are said to be very largely Unitarian.

The Episcopal Church only comes seventh on the list of religious bodies, but it has over a million actual communi-cants, and is increasing with a healthy rapidity.

Religious life is much disturbed, both in the Episcopal Church and still more among the non-Episcopal communities, by the extravagant contest which is being waged between " Modernists " and " Fundamentalists." We all know what Modernism is, and we may be sure that it is not watered down in the land of superlatives. Fundamentalism is what on this side of the water we should call Obscurantism.

It is, in fact, the policy of Prohibition in the sphere of historical criticism.

In Canada the position is somewhat different. Roman Catholicism is again very strong, but it is largely concentrated in the French provinces, where the population is rapidly growing. It is of a quieter and more normal type than that of the United States. In the rest of Canada matters are fairly evenly divided between the " Church of England in Canada " and the new United Church, consisting of an amalgamation of the Presbyterian, Methodist and Congregational Churches. This union has come about as the result of twenty years' negotiations. The terms of union are based on evangelical standards of orthodoxy, and have even a slightly old-fashioned ring. We hear about " our first parents " and " conscious assurance," quite in the traditional manner. The Catholic Creeds are accepted. On the other hand all are admitted to the Lord's Supper who make a credible profession of faith in the Lord Jesus Christ and of obedience to the Law of God. The latter phrase must presumably be interpreted to mean an *intention* to obey the Divine Law. But we cannot help noticing that extraordinary laxity about Baptism which is unfortunately characteristic of the non-Episcopal churches of the present day. Union has only been achieved at the price of the disruption of the Presbyterian Church, a strong minority of whom remain outside.

In India we are faced at the moment with an extraordinary state of affairs so far as the Anglican Church is concerned. Most of the theories on which it has been built up imply that it exists as an Establishment to minister to English people resident in India. But in fact it is, of course, very largely a missionary body. However, the Indian Church seems to be in process of securing its own disestablishment, and this will automatically bring the many anomalies to an end. One striking result of the growth of the native Church has been the strong desire for Christian unity which has sprung up among the native Christians themselves. We have already considered the details of the scheme by which it is hoped to bring about a partial unity in Southern India.

In Australia the Anglican communicants number about 170,000.[1] In New Zealand the Anglican Church claims 44 per cent. of the population.

South Africa, like India, is a land where the same ecclesiastical arrangements have to be adapted for a white population and for native converts ; but there is no hampering and obsolete code binding it to hard and fast Anglican traditions. It is in fact an autonomous National Church.

A book on Reunion would be very incomplete without some account of the Uniate Churches. A Uniate is a Catholic who is " Roman " in the sense of being in communion with the Pope, but non-Roman in the sense of using a different liturgy and following different religious customs.

The Uniate Churches represent the ancient Patriarchates, other than those of Rome, in so far as they are in communion with the Roman see. When the East and West separated in 1054 the Oriental Churches ceased to hold communion with Rome. Up to that time there had been churches with married clergy, leavened bread and a totally different form of service from that of Rome, in full communion with her. Nor had the Papacy ever made any attempt to press the Eastern to follow her customs in these matters. We may think that on the whole the East was in the right in the matters which caused the final separation, but to do Rome justice it was the Easterns, not the Romans, who made all the pother about externals.

As is natural, Rome has always made efforts to bring the Easterns back to unity with herself, and always it has been

[1] Attempts on the part of the Presbyterian, Methodist and Congregational Churches in Australia to unite into a single Church have broken down after twenty-one years' negotiations. As in Canada, Presbyterian opinion was much divided, and Australian Presbyterians were not prepared to face disruption.

unity in doctrine that she has pressed for, not uniformity
of rite or ceremonial. Consequently, whenever a body of
Easterns, however small, has shown itself ready to enter her
fold, it has always been allowed to keep its own rites and
customs. Nor does this mean simply that there are
" Roman " Catholics who use the Byzantine rite. It is quite
true that this is the only rite used in the Orthodox Church ;
but that is because the Orthodox have in the past made such
a point of absolute uniformity. But the Oriental Churches
who separated from the Orthodox on points of doctrine took
this step in most cases before the Byzantine liturgy had
ousted all other rites. Thus it comes about that the Chaldees, the Copts, the Syrians, the Abyssinians, the Armenians,
the Malabar Church, have each their own rite. Consequently,
when any group within these bodies has come into union with
Rome, their own rite has not been suppressed in favour
either of the Roman or the Byzantine liturgy : there was
nothing heretical in the rite, or if there were it could easily
be amended, and no objection was made to its continuance.
The theory was that Patriarchate and rite went together.
The Westerns were in the Roman Patriarchate, and so were
to follow the Roman rite : the Easterns, though subject to
the Pope *as Pope*, were not under his Patriarchal jurisdiction
and so were not obliged to follow his rite. As a matter of
fact, attempts have been made at various times to Romanise
the Oriental rites of the Uniate Churches, and rather grotesque
hybrid rites have resulted ; but this is now recognised as
an abuse, and the policy of the Vatican has rather been to
press in recent years for a scrupulous accuracy in the render-
ing of Eastern services in an Eastern way.

   In most cases the Uniate Churches are portions of an
Orthodox or Heterodox Eastern Church which has entered
into unity with Rome, but the small group of Byzantine
Uniates to be found in Southern Italy and Sicily can show
continuity of jurisdiction, although in *personnel* they now
consist almost entirely of Albanian immigrants. The Roman

authorities claim that the Melkites, Chaldees and Malabar Uniates are the ancient stock, and that the Orthodox Syrians are a schism which broke away from the old Church on its returning into communion with Rome. However this may be, it is the case that at this moment every Eastern Church, Orthodox, or Heterodox, has its Uniate counterpart, hardly differing externally at all from the non-Roman corresponding Church. The Uniate clergy are married : Holy Communion is given in both kinds : the services are in the vernacular, or at any rate not in Latin ; and it would be impossible to tell by mere inspection that the congregation looked to the Pope as their spiritual head.

There is also one small body of Uniates who have no corresponding non-Papal Church. These are the Maronites of Mount Lebanon, who after having held to the Mono-thelite heresy since the seventh century (being the only permanent schism which was founded on that belief), were persuaded in 1182 by the Crusaders to return as a body to the Catholic faith, and accept the supremacy of the Pope.[1]

The fact that so many of the Uniates represent a returned *Heterodox* church accounts for their very curious grouping. In the Uniate organisation the old Patriarchates of Alex-andria, Antioch and Jerusalem have practically disappeared, and the Uniate Patriarchs represent Rites rather than geo-graphical areas. Thus there is a Coptic Patriarch, a Melkite Patriarch, a Syrian Patriarch, a Maronite Patriarch. In each case he is technically a Patriarch of one or more of the ancient Patriarchal sees ; but for practical purposes he is the head of a liturgical group.

Of the Uniates the following groups use the Byzantine rite, *i.e.* the same rite as the Eastern Orthodox : Italo-Greeks, Greeks, Georgians, Melkites, Ruthenians, Serbs, Bulgars, Rumanians. The Italo-Greeks have in the past

---

[1] The Maronites have deliberately adopted unleavened bread, Com-munion in one kind, and Western vestments.

admitted an extraordinary amount of Latinisation into their rite, even including the use of unleavened bread ; but the tide is now setting strongly in the other direction. The Greek Uniates are few in number and are discouraged by the government, who insist on all converts to Rome changing their rite and becoming Latins. The Melkites owe their name (which means " imperialists ") to the fact that when most of Egypt and Syria embraced Monophysitism in the sixth century, the Orthodox remnant held with the faith favoured by the Emperor. So the name stuck ; and when in later days this remnant was again divided into " Orthodox " and " Catholic " it so happened that the name Melkite was appropriated to the latter. The Ruthenians are Russian by race, but until the war were mostly domiciled in Hungary. The Magyars made no attempt to civilise them, or to influence their religion. In Russia itself Uniatism was persecuted out of existence : but at one time the Metropolitan of Kiev and nine Bishops were in communion with Rome. Uniates are rather numerous in Serbia and Rumania : in the latter country, however, converts to Rome are encouraged by the Roman authorities to adopt the Latin rite.

The other groups of Uniates have their own peculiar rites : the Copts using an Alexandrian type, the others worshipping according to variants of the ancient Syrian liturgy which had its headquarters at Antioch.[1]

The connection of the Uniate churches with the wealth and culture of the West makes it true to say that on the whole their adherents enjoy a political, educational and secular position superior to that of the Orthodox. But it may be doubted whether the Uniate bodies really do much for the cause of Reunion. Their propaganda is very bitterly resented in the East, and to Orthodox eyes they seem to be not indigenous bodies who have joined hands with another

[1] Most of this information is extracted from Dr. Fortescue's *The Uniate Eastern Churches*, a work which his untimely death prevented him from finishing.

part of the Church so much as creations of the Vatican seducing the children of the East by specious imitation and worldly advantages.

But for those who are trying to solve the problems of Reunion the Uniates are a continual reminder that the problem is ultimately one of doctrine and not of practice.

XVII

THE POSSIBILITY OF REUNION

IT is time to bring our historical survey to an end and to see whether in its rather lurid light we can discern the dim outline of the future solution of our problems.

The first and most important conclusion to be drawn from history is certainly this : that we are none of us, as corporate bodies, free from very serious blame. That this seems a platitude is the most hopeful feature of the very difficult situation.

The second and complementary conclusion is that we are none of us *altogether* blameworthy. On our principles, which, however exaggerated, were seldom entirely false, we all had to take some such action as we did take. Inevitability seems to be written all along the course of events. Having gone so far on a course which in part was mistaken, and in part sinful, there could be no turning back. That is what gives the solemn note of tragedy to our schisms. What else could the actors have done in that mystical Passion Play which is Church history ? *Something* else doubtless ; the parts could have been more nobly played. But, when things had gone so far, can anyone suggest how any particular schism could have been avoided ? Less harshly, less blindly, less passionately men might have broken unity, but who will tell us how, persons and things being what they were, unity could have been maintained ? So schism was our punishment ; and the punishment consisted in our being left to experience the natural result of the past misdoings of the Church.

It may be that our place of repentance is not yet. Corporately we must go on in sin. But personally our sin will not be imputed to us, unless, which God forbid, we have the schismatic mind and heart.

And if schism has been penal, that means that it has been the lesser of two evils ; sometimes, even if not always. And this we can dimly see, by asking the question, What would have been the result if such a schism had not taken place ? Supposing, for instance, *things being what they were*, John Knox had been content to preach reform, and then submit himself to the hierarchy, are we quite sure that it would have been better than the revolt which in fact he did inflame ? It is easy to point out how much more Christian-like he might have shown himself ; but on the main point, Reform or Revolution, it is not easy to see how the Scottish Church of those days could have been purified with rose-water. Or to put a broader question, What would the Catholic Church be like to-day if there had been no Protestant Reformation, with the schisms which were inevitably connected with it ? Would the Counter-Reformation have been even as thorough a reform as it was ?

If, then, schism is in some sense providential, if, that is, it is in accordance with the *secondary* will of God, evil and accursed though it is, we must deal with it patiently, and not insist on getting rid of it at all costs. The remedy might turn out to be worse than the disease. But we must look at the matter every way, with sympathy, penitence and love ; we must explore all avenues ; we must try to put away prejudice. Having done this much as the minimum of our duty, we may be able to surmise at least from what direction to expect the dawn.

Reunion with the Roman Catholic Church

We must begin here. It is the fundamental problem for an English churchman. The breach with Rome was the beginning of our isolation, and the root of our subsequent

(or their)

disunion. Rome stands for unity. However much her
actual policy has been the cause, even the justification, of
schism, it is almost impossible to conceive of any other
centre for a reunited Church. " Hers," we might almost
say, in S. Paul's words, " is the adoption, and the glory, and
the covenants, and the giving of the law, and the service of
God, and the promises ; hers are the fathers ". . . Anglicanism looks provincial beside the majesty of Rome. That
of course is only one side of the question, but it is a side
which we cannot ignore. It is not always realised by
Anglicans how strong and ancient is the tradition, apart
from any question of dogma, of asking, as a rough and ready
test of Catholicism, " What does Rome say ? " or " Is he in
communion with the Apostolic See ? " It does not follow
that that is the only test that can be applied. If it did, there
would be no further question. We should all have to " go
over to Rome," and be done with it. But there are limits
to a mother's privileges, and Anglicans hold that these
limits have been transgressed. The question is : Can we
see any possibility of the matter being accommodated ? At
first sight it looks as though there was no choice between
complete submission and the continuance of the schism.
But the history of the seventeenth and eighteenth centuries
has taught us that some Roman Catholics at all events have
been prepared to modify their intransigeance, and the
twentieth century shows us once more the spectacle of Roman
and Anglican Catholics sitting down to discuss the question
whether anything can be done. The matter is, of course, made
immensely more difficult by the existence of the Vatican
decrees, which we shall have to consider in considerable detail.
On the one hand they seem at first sight to express the Papal
claim in its most uncompromising and ultramontane form.
It looks as though they had been so framed as to exclude
the possibility of any " Gallican," for instance, remaining
in communion with the Pope. *A fortiori* no Anglican
could enter into such communion. We may be driven to

the conclusion that this is so. In that case we can see no way out, either now or in the future. On the other hand, we must recognise that the Roman Church cannot be expected to commit suicide. Supposing, for the sake of the argument, that her most enlightened sons would wish the decrees dealing with the supremacy and infallibility of the Pope to have been very differently expressed, they cannot now be contradicted. It would be ungenerous for anyone to press that they should be, unless we can show that there is no tolerable meaning which they can be made to bear. Rome cannot contradict herself. But she can explain. And if it seems that the only tolerable way of explaining the Vatican decrees goes near to explaining them away, well, we cannot help that. Our Mother is perhaps a little hasty, and much as we love and admire her, great as is our veneration for her apostolic throne, and our gratitude for her gift of the Gospel to our forefathers, we cannot in so serious a matter compromise our honesty. Nor, of course, should we be asked to. That is why there would be little advantage in discovering some sense in which we think we might accept the decrees, unless we could have an assurance that that is a sense which the Roman authorities would tolerate. It would be far better that the explanations should come from those who are themselves responsible for the terms of communion which are proposed.

It may, of course, be said that there is an air of unreality about the whole discussion. Even supposing, a large supposition, that agreement could be come to between Roman Catholics and the Anglo-Catholic party, is it conceivable that the English Church as a whole would accept it ? We know quite well that the majority of Englishmen have no more wish to be reconciled to the Pope, than, in the carefully chosen words of the Dean of S. Paul's,[1] they have to the Grand Lama ; and neither Rome nor any section of English churchmen has any wish for the creation of a small Uniate

[1] In *The Review of the Churches.*

church, in communion with the Pope, but in schism from
Canterbury. We can just conceive circumstances in which
that would be a possible resort ; but it could never be other
than a hateful necessity. Still, even if we can see no likelihood of any immediate result, it is none the less a duty to
clear our minds and see where we stand.

What then would be the difficulties about corporate reunion with the Latin Church, supposing that the whole of the
Church of England were of one mind as to general Catholic
principles ; supposing, to put it roughly, that all the Anglican
Bishops could be relied upon to accept those doctrinal
standards which are common to East and West ?

We should have to face, first, the matter of the decrees of
the Vatican Council of 1870. These, of course, are the crux
of the matter. Rome is ready to " explain " them : is there
any explanation which would be satisfactory to us on our
side ?

We are encouraged by some Roman Catholic Divines,
notably by that learned, courteous and charitable Dominican,
Fr. McNabb, to consider what the decrees say, and not what
has been said about them. The decrees, we are told, mean
what they say, *and no more*. What then do they say ?

First, that S. Peter received from Christ directly and
immediately a primacy of true and proper (*propria*) jurisdiction.

Secondly, S. Peter has perpetual successors in his primacy
jure divino ; and that the Pope is the successor to S. Peter
in that primacy.

Thirdly, the Pope has full and supreme power of jurisdiction over the whole Church, as regards faith, morals,
discipline and government, and ordinary and immediate
jurisdiction over clergy and laity.

Finally, " the Roman Pontiff, when he speaks from the
Chair " (of Peter), " that is when fulfilling the function of
Shepherd and Teacher of all Christians, he defines by
his supreme Apostolic authority that a doctrine of faith or

morals is to be held by the whole Church, through the
Divine assistance promised to him in the person of Blessed
Peter, is strengthened by that infallibility with which the
Divine Redeemer willed His Church to be instructed in the
defining of a doctrine concerning faith or morals ; and
therefore the Roman Pontiff's definitions of this kind are
irreformable in themselves, and not from the consent of the
Church."

These seem stupendous claims : let us examine them
more closely.

First, let us see what they do *not* say.

They do not say that the Pope's *jurisdiction* is *jure divino*.

It would be the natural deduction to make from a combination of the first three decrees, but the deduction is
not actually made : it might conceivably be maintained
that though the Pope inherits S. Peter's position the extent
of his powers need not by Divine appointment be precisely
the same as that of S. Peter, and has in fact been extended
by the Church. Nor would it be inconsistent with the
wording of the decree to hold that our Lord merely ordained
that there should be a perpetual primacy, and the Church
attached it to the Bishopric of Rome. Presumably, therefore, the Church could transfer it to some other see ! It has
probably never occurred to any one to hold exactly this
opinion ; but the point of the second decree seems to be
that the Papacy itself, rather than its identification with
the Roman Bishopric, is a Divine ordinance. It was, on the
Papalist showing, S. Peter, rather than our Lord, who
connected the Primacy with Rome. Is this irreformable ?
Not that anyone wants it reformed : any more than anyone
wants any other family than the House of Windsor to sit
on the British Throne. But just as the fact that the nation
has ultimately *chosen* its Royal Family makes all the difference
to the temper of its loyalty, so if it could be thought that the
Church in the person of S. Peter *chose* a particular see to be
endued with the divinely ordered Primacy, it might make

all the difference to the prospect of that Primacy winning general acceptance.

Nor do the Vatican decrees actually say that the Pope's infallibility is *jure divino* ; though indeed the preamble to the fourth decree says that it is a dogma divinely revealed.

Further, it seems to be the case that no one is *obliged* (on grounds of Roman theology) to believe anything which is not propounded under anathema. And the anathema attached to the fourth decree is curiously vague. It is only directed against " anyone who presumes to contradict this Our definition." What is the exact effect on conscience of the difference between the anathemas of the first three decrees and that of the fourth is one of the points which we should have to ask the Papal theologians to explain.

Further, the fourth decree does not state that the consent of the Church is unnecessary *before* the definition is made, but merely that when it has been made it is valid apart from any *subsequent* consent of the Church. This might conceivably be interpreted to mean that the Papal confirmation, either of the decree of a General Council or of the opinion of the Teaching Church however obtained, is the *ratification* of that decree or opinion, and no further question can be raised about it. In other words, the Pope would be in the position of a constitutional monarch or the chairman of a corporate body whose signature is necessary for the validity of its *acta*. The Pope would in this respect hold the same position in relation to the universal Episcopate as the Primate of all England does to the Convocation of Canterbury.

It is not probable that any accredited Roman Catholic theologian would go to these lengths in explanation of the Vatican decrees ; but a time may come when minimising will be the word, and it seems therefore to be worth while to consider what is the mildest interpretation which can be put on the actual text of the definitions. And Roman Catholic theologians do remind us that the exercise of infallibility is strictly limited. The Pope does not act without the Church, or in independence of it. The Infallibility definition itself is fortified by an appeal to the approbation of the Sacred Council.[1] Nor are the casual statements of the Pope endowed with infallibility. It is only when addressing the whole Church in the most solemn and official manner possible that the Roman Pontiff claims this privilege.

Nor must the apparent strength of the language used lead us to suppose that the result of the Vatican Council simply represents the decisive victory of the extreme Ultramontanes. *Ex Cathedra* is a limitation which did not meet the approval of the extreme party. The Pope does not appear as the living oracle of Divine truth, still less as the possessor of a blank cheque-book by means of which he can obtain new revelations from God. As Fr. McNabb points out, " assistance " does not mean inspiration or omniscience : and the Pope's authority does not mean that he can promulgate an eleventh commandment, or add an eighth Sacrament, or a second sacrifice.[2]

Let us imagine, then, some future Synod of Anglican Bishops, say in the year 2000. They have *ex hypothesi* been satisfied that a minimising interpretation of the Definitions will be acceptable to the Vatican. They have to consider whether for the sake of unity they can or ought to accept them under such an interpretation. We should have to assume that the Church of England had been freed from the patronage of the State, and that the Bishops had been freely elected by some canonical body, and were truly representative of the Anglican Communion as a whole. We should assume also that the Catholicising of the tone and temper of the English Church had gone on at an equal rate to that

---

[1] But for the first time a conciliar decree was issued in the name of the Pope, not of the Council. The course of the debate makes it clear that " *definimus* " is a " royal plural," and does not mean that the Council as a whole was the authority for the definition.

[2] McNabb, *Infallibility*.

at which it is now proceeding.[1] Would it be conceivable that the Bishops, or a majority of them, would consent to sign the decrees ? Ought we even to wish that they should do so ? The questions are far easier to ask than to answer ; but let us proceed with our imagined situation.

About the question of Primacy it may be conceived that there would be no difficulty. On Catholic principles we cannot avoid the conclusion that the Bishop of Rome is in some sense the leading Bishop of the Church. The Oecumenical Councils and the practice of the Church are decisive on the matter.

Nor should we be involving ourselves in any difficulty with the Eastern Orthodox by acknowledging a Primacy *jure ecclesiastico*. Here are the words of M. Glubokovsky, the eminent Bulgarian professor, at the end of his controversy with Mgr. Batiffol in *The Christian East* (Dec. 1924) :

" I should not like to leave an impression that I am an enemy, on principle, of every kind of Papacy, or of the Papacy as it has existed throughout Christian history. This would correspond neither to my Orthodox convictions nor to my scientific knowledge. I differentiate the historical Papacy from the dogmatised Papacy. . . . With such a Papacy . . . I do not foresee any peace. . . . But I accept the historic Papacy, and we Orthodox are ready to return to it."

So in February 1923, in the course of a lecture at Belgrade, the Metropolitan Antony of Kiev, representing the most conservative school of Orthodox theology, used these words : " In the circumstance of the renunciation by Roman Catholics of their pseudo-dogmas, and in particular of that absurd one of theirs which ascribes infallibility to the Pope in matters of faith, the Holy Church in restoring them to unity with

---

[1] This does not mean that " Rupert's Horse " would have charged still further in front of the main body ; but that the main body itself would have consolidated the position which the devotion and dash of the light cavalry had won for it.

herself would not only certainly restore to the Roman Primate that primacy which was assigned to him before his falling away into schism, but would probably invest him with such authority in the Oecumenical Church as had never hitherto been assigned to him." [1]

But is this a primacy of honour only or of jurisdiction also ? That is a more difficult question.   It would probably be conceded that from the earliest times the Roman Bishop has a certain relation to the whole Church.   He had an importance throughout the Church which cannot be predicated of any other Bishop.   To be out of communion with him was a disaster, and exposed a man to the imputation (no more) of not being a Catholic.   This was a risk which no one would willingly run, and consequently the first thing that occurred to a Bishop involved in a theological dispute was to get the Roman Bishop on to his side.   This state of things developed so rapidly into an appellate jurisdiction that it might not unfairly be called jurisdiction in germ.

But could we honestly say that this has anything to do with S. Peter and his primacy ? or, in the words of the decree, that " it was by the institution of the Lord Christ Himself, or *jure divino*, that blessed Peter should have perpetual successors in the primacy over the whole Church ? " Our imagined Anglican Bishops would no doubt be inclined to say that this seemed very doubtful.   But if the path were made easy for them they might perhaps agree that, though there is no evidence that S. Peter or his immediate successors had any idea of perpetuating his primacy in the person of the Bishop of Rome, yet through the Apostolic prestige of the city of Rome it did turn out that the prophetic promise of our Lord to S. Peter was in this way fulfilled.   Mgr. Batiffol seems to hint at some such interpretation when he claims that " the historian has a right to say that subsequent history makes clear the meaning of terms which without it

[1] *The Christian East*, February 1924.

would remain obscure."[1]   This does not seem quite the same as to assert with the decree that our Lord instituted a perpetual primacy ; but we might perhaps agree that if our Lord used words which were afterwards discovered to be fulfilled in a perpetual primacy in the Church, that is equivalent to saying that the primacy is there by His institution.   It does *not* seem quite satisfactory, but our imaginary Bishops will say to each other, " *We* did not make this definition : if we had been there it would never have passed ! we are only trying to get some tolerable meaning into it."

Then there is the Supremacy.   Fortunately they will not be asked to say that this is *jure divino*.   All the same a great deal of explanation will be necessary here.   Presumably this will take the form of making it clear that the definition does not mean that every Christian owes an *absolute* obedience to the Pope.

In other words it would only be a *canonical* obedience which would be due.   We should not be accepting the Papacy as an absolute monarchy : we should only be agreeing that the Pope has a right to call on us to observe the law. He cannot make laws *motu proprio* : only there is no appeal from his decision as to what the law is.   A cynic might say there is no difference ; but in fact we do trust a court of appeal to declare the law and not to make it : and they do not often betray our confidence.   The English Church would never accept a Papal autocracy.   If anything in the whole debate is clear, it is that.   But the present theory of Papal supremacy does give a Papal decree the force of Canon Law.   And if we ask what protection we have against an unscrupulous use of the Papal prerogative it must be confessed that we do not receive very satisfactory assurances. The *Catholic Encyclopedia* gives the following answer to the question, What limitations has the power of the Pope ?

[1] At the Anglo-Catholic Congress Anniversary in July 1925 Lord Halifax seemed to substitute the phrase *Providentia divina* for *Jure divino*. If this interpretation were accepted it would go most of the way towards bridging the gulf between *divinum* and *ecclesiasticum*.

" It is circumscribed by the consciousness of the necessity of making a righteous and beneficent use of the duties attached to his privileges : by the spirit and practice of the Church, by the respect due to General Councils and ancient statutes and customs, by the rights of Bishops, by his relation to the civil powers, by the traditional mild tone of his government . . . by the respect indispensable in the spiritual power towards the spirit and mind of nations."

This is not very helpful. We are not likely to forget that there were such people as the Renaissance Popes, and such an institution as the Spanish Inquisition. Nor, to come nearer to our own times, can we forget what Pius IX. called the " *coup d'état* of the Lord God," [1] when, in opposition to the Canon Law, he compelled Mgr. Errington to resign his right of succession to the Archbishopric of Westminster. We must have canonical and constitutional protection. And it is difficult to imagine that Anglican Bishops could submit to the present system by which every Diocesan in the Papal obedience has to take out fresh faculties every five years to enable him to exercise jurisdiction over his own Diocese, while a Metropolitan cannot even govern his Diocese until he has made a journey to Rome to receive the pallium. It is quite true that in the Roman theory the Bishops have " ordinary jurisdiction," that is to say, they function of their own right, and not as delegates of the Pope. That is acknowledged by most people on both sides. But the quinquennial visit *ad Limina*, not only to report, which would be reasonable enough, but to receive permission to do the very thing which they were consecrated to do, seems, to the outsider, an intolerable derogation from the episcopal dignity. Nor is it necessary in the interests of unity. The Pope, even as Bishop, can always threaten to excommunicate in the last resort ; or, as Pope, can take steps for a canonical deposition. Still this is comparatively a detail. The point we should wish to be reassured about is this : that the Pope, to

[1] *Il colpo di stato di Dominiddio ;* it sounds less profane in Italian !

take the rough analogy of the civil law, only claims to be the head of the Executive and supreme court of appeal ; that he is not a dictator, or even an independent lawmaker.

Finally we come to Infallibility. The greatest thing we should all want to know, if Reunion really came above the horizon, would be this : Is it an essential part of the Pope's claim that he can, if he desires and makes it clear that he so desires, make an infallible definition on a point of faith or morals, without consulting the Bishops and obtaining their approval ? The present attitude of moderate Roman Catholics seems to be that he *could*, but never does. This could hardly satisfy our scruples. We can appreciate the point that the ratification by the Pope of a Conciliar decree has come by a natural development to be the equivalent of the subsequent consent of the Church. We can follow the argument that Councils are not themselves a divinely appointed method of ascertaining the faith of the Church. Our Lord appointed Apostles, not Councils. The General Council was an invention of the Emperor Constantine. Nor is it quite obvious historically that Councils are the best means of obtaining the sense of the Church. Council-chambers have been the scenes of some of the most distressing incidents in ecclesiastical history. S. Gregory Nazianzene roundly accuses the Fathers of Constantinople of being " liars, gluttons and time-servers." The turbulence of Ephesus hardly redounded to the good name of the Church. The Council of Constance covered itself with infamy by an act of treachery hardly surpassed in the whole course of history. Nor was the Vatican Council itself exactly a model of fair play. It must be confessed that ecclesiastics do not show themselves at their best on occasions of public controversy. There is a great deal to be said for Pius IX.'s method [1] of consulting the Episcopate by correspondence. It does not matter in the least by what means the consensus of the Episcopate is obtained.

[1] Employed in 1854.

But it is one thing to say that the ruling of the Episcopate is not valid until their chairman has signed their resolutions, as Fr. Walker does on p. 246 of *The Problem of Reunion*, but quite another to assert, as he seems to do on the following page, that this shows that it is only the final signature which is really operative, and that therefore the resolutions are not necessary at all. By such means it would be easy to prove that the British Constitution was an absolute monarchy. Of course no Roman Catholic would assert that the infallibility of the Pope was a personal endowment, independent of the infallibility of the Church : the theory is rather that this is the way, or even *a* way, in which the infallibility of the Church is exercised. But the idea that the Pope can at any moment say, " I am about to propound an infallible definition," and that when he has done so, it binds the Church for ever, seems to Anglicans, if we may be permitted to say so, simply grotesque. We do want to be sure that this is not the meaning of the definition. It would inevitably lead to what a somewhat rebellious Roman Catholic once referred to as the " cult of the Papal mind."

Again, we on the Anglican side should have to ask for information as to the tests by which it can be ascertained whether the Pope is speaking infallibly or not. There seems to be great uncertainty on this point. The minimiser appears to hold that there are only two Papal utterances so far which satisfy the conditions of infallibility. Clearly the Papal prerogative is not recklessly employed ; but we ought to have more information as to what the approved theory is in this matter.

But it would not be honest to conceal the fact that distrust of infallibilities in general is rather widespread in the Anglican Communion. The infallibility of the Bible in the old-fashioned sense has almost disappeared ; and if you ask almost any theologian if he believes in the infallibility of the Church or of the Apostles he will not find the answer easy. But although the giving of " a straight answer, Yes or No," would be in this instance, as in almost every other, very properly declined, it does not seem as though Catholic theologians ought to refuse the word altogether. " Whatever prevents error causes infallibility," says Fr. McNabb. If we can have certainty, the *moral* certainty of faith, the kind of certainty which will act unhesitatingly on the conviction that something is true, without " hedging," the " determination to stand or fall by the noblest hypothesis "— then whatever are the conditions which rightly produce that certainty are likewise conditions of infallibility. We are infallibily assured, *e.g.*, of the Resurrection of our Lord, not in the sense that the opposite is inconceivable, but in the sense that if that opposite were to be true our whole life would be wrongly based : our faith would be vain. We should rightly feel that the Church had deceived us ; we should, if we became convinced of the entire falsity of the Resurrection, cease to profess ourselves Christians. Now anyone who is prepared to say that his certainty of this or any other doctrine rests ultimately on the authority of the Church may be said to be ascribing infallibility to the Church. And our desire to get other evidence of the truth is based partly on the fact that we feel that God would not wish us to take in our doctrine without digesting it and making it our own, partly on the wish to be able to *defend* the Catholic position, and partly also on the fact that we wish to test our own faith, as children prove their sums by doing them backwards. But there is nothing unreasonable in declining to believe that our Lord would permit His Church as a whole to commit itself to error. If we are sure that the Catholic Church does unquestionably teach a doctrine, then we may rightly believe it, *sine timore oppositi*, for that reason only.

Of the two clear cases of the exercise of the Papal claim to Infallibility one must certainly be the definition of the dogma of the Immaculate Conception in 1854. This dogma is so generally disbelieved in the Anglican Communion that it forms a very serious obstacle to propositions for Reunion. No doubt anyone accepting Papal Infallibility would *ipso facto* have accepted the Immaculate Conception, but so strong is the feeling among Anglicans generally on this point that it might well be that some of our imagined Bishops of the year 2000 might bring it as an objection to accepting Infallibility in any sense that it would commit them to something so uncertain as the doctrine of the Immaculate Conception.

But granted a liberal interpretation of the doctrine—and of course we have already assumed an amount of Liberalism which does not at present exist among the authorities of the Roman Church—there is little difficulty in presenting it in an acceptable form. The chief difficulty arises from the somewhat materialistic way in which we generally look at original sin. We speak of it metaphorically as a *poison*, and say that it is removed at Baptism. This will serve as a metaphor; but the fact is that original sin has no *present* existence at all. It consists in the condemnation which God cannot but pass on a soul which will, if left to itself, fall into sin because of the character of the nature it inherits. Until Baptism is accomplished, or at least intended, there cannot but be, in one sense (though not in another), a hostility between God and the soul. Through Baptism a change is effected in the relation of the soul to God. Now the relation of our Lady to God cannot have been in any sense one of hostility. Surely she cannot have been less favoured than the baptized child. But she was never baptized. Then what was it that brought her into this relation of love and favour with God? Surely God's choice of her: His predestination. In other words, in so far as she existed at all before her birth she was already the object of God's favour and choice.

To say this is not to approve the promulgation of the doctrine. On Catholic principles we may still hold that Pope Pius IX. would have been better advised to follow the counsel of the large number of Bishops who answered his enquiry with the opinion that though the doctrine was true it was not desirable that it should be made an article of faith. Nor have we really solved our difficulty : we have only relieved it. For Roman principles would require us to say not only that we believed the doctrine, but that it was part of the faith of the Church, and that this fact endangered the salvation of those who denied it. That is a different matter, and it is difficult to see how anyone on the Anglican side could say that. We should, for one thing, be accusing the Eastern Orthodox of heresy. But the whole thing is really in the future, and we have to imagine a state of things in which both Rome and the East would accept some such slightly liberalised statement of the doctrine as that which is outlined here : and in that Utopia (οὔπω, not οὔποτε) we should not be as hard upon each other as now we tend to be. The Archbishop of Syra, in conversation with the Bishop of Ely about the year 1870, informed him that the Easterns considered the doctrine " blasphemous." As long as we are in this state of mind it is clear that we can make no progress. But if we could agree that there is a way of stating the doctrine in which it represents no more than a fair development, then we have reduced the gravamen against the Roman Church to the lesser one of innovating on the *statement* of the faith. And if she had been, as of course she claimed to be, the whole Church, then it might be maintained that she had the right to draw up a new statement, not indeed of fact, but of the best way of putting the acknowledged truth of Mary's predestination and acceptability with God. But it would have to be made clear that the doctrine was being accepted in this sense ; otherwise we should again have the Easterns accusing the Westerns of obtaining their consent " treacherously " to an ambiguous statement. And both sides would presumably have to agree not to raise the question which Church has been the true Catholic Church all these years, or whether both alike have

been divided portions of the one Church.   Certainly there
will have to be a very great change of mind before such a
situation can be expected.

The third great question which will have to be settled
before Anglo-Roman unity can be achieved is that of the
validity of Anglican Ordinations.   Until 1920 we seemed to
be in an *impasse* on this point.   Then came the Lambeth
appeal with its astonishing declaration, as interpreted by
the " Three Bishops "—an interpretation which has never
been disavowed—that if Orders were the only point remaining to be settled, the Anglican Bishops would be willing
to submit to the repetition of the ceremony according to
the Roman rite.   It is said of a well-known Italian Cardinal
that he was moved even to tears by this declaration, as
the greatest exhibition of Christian humility he had ever
heard of !

Now it is hardly necessary to say that there was no uncertainty in the minds of the Bishops as to the validity of
Anglican Orders.   To Anglicans the grounds on which the
Pope condemned our Orders seemed baseless.   But although
the Pope cannot make our Orders invalid by pronouncing
against them, and although we know that an examination
of the evidence led distinguished Roman theologians to an
opposite conclusion, it is idle to deny that such a pronouncement is a serious fact, in view of the representative position
which the Pope does hold.   If conditions were normal this
is just the sort of question which would naturally be referred
to him for decision.   Conditions are not normal, and moreover we are convinced that anti-Anglican bias did affect
the decision.   It was made under the assumption that the
Anglican Church was in any case both schismatic and
heretical.   But, if these matters of schism and heresy had
been got out of the way, then in view of the fact that our
Orders had so long been *considered* invalid by the greater
part of the Western Church, would it not be the Christian
part, for the sake of the unity of Christendom, to aver our

willingness to satisfy all men's consciences in the matter? The sacrilege, if sacrilege it were, would not be ours; and it would be necessary that the Anglican bishops should be allowed to make a solemn declaration that they themselves had no doubt of the truth of their own Ordination and Consecration. The precedent of S. Chad is before our eyes.[1] Unless we are prepared to say that he was wrong we cannot condemn our own Bishops for their willingness to have their Consecration repeated, or its alleged defects supplied.

But indeed, if Reunion were really being arranged, the Roman authorities would already *ex hypothesi* have conceded so much that they would probably consent to a consecration *sub conditione*, to which no reasonable objection could be offered. If serious theologians have scruples about the validity of any Sacrament which confers " character," the obvious way out of their difficulty is to have the Sacrament repeated with a declaration that it is only intended to confer it *in case it has not already been conferred*. Then the question of sacrilege does not arise.

There would still remain the definitions of the Council of Trent, but the difficulties connected with them are less serious, and they could probably be presented in such a way that we could accept them.

It may well be thought that all this discussion is utterly unpractical. It deals with the Reunion of a Church of England and a Church of Rome utterly unlike the bodies which we know under those names. To some extent this is true. Both Churches would have to be different. But the discussion must go on all the same, if the suggestion that we are willing to consider the matter of Reunion with the Holy See is to be taken seriously. It is no good talking about Reunion unless we are willing to consider what it would involve. Of course it is open to anyone to say, " If it involves that, it is impossible."

But is there any possibility of such changes coming about

[1] See p. 42.

in the character of Anglican and Roman theology as would bring the matter into practical politics ?

It is necessary to be on our guard against the tendency to personify a continuous and corporate body. " Rome " is not a person with a definite character which only hardens into something more and more unchangeable. " She " consists like every other society of many individuals : generation follows generation ; and, conservative as she is, she is not impervious to the *Zeitgeist*, nor unamenable to the influence of the Holy Spirit of God. Pope succeeds Pope in rapid succession. Confined as he is to a single house in an unhealthy city, with labours and responsibilities unequalled, the life of a Pope is not likely to be long. And every change in the Papacy makes itself felt throughout the Roman Catholic world. The last ten years has seen a revision of the entire *corpus* of the Canon Law, the Missal and the Breviary : the last twenty a revolution in the habits of devout Romanists in regard to frequency of partaking of Holy Communion. A steady change is observable in the attitude of the Papacy towards nationalism, towards the study of Holy Scripture, towards this very problem of Reunion itself. The Anglican mind revolts with some justice from some of the curious particularities of cult which seem to rejoice the heart of Romanists on their more sentimental side ; yet almost all that is most hopeful and most helpful in the devotional life comes to us from the Roman side of the border, and there is no sign of the stream of practical devout methods drying up. Again, it is the last few years that have seen the development of the " Retreats for the People " movement which is our envy and our guide. The picture of the Roman Church as stagnant, or as merely moving from corruption to deeper corruption, is the product of a deeply prejudiced imagination. Rome does change, and sometimes for the better ! And it is said that it is the desire of the heart of Pius XI. to be the Pope of the Reunion of Christendom. God forbid that we should throw cold water.

What are the changes then that we must look for some day on the Roman side if our Divine Lord's desire for the unity of His Church is ever to take effect ?

First, we must look to see the Papacy become more truly international, and at the same time more appreciative of the national spirit. Nationalism in religion, as we have seen again and again, is a danger to unity, but national feeling is too powerful a thing to be simply ignored ; and the unity gained by sheer centralisation is not really international at all. It tends to become Italian. It is surprising how slight are the effects of the Latin character of the Papacy, but they are there. The Papacy, if it is to be international, should be open to all nations. The Italian government would probably be as unwilling to have a Pope at the Vatican who was *not* an Italian as the Turks are to have a non-Turkish Patriarch ; and that is what would give force to the Papal demand for an internationalised area as the *locus* of the Papal government. It is at present only by courtesy that the Pope is treated as a Sovereign prince, and that the Vatican is considered non-Italian. But on the ecclesiastical side also it always seems that nationalism is considered to be the enemy. From this arise two deplorable facts. One is the excessive centralisation of the Roman Church as a whole, of which Newman complained so bitterly. " In former time," he says, " primitive or mediaeval . . . if a private theologian said anything free, another answered him. If the controversy grew, then it went to a Bishop, a theological faculty, or to some foreign university. The Holy See was but the court of ultimate appeal. Now, if I, as a private priest put anything into print, Propaganda answers me at once. How can I fight with such a chain on my arm ? It is like the Persians driven to fight under the lash. There was true private judgment in the primitive and mediaeval schools —there are no schools now, no private judgment (in the religious sense of the phrase) no freedom, that is, of opinion." [1]

[1] Quoted by Dr. Headlam in the *Church Quarterly Review*, July 1920.

This seems unanswerable. How can it be possible for an Italian Congregation of Cardinals—and the *personnel* of the Roman Congregations is overwhelmingly Italian—to understand at the first enquiry the *ethos* of a foreign country ?

The other fact arising from the exclusively anti-national policy of the Roman Church is that national feeling is in almost every country arrayed against Catholicism.

Now it is quite true that nationalism by itself is the fruitful parent of schism, and indeed of hatred, oppression and war, and there is much to be said for the mortification of it. That is one object of the existence of a Catholic Church, to neutralise the strength of nationalism. But in trying to destroy it the leaders of the Counter-Reformation set themselves an impossible task.

Further, it looks as though the Roman Church must, before Reunion is possible, come to terms with the critical spirit. If undiluted nationalism leads to schism, undiluted criticism is the mother of heresy. The judgment of the Catholic Church is a greater thing than the judgment of an individual, and the Catholic mind shows itself in a humble willingness to be corrected. But the policy of Rome has always been *suppression* of criticism. If Rome had had her way we should be living to-day in an obscurantist twilight. Questions which we *know* are still open would have been closed by her oracular voice, without free discussion or real intellectual authority. We cannot unite with Rome while she is in this mind. Students cannot be expected to throw their thinking caps over the windmill for the sake of the *beaux yeux* of Propaganda.

But there may come, perhaps almost imperceptibly there is coming, a change.

In regard to nationalism it is certain that great concessions would be made to a Church which desired to unite with Rome and yet maintain its national characteristics. The Anglican Church united to Rome would retain its married clergy, its vernacular service, its Communion in both kinds.

Its chief Archbishop would have a Patriarchal position in addition to that office of *Legatus natus* traditionally associated with his position. And the existence of the Uniate Churches is perpetual evidence that union with Rome does not necessarily mean the passing of a sponge over everything which distinguishes one church from another. And in minor ways we have evidence of the dawning of a new spirit. Roman Catholics are no longer forbidden to vote in civil elections. In 1922 the new Pope, for the first time since 1870, gave his first Pontifical blessing *urbi et orbi* from the balcony of S. Peter's, instead of to the faithful alone from the interior of the Basilica. In 1925 the dome of S. Peter's has been again illuminated externally on the occasion of a canonisation. These are little things ; they may even seem puerile ; but they are symbolical, and are meant to be so.

Nor is it the case that no progress has been made in accepting the critical spirit. Roman Catholics are freely permitted to study in the universities, where they more than hold their own. Roman Catholic scholars are doing first-class work in the domains of philosophy and history. We hear occasionally of authoritative condemnations ; but we need not be in a hurry to assume that they are unjustifiable. M. Loisy would have had to be disavowed sooner or later, and Fr. Tyrrell, in spite of the sympathy felt for him by Anglicans, would have been a difficulty in any church. The most hopeful fact about the Reunion discussions is that they have been raised to the level of pure and self-respecting history. It is this which has led Dr. Gore to speak of a " new orientation " in the controversy. Mgr. Batiffol uses fair arguments and draws moderate conclusions. His view of the development of the Papacy is very far removed from Leo XIII.'s assertion that the Vatican decrees represented " the venerable and constant belief of every age." It is not beyond the bounds of possibility that a change may come over the characteristic Roman spirit, as we have hitherto apprehended it.

Nor are external influences wanting which may hasten the process. Revolts and defections occur from time to time, sometimes personal, sometimes on a national scale, which must weaken the extreme Papalist position. The number of Anglican priests who have actually submitted to the Roman claims and have afterwards withdrawn their submission is considerable. The Czecho-Slovakian revolt, deplorably as it seems to be working out, is evidence for the exasperation which refusal of reform may cause quite suddenly and on a wide scale. Nor is Old Catholicism in Germany, Switzerland and Holland a negligible force. There must come a point at which such influence will invade the Vatican. Then we shall have a reforming Pope and shall see what we shall see.

REUNION WITH THE EASTERN ORTHODOX CHURCH.

The Dean of Canterbury, preaching on the subject of Reunion with the Orthodox, recently used these words :

" The Anglican is prone to fix his mind on finding dogmatic agreement with a view to full Reunion. The Orthodox considers how, no such Reunion being imminent, the churches may get into the fullest comity and amity possible, and so into active co-operation."

Our negotiations with the Orthodox East have been so full of promise that such words seem to come as a cold douche, and to require some explanation. They might seem to imply that all that we can hope for from our relations with the Orientals is the same sort of co-operation in good works and mutual sympathy as we have already with our friends of other denominations in England. The true meaning of them can only be understood if we will be at pains to enter into the mentality of the Eastern Church. Quite as firmly as the Roman Church the Eastern Orthodox are convinced that they are *the Church*. When the Pope thought that he was excommunicating Cerularius, he was really excommunicating himself, and all who held with him. And by so doing he was falling away from grace even more deeply than according to the Roman view the Easterns were. For the Roman Church acknowledges that the Sacraments of the Orthodox are entirely valid ; but the Easterns consider that the Roman Sacraments in themselves have no validity at all. Some of them hold that if the Pope were to " join the Church " he would have to be baptised ! Quite as definitely as the Romans the Easterns hold that the primary unity of the Church is dogmatic ; and that to fail to hold the dogmas of the Church *ipso facto* excludes a man from that unity. But to the Easterns those dogmas are the decrees of the Seven Oecumenical Councils : those of the later supposed Oecumenical Councils are at best not binding, at worst the expression of heresy. And to the Eastern mind comparatively little turns on the question of the conditions of validity of Sacraments. The Sacraments belong to the Church : if a man is outside the Church he cannot expect to have any Sacraments. And to be inside the Church is more a matter of holding the faith than of being in right relations with the hierarchy. There is, therefore, no possibility of any union other than dogmatic union ; and if that is attained, the rest follows. It would seem, therefore, that we have here a position at least as intransigent as that of Rome herself, except for the fact that our dogmatic standards require less accommodation to make them fit in with those of the Orthodox East than with those of the Romanised West. That this is not so is to be accounted for by the Orthodox theory of *Economy*. Economy means the power of the Church to *validate* for particular purposes, and at her own discretion, sacramental and other acts of Christians who stand outside the Church. It is an unfamiliar view to most of us, but in truth perfectly logical and consistent, if we grant the premise that Orthodoxy constitutes the unity of the Church.

The importance of it for our present purpose is this. Whereas in the case of the Roman Church it is all or nothing in the matter of Reunion, with the Orthodox there is a half-way house. Even though dogmatic unity may not be attainable for the moment, there is theoretically no limit to the power of " the Church " (*i.e.* the Orthodox) to recognise the ministrations of Christians who in the main believe with the Church. There is, therefore, something immediate and tangible to work for.

Now if the Anglican Church consisted entirely of those who adopt the " Catholic " attitude we could probably arrive at a true dogmatic union. But of course it is clear that it does not. As Dr. Douglas points out in his book, *The Relations of the Anglican Churches with the Eastern Orthodox*, it is idle to expect that the Anglican Church to-day would bind itself to the Seven Oecumenical Councils. Some of us believe that we are obliged to accept them, but if we presented some of our brethren, *e.g.* with the decrees of the Second Council of Nicaea, it is not likely that we should win from them a ready assent to its teaching on the veneration due to sacred images. Nor would the more Protestant-minded members of the English Church accept Eastern doctrine on many other points : the number of the Sacraments ; the Real Presence ; the Eucharistic Sacrifice ; the need for sacramental Confession ; the invocation of the Saints. Unless we are prepared to have a breach with our brother-Anglicans on these points, which have not hitherto been pressed in the post-Reformation Anglican Church, it is no good thinking of dogmatic union with the East. That will come when the Anglican Church has made up its mind that it can rightly insist on such things as these, and not before. For the Eastern Church does not change. There is no sign whatever that she is likely to relax any point of what she holds to be the authentic and essential Christian faith. Nor is there any reason for her to do so. She is right in holding that these things belong to *authentic* Catholicism, and, not being face to face with " reduced " Catholicism (to adapt Dr. Sanday's phrase) within her own borders, there is no obvious need for her to revise her estimate of what is *essential* to the Christian faith. Our position is different. We could only insist on these doctrines to the point of asking for explicit acceptance of them, if we were willing to break off communion with those who do not hold them. That we see no reason to do. We must hold to the Oecumenical Councils ; but, fortunately, the Oecumenical character of the Second of Nicaea is disputed ; fortunately, for we should indeed be in a miserable position if we had to take our choice between counting the solemn decisions of an Oecumenical Council a thing indifferent, and refusing to hold communion with our fellow-Christians because they could not bring themselves to think it right to pay external reverence to sacred images. The second alternative has only to be stated to show its impossibility, and Dr. Douglas states that the result upon his mind of many conversations with Orthodox theologians has been to confirm him in the opinion that the Orthodox themselves have no wish to hurry matters. " They would find no gratification," he says, " in seeing a section of the Anglican Church break off and form an English Western-Orthodox Church."

All this means that the hope of dogmatic Reunion with the Orthodox is almost as remote as with Rome. All that we can do is to go on trying to teach our countrymen the Catholic faith as we have learned to hold it, in the *hope* that when at last the Church of England can come to one mind on sacramental doctrine it may then be found that that doctrine is simply the doctrine which is already held in common both by East and West. As Catholics we do hold that. We think that it belongs to *authentic* Catholicism ; it seems to be in the true line of development. But that is a different thing from saying that it belongs to *essential* Catholicism ; *i.e.* that a man who does not hold it is a heretic. By what steps our hope can be realised it is not for us to say. The change in the general attitude to Catholic doctrine, as the " Anglo-Catholic " school apprehend it, has been so astonishing during the past ninety years that, if there were nothing else to consider, it might well be supposed that another half-century would see the Anglican Communion ready to accept as Catholic doctrine what she now treats as matter of controversy.   But of course things are not as simple as that.   There is such a thing as reaction.   Moreover, any comparatively new movement lays hold quickly of those who are naturally disposed towards it; but the conversion of those who are temperamentally on the other side is a slower business.   Nor is the Catholic movement the only one which is active within the Anglican Communion.   There is the movement of the critical spirit, which is called Liberalism.   This critical spirit is like salt.   A seasoning of it seems to be necessary to prevent our Catholicism from becoming morbid, either from stagnation or unwholesome growth.   But an excess of it will turn the waters of life into the Dead Sea.   To vary the metaphor, criticism may be either surgery or mere dissection.   It is difficult to foresee the end of this liberalising movement which is going on *pari passu* with the Catholic movement. Some Catholics are in sympathy with it, others think it the thin end of the diabolical wedge of Modernism.   Evangelicals are divided in the same way ; and though at present the " Liberal Evangelical " group seems to have made an alliance for a particular purpose even with the extremer Liberals who are now known as " Modernists," the union is not really a natural one, and is not likely to be permanent. The real division in the Church of England is between those who are primarily rationalisers and those who believe in the supremacy of grace.   The ultimate tendency of the former seems to be towards " reduced Christianity," of the latter towards Catholicism.   And in the Free Churches the same division has a place.   There, too, there are Catholic-looking men, as well as those who have turned their faces definitely in the opposite direction.   It may be that in the future, not in this generation, the distinction will have become so clear that men will have to choose whether they will be on the one side, that of Catholicism (whether above or below the " salt ") or on that of *negative* Liberalism, which is Protestantism when it ceases to be Evangelical. If this does happen there *ought* to be a disruption, and the Christian world would then be grouped according to its natural lines of division. There would no longer exist a community astride of the great watershed of Christianity, which lies between Protestants and Rationalists on the one hand and Catholics and Evangelicals on the other. But all this is the purest speculation. At present this sharp line does not exist. Our Protestants are seldom purely rationalistic : our Evangelicals have not yet advanced to what we know as Catholicism. And most of us believe that the present position is providential, and that it means that we have still a good deal to learn from each other, and that God does not mean the parting of the ways to come at present.

It seems then that it is not our business to hurry on this matter of Reunion with the Great Church of the East until it is indicated that the time for it has arrived. At present the union of Christians of different kinds within the English Church is one of the most valuable assets of Christendom. Whether it will be possible or desirable to maintain it when the movements of to-day have reached their natural conclusion it is impossible to say. But the Church of England is the nearest thing there is to a microcosm of the Christian world, and displays to that world the extraordinary spectacle of what is possible in the way of unity between men whose beliefs and temperaments are as different as ours. It is not a unity to be lightly shattered.

But the Eastern theory of economy gives us an immediate goal to work for. There is in theory no limit to the extent to which the Orthodox Church could permit economic inter-communion. And on the strictly practical side this is all that is urgently needed. From what has happened already it is clear that no Anglican and no Orthodox need ever in future be permanently deprived of the Sacraments so long as a Priest of the other communion is available. Herein lies the great importance of the qualified recognition which Orthodox theologians have given to our Orders. It will be remembered that the sacred Synods of Constantinople, Jerusalem and Cyprus have agreed that Anglican Orders have the same validity as those of the Roman Church. That is to say, they have all the conditions of validity except the all-important one of being within the Orthodox Church. But the fact that the external conditions of validity are present makes it a simple thing for the Orthodox Church to treat them as valid by economy ; and this has already been done on very numerous occasions. It is true that some of the Eastern theologians hold that in theory the Church *could* give the same recognition to non-Episcopal Orders ; and indeed that seems to be the logical conclusion of their doctrine in the matter. But if there is one thing which an Orthodox theologian is more suspicious of than another it is a logical conclusion in theology ; and it seems to be generally acknowledged that there is not the faintest chance of the Eastern hierarchy granting economical recognition to any Orders which seem to be obviously founded on a doctrine of the Priesthood which differs widely from their own. What we can look and work for, then, is a friendly mutual recognition between the Orthodox and ourselves, such as will lead to the practical advantages of intercommunion, when and where it is needed. This is not Reunion, and it is no good pretending that it is. The scandal of division will still continue : there will still be no organic connection acknowledged on both sides and recognisable by the world. But a long step forward will have been taken.

It will have been noticed that we have again to meet the question of Infallibility in trying to come to terms with the Orthodox ; but Dr. Douglas points out that the Orthodox idea of the infallibility of an Oecumenical Council is not quite the same as that held by Roman Catholics. It is not only that, as we have seen, the Roman view is that the consent of the Church is given by the Papal confirmation. But there is also this very characteristic difference. A Roman theologian is prepared to say under exactly what conditions a Council attains oecumenicity, and such Councils are part of the regular machinery of the Church, an ecclesiastical method for getting at the mind of the Bishops, which if approved by the Pope *is* the mind of the Church. But to the Orthodox mind such Councils cannot be called into being at the will of the Church at all. Councils can be summoned, but they are not Oecumenical unless the Church subsequently recognises that the Holy Ghost has spoken through them. The Church does so recognise the Divine Voice in seven such Councils ; therefore of course these seven are infallible. But there is no reason to suppose that there will ever be any addition to the number. That depends entirely on the will of God. Thus we get rid of the fear that anything may be infallibly declared at any moment ; but it is at the cost of a somewhat static conception of the possibility of development in the apprehension of Divine truth.

Reunion with other Episcopal Churches.

We must briefly consider the possibility of closer relationships with the following churches : the Eastern Separated Churches, the Swedish Lutheran Church, the Old Catholics, the Moravians. In so doing we need do little more than summarise the conclusions of the Lambeth Committee on Reunion, and the corresponding sections of the Lambeth Encyclical.

There would probably be little difficulty in entering into relations of intercommunion with the remnant of the Armenian Church. It is true that they have not hitherto accepted the Council of Chalcedon ; but that does not mean that they are Eutychians. Nor do they themselves allow that they are Monophysite, though they have been supposed to hold that our Lord's two Natures are mingled into one. It is probable that their heresy is more nominal than real.

The East Syrians are commonly known as Nestorians, and venerate the name of Nestorius in their Liturgy, while anathematising S. Cyril of Alexandria. It seems, however, that though rejecting the decrees of Ephesus they do not really make any separation of Person between Jesus Christ and God the Son, and that the peculiarity of their theological statements is more a matter of patriotic tradition than anything else. It is greatly to be wished that they could be induced to put themselves right with the rest of Catholic Christendom on these matters, but the essential correctness of their theology seems to be secured by their acceptance of the Christological clauses of the *Quicunque vult*.

The West Syrians, Copts and Abyssinians are all in full communion with each other, and there does not seem any reason to think that they are really any more Monophysite than the Armenians. The Lambeth Committee suggest that we should take steps to examine their liturgical books as a preliminary to entering into closer relations with them.

The Church of Sweden presents a problem more difficult, and also, because of our close neighbourhood, far more important. Theologically the Swedish Church is undoubtedly orthodox, and holds firmly to the Catholic Creeds. Her emphasis, however, seems to be less on theology than on soteriology, and in this matter she shows as we should expect a Lutheran bias. The Augsburg Confession perhaps lays a disproportionate stress on justification by faith alone, and goes near to teaching that a man is justified when he believes himself so to be. But there is nothing in this to make Reunion impossible. Moreover, there seems little doubt that the Episcopal succession has been maintained. In some ways Swedish practice is nearer to Catholicism than that of the majority of English churchmen.

On the other hand, there are matters which make us hesitate. The Swedish Church is in full communion with

other Lutheran churches which have not retained the transmission of Orders by imposition of hands. The Diaconate
has been abolished. Confirmation has been transformed
out of recognition by having attached to it *neither* of the
outward signs used in other parts of the Church. Swedish
theologians tell us that they have no objection to imposition
of hands, but that they would strongly resent its restoration
being made a condition of Reunion. So with the Diaconate.
Holding as they do that all distinctions within the ministry
are *jure humano*, they see no reason why they should be
pressed in such a matter. Their liturgical customs seem to
be open to criticism. Though retaining much Catholic
ceremonial the actual rite employed in the celebration of
Mass (always known by that name) has several abnormalities.
"The liturgy lacks a definite prayer of consecration, and the
celebrant is not obliged to communicate : these two facts
are in accordance with the Lutheran view that the presence
of Christ is effected at the distribution of the Sacrament
rather than at the words of Consecration spoken by the
celebrant." [1]

The Bishops at Lambeth recommended that Swedish
Lutherans should be allowed to communicate at Anglican
altars, and that Anglican Bishops should take part, if invited,
in Swedish Episcopal Consecrations. The latter recommendation has been carried into effect.

It is clear that we ought to wait for full Reunion with the
Swedish Church until her purely Lutheran peculiarities
have been modified ; but it is impossible to find fault with
the Lambeth recommendation to admit members of the
Swedish Church to Holy Communion on exceptional
occasions. It is more difficult to be enthusiastic about our
Bishops going out of their way to join in Swedish Consecrations seeing that it is in the very matter of the Sacrament
of Holy Orders (the abolition of the Diaconate) that the
Swedes show themselves so far from Catholic practice.

[1] Pullan, *Bampton Lectures*, p. 265.

With regard to the Old Catholics, it is very greatly to be hoped that the "friendly relations" spoken of in the Lambeth Encyclical may develop into a far closer unity. The Old Catholic position is so closely akin to that of the Anglican Church that there seems nothing on our side to hinder a real union. The so-called "Old Catholic Church of Great Britain" has been definitely repudiated by the Old Catholic Bishops in Synod; and thus the only cause of dispute is removed.

Negotiations for Reunion with the Moravian brotherhood in England have been held up by the discovery, only recently made, that their Deacons are permitted both to administer Confirmation and to celebrate Holy Communion. The Lambeth Encyclical recommends that if these irregularities are brought to an end the doubts about the validity of Moravian Ordinations might be set at rest by Anglican Bishops presiding at the Consecration of a Moravian Bishop. Care is to be taken that such Consecration is unquestionable; but nothing is said about reconsecration of existing Bishops or reordination of existing presbyters. They are, so to say, to be given the benefit of the doubt which exists as to the validity of their status.[1]

[1] The *Church Times* of Sept. 4, 1925, states, on the authority of a Greek newspaper, that the Old Catholic Archbishop of Utrecht addressed the following letter to the Archbishop of Canterbury in June of that year. "Until the present, the Old Catholic Church of Utrecht has hesitated concerning the validity of Anglican ordinations. On the one hand, it had no doubt as to the actuality of the consecration of Archbishop Parker, but it had doubt as to the sufficiency of the Rite of Edward VI., in that it had anxiety as to whether that Rite expressed the Catholic Faith sufficiently. But after lengthy investigation and careful consideration, and having taken counsel thereupon with our clergy, we have reached the conclusion concerning which we notify your Grace by this letter. We are convinced that the Anglican Church has at all times willed to preserve the episcopal government of the Primitive Church, and that the Edwardian Rite of ordination must be reckoned as valid. Accordingly, we declare our opinion readily as that the Apostolic Succession has never failed in the Anglican Church."

Reunion with Evangelical Protestants.

It is often said that the Church of England must really make up her mind with whom she wishes for Reunion. At present she is engaged in inconsistent parleys with both sides in the great dispute. She is like a Balkan state in the early days of the Great War, with a pro-German and a pro-Ally party, each trying to commit the government to some action which would be compromising. Of course, the first answer is that disagreements between Christians are not to be compared with a war. If they are to be likened to worldly controversies they rather resemble political disputes between two parties, the patriotism of both of which is beyond question. The Anglican Communion sits on the cross-benches; not, it is hoped, on the fence !

The rest of the House of Faith is divided into complex parties. Untempered Catholicism is presented by Rome : Nationalised Catholicism by the Eastern Orthodox : sectarianised Catholicism by the Eastern Heterodox (though this sectarianism is nominal rather than real) ; and on the other side of the house an immensely strong and vigorous Coalition in which is incarnated in various degrees the spirit of sectarianism. The word is used simply to express facts, and without a suspicion of a derogatory sense. It simply expresses the opposite conception to that of the one great organised Church, which is our Home and to the discipline of which we must submit.

It is not surprising that the Anglican Church has found it difficult to coalesce with other bodies, for she herself represents what is certainly the maximum amount of coalescence which has ever been attempted. Whether it is a complete success or not may be open to question, but it is an amazing fact ; and it may be reasonably questioned whether the limits of comprehensiveness have not been reached, and whether we must not in the nature of things let further appetite wait on good digestion. Can we really at this moment try to assimilate anything more ?

Now, if we were actually in treaty either with Rome or with any of the Protestant churches for immediate Reunion, that would probably be for the time the end of any suggestion for Reunion with the opposite party. But it has not come to that nor to anything like that. All that we are trying to do is to clear our own minds first, and then the minds of others, and to come to an agreement as to what we think essential in the doctrine, discipline and worship of the Christian Church, and what merely desirable, and what indifferent. One very useful means of arriving at a clear mind on these points is to talk them over with those who are not at present in communion with us ; but the question has not really gone beyond the informal stage. These conferences with those from whom we are separated are *pourparlers*, and in no sense meetings of ambassadors.

Our conferences with the English Free churches have, however, had a more official character than those with the Roman Catholic representatives ; and although it is becoming clear that no Reunion is likely to spring from them at present, the general opinion would probably be that " Home Reunion," as it is called, is a more living question than any other. It is difficult to say why Reunion with our Protestant brethren should be considered " Home," while that with our fellow-Catholics, as we believe them to be, should be thought of as " foreign." It is presumably a legacy from the days when the Roman Church in this country was referred to as " The Italian Mission " ; but there are no more patriotic British subjects than our countrymen of the Roman obedience.

The question of Reunion with Nonconformists generally comes in the end, too often in the beginning, to a discussion of the necessity of Episcopacy. That indeed is the point on which it looks as though the discussions were likely to break down. Just in the same way our discussions with

Rome tend even to exaggerate the place which the Papacy occupies in the Roman system. Indeed the fact that our attitude to the Free Churches is in so many ways similar to that of the Roman Church to ourselves ought to give us much sympathy in trying to meet the reasonable demands of Nonconformists. It is best to begin by acknowledging very frankly that there are points in which we would wish to emulate the achievements of Nonconformity : their strong sense of church membership, their careful intellectual preparation of candidates for the ministry, their freedom from the interference of the State in appointments to office in the Church, their sense of responsibility for the finances of the Church, their serious value attached to the " ministry of the Word." These are all qualities of the very highest value, and Reunion, if it was to be fruitful, would have to conserve them, and give us also the benefit of them. It is to be hoped that no one on our side of the line is so foolishly conceited as to suppose that we have nothing to learn from those who by our mutual fault and to our common loss have gone out from us or been driven out.

Then there are the vastly important doctrines that we hold in common, difficult though it is to discover in some cases what are the doctrines to which Nonconformists are really pledged. That is a point to which we shall have to return. But it must surely be taken for granted, as it is by our most influential advocate of " Home Reunion," the Bishop of Gloucester, that we are not thinking of the possibility of Reunion with any except " Orthodox Nonconformists," those, *i.e.*, who are orthodox on strictly theological or Christological questions, and believe in and make use of the two Sacraments which the English Catechism calls " generally necessary to salvation." We are thinking of the type of Nonconformity represented by the Free Church Catechism.

Here is at any rate a broad common basis of highly developed doctrine, held for truth apparently because it *is* orthodox ; for apart from ecclesiastical authority of some kind it would hardly be possible for men to agree in a statement so detailed and elaborate. If it were not for the unhappy experience of the Church one might have thought it would be simple to go together the rest of the way. Our first principles seem to be identical.

And indeed in many of the things which do in fact separate Catholic Churchmen and Protestants, the things which actually determine men in " choosing their religion," as they say, it is impossible to maintain that Catholic methods are the only ones. When a man says, " I am Chapel," in nine cases out of ten it means that he likes what we call a " mission service " with a good rousing sermon as the climax of it, and that he does not care for the more formal evening service of the Church of England, with the more doctrinal but less elaborate sermon which is characteristic of our methods. It is obvious to anyone who knows that this has nothing to do with our Reunion difficulties. Rightly or wrongly many of the Anglican clergy would agree with this " Chapel " *habitué* that Evensong as the chief Sunday evening service, though indeed representing the soberness and moderation of the Anglican genius at its best, yet was lacking in emotional and devotional appeal : some of them want to supplement it with " extemporary " prayers, some with an " after service," some with Benediction. Fixed liturgical forms are a Catholic custom, but not (except within very narrow limits), a necessary Catholic principle. And this fact that the most obvious external feature of " Church " is not a necessary part of her principles suggests that it may be worth while to mention some other things which bulk large in the popular conceptions of churchmanship, but are not really necessities at all. It is not a question of whether they are good or bad ; nor a question of whether we ought to alter them : we are only asking, " Could we be in union with a church which did not observe them, and recognise it as a part of the Catholic Church ? "

Here, then, is a list of persons and things which are as a fact found in " Church " but not in " Chapel," yet are in no sense *necessities*. Archbishops, Deans, Archdeacons, Rural Deans, Rectors, Vicars, Curates, Canons, Chancellors, Registrars, Churchwardens, Sidesmen, Church Councillors, Prelacy, Patronage, ecclesiastical vesture, ceremony, crosses, lecterns, reading pews, church ornaments, particular postures for prayer, Church seasons (except perhaps Easter), Saints' Days. It is clear on consideration that none of these persons and things can really claim universality [1] : if we make any of them necessities we are excommunicating not only the Dissenter who does not have them, but the Catholic of some period or other who did not have them either. But we must make it quite clear what we mean when we say that these are unnecessary. No group of people could organise themselves for worship and Christian discipline and leave all these in suspense, neither abolished nor retained ; and if we cannot come to an agreement about them the only form of Christian unity left is that we should still remain in our present separate group organisations, but yet be in communion with each other. That is to say, a man would still say, not indeed we hope, " I am Chapel " ; but " I go to the Methodist church," and his external religious life would go on much as at present. But his minister and the " Anglican" minister (if that name survived) would on occasion communicate together at the same service, and he himself if he wished could attend the services and Sacraments of the Anglican Church without any sense of disloyalty. The same would apply conversely of course to the man who now says, " I am Church." The ministers of the two bodies would probably preach occasionally in each others' churches (this, of course, implies that there is no difference in their ultimate doctrinal standards), and on exceptional occasions no difficulty would be raised about a similar exchange of Altars, or

[1] Except indeed the Saints' Days ; but these, ancient and universal as they are, are obviously " indifferent " in the last resort.

reading pews. (This could only be exceptional, for *ex hypothesi* the liturgical standards of the two bodies would be different, and the spectacle of a clergyman attempting as he goes along to familiarise himself with a manner of conducting services fundamentally different from his own is unedifying, and ordinarily quite intolerable.)

Things would go on then externally much as they do at present, except that there would be full co-operation instead of rivalry, and—a most important fact for those who realise the doctrine of One Holy Catholic Church—there would be the sense that we are really one in Christ, One Bread, One Body, as well as One Lord.

That seems to be the plan envisaged by the Anglican Bishops, and worked out in detail by the Bishops, as they then were, of Peterborough, Hereford and Zanzibar in their book entitled *Lambeth and Reunion*. It differs in an important respect from the plan outlined by Dr. Headlam, now Bishop of Gloucester, in his *Bampton Lectures* (written and delivered, of course, before the Lambeth Conference). The Bishops' plan would seem to fall under his rather severe strictures on those who by " Reunion " really only mean a loose federation, with occasional interchange of pulpits, and joint Communion. They would, he says, " substitute for the Catholic Church a glorified Free Church Council." Dr. Headlam then thinks, or thought, that a much closer union is possible, in which the Dissenters, as they now are, would come into the Church of England, as it now is, and simply form what we may perhaps without offence call the Left Wing of the Low Church party. They would apparently be obliged to use the Anglican Liturgy, or some new alternative Liturgy agreed to by the reunited Church, but without being pressed to state in what sense they used the liturgical words. The difficulty of the situation thus created would prove too much, we may take leave to think, for any Bishops of a less forcible and determined character than Dr. Headlam. Hampton Court would have to be taken on a long lease.

The difficulties of the scheme propounded at Lambeth are less obvious, but it cannot be denied that they are formidable from the point of view of doctrine, practice and validity.

But first we may lay it down that the Lambeth plan has this great advantage, that it takes full account of things as they are. The actual occurrence of Reunion would not at once, according to this plan, cause a whole series of startling changes in the religious life of the devout Christian. It would rather be the recognition of the unity which does exist than the artificial piecing together of broken fragments. And it is important to notice that even if we cannot attain at the moment to outward unity there is between us already a very large measure of agreement. We have but to consider the Free Church Catechism, and compare it with such a statement of faith as would be put forth by Evangelical members of the Church of England, to see how very real a basis of agreement it provides us with. The ground plan of unity is already in existence. And if we could but agree on the dogmatic basis it is surely true to say that sufficient agreement in practice and in the conditions of validity *ought* to follow. They may not do so at once ; and these things cannot safely be hurried, but we must surely feel that where the faith is one it is no less than a scandal that these lesser things should not be one also.

The Lambeth Fathers recommended that there should be no general interchange of pulpits until such time as, in the opinion of a Diocesan bishop, it could be said that a particular minister was definitely working towards such a plan of Reunion as was sketched in the Appeal. It would have been better if this recommendation had been more carefully followed. The preaching of a sermon implies ministerial authority, almost as much, and just as truly, as the ministration of a sacrament. It is true that a deacon or a layman may be permitted to preach, but only under a licence from the Bishop, who has first satisfied himself by elaborate precautions that the preacher holds the doctrine of the Church of England. But a Dissenting minister from the very fact that he dissents from that doctrine is surely incapable of speaking with authority to members of that Church, and it is little less than an outrage on the faithful laity that they should be put in the position of having to sit as pupils at the feet of one who definitely rejects what they have been taught to hold as necessary truth. This sharp distinction between the ministry of the Word and that of the Sacraments tends to destroy the balance of the Christian life. Of course, if it is made clear that the Free Church minister is not preaching a sermon with authority, but merely giving an address on some particular subject of interest, the difficulty is less acute.

The doctrinal basis of Reunion put forward at Lambeth is Holy Scripture and the Nicene Creed. This at once raises a difficulty. Nonconformists are not accustomed to deal with formal creeds. No Nonconformist layman is under any formal obligation of belief at all. He may, before being admitted as a member of a congregation, have to satisfy the minister that he is rightly disposed towards God : and in this disposition it might be maintained that a true doctrine of God is implied. But there is nothing explicit ; and we do look for some assurance as to whether it is possible for a man to be a devout communicant at a Nonconformist church while disbelieving in the Holy Trinity or the Deity of Christ. It may, of course, be said that in the Church of England no explicit affirmation of these doctrines is required. The Baptismal affirmation only binds a man to the Apostles' Creed, which does not contain either of them. That is quite true. The use of the Nicene Creed at the Eucharist is certainly not to be thought of as a test of faith, and it is by no means a necessary liturgical feature. But in our liturgy Catholic doctrine is so fully expressed that it would be difficult to imagine the case of a man who was definitely and explicitly incredulous of it continuing to associate himself with us in worship. The fact that Nonconformist worship is at the discretion of the minister makes it difficult to be sure that the faith is as amply safeguarded.

Still, where there is a ministry which is theologically orthodox, this could no doubt be adjusted. It would not be difficult to get an assurance that some steps were taken to make it clear that the receiving of Communion does imply that in fundamentals of the faith the communicants are at one.

But what about the orthodoxy of the ministry ? Supposing that we are satisfied that subscription to the Nicene Creed is a sufficient test of orthodoxy for purposes of inter-communion,[1] can we expect that Nonconformist ministers as a whole would be willing to accept it ? Probably we can in the case of the Presbyterians and the Wesleyans ; certainly we cannot in that of the Congregationalists, Baptists and Quakers. Dr. Garvie has told us that the furthest that the Congregationalists could go in this matter would be to approve the creeds as historical documents expressing the substance of the Christian faith, and to give a statement of what in fact they do themselves believe. It seems impossible to be satisfied with this. It is true that we have the Free Church Catechism ; but this binds no one. And it is notorious that the present day drift in Congregational circles is *not* towards orthodoxy. As regards the Baptists, it is said that there is less tendency to extreme Liberalism ; but the difficulty of the refusal of subscription to any creed remains, with the further complication of the refusal of Baptism to children. This need not in itself be a final obstacle to intercommunion : there is, of course, plenty of precedent in the history of the early Church for the deferring of Baptism ; but the question might have to be raised whether the doctrine made explicit by the confining of Baptism to

[1] A question may be raised at this point as to whether the mere signing of the Nicene Creed is necessarily in itself a sufficient test of orthodoxy. Before giving Ordination (as we consider it), the Bishop would have the right, and in some cases the duty, of satisfying himself that the candidate was not simply accepting the Creed in an esoteric sense of his own, and that he was orthodox in the sense, *e.g.*, of not being a Nestorian.

adults was really compatible with our fundamental convictions as to the relation of the human soul to God.   It is an easier question to ask than to answer.   Moreover, both Baptists and Congregationalists seem to have a fundamentally different conception of the Church from that which is connoted by the " One Holy Catholic and Apostolic Church " in the Nicene Creed.   It is true that they have pretty generally moved from the conception that every congregation is *a* Church to the far preferable one that every congregation is *the* Church, *i.e.* the local embodiment of the universal Church.   This change may seem to remove the question from the sphere of doctrine to that of discipline and Church order.   But the difficulty does remain.   For the independence of the congregation is a fundamental principle, and it is difficult to see how any organic union could take place with a community to which the Church is not one organic unity at all.

On the whole, then, it appears that the Congregationalist principle, which is common to Congregationalists and Baptists, coupled with the rejection of the Catholic creed, does really preclude any possibility of Reunion, especially when we feel suspicious of the tendency of theological opinion among them.   Enquiries as to heretical teaching would inevitably arise, and we should be in the impossible position of having no standard by which to investigate them.   With the Presbyterians there would be much less difficulty on the score of doctrine.   It is true that the Westminster Catechism does want some explaining away ; but it is probable that the Scottish divines would make short work of that, and find little difficulty in satisfying our scruples.[1]   With the Methodists the same is probably true.   We ought to be able to satisfy each other of our essential orthodoxy.   It is probable that there is no difference at all, theologically, between the

---

[1] Dr. Headlam, dealing generally with the sixteenth century Confessions of Faith, says : " There is no doubt that one of the first steps towards Christian union must be to recognise that these formularies are obsolete."

general body of Methodist Ministers and the Evangelical section of the Church of England. They have a reputation for Liberalism, but if we are right in supposing that their general theological outlook is really modelled on John Wesley's sermons, making allowances for the changed outlook of the present day, then doctrinal difficulties ought not really to stand between us. Many of us may feel that Churchmanship *ought* to mean the acceptance of a good many positions which it is notorious that Evangelicals do not accept ; but anyone who remains in the Anglican Communion at all does by the very fact of his doing so assert that he wishes to be in communion with a great many people whose ideas of the *implications* of the Creed are very different from his own.

Of course the question may be asked, Why insist on the Creed when you assert that all that is necessary for belief is to be found in the Bible ? It seems impossible to believe that anyone who asks this question can really have considered what the modern critical attitude to the Bible really implies. It was always a highly artificial proceeding to treat the Bible as though it was a compendium of doctrine. Quite clearly it is nothing of the kind. The primary source of doctrine is the teaching of our Lord as interpreted and handed down to us by the Apostles. But because a tradition is liable to corruption, the critical spirit of the Reformation taught us that the tradition must be tested by the unchanging touchstone of Holy Scripture, which represents the tradition at its source. But although this was really a *critical* principle, the use that was made of it in earlier times was uncritical in the highest degree, even to the extent of treating all parts of Scripture as of equal value. But now that critical principles have been applied to the Bible itself it is quite impossible to found our religion on the uncriticised text of the Scriptures. It is open to anyone—and the modern theologian seldom hesitates to make the fullest use of the privilege—to say that such and such a book is not authentic, that this event did not occur, that such a saying may have been altered in transmission. We are thrown back on the tradition of the Church as a necessary means of discovering what the authentic Christian religion has been from the beginning. Of course we must treat tradition scientifically also : modern theology consists very largely in such sifting of the traditions of the Church. We can never go back to the old way of saying, " The Church says so," without asking also, " When, where and why did the Church say that ? " But neither can we say, " The Bible says so." It is a first principle of modern criticism that the Bible is a part of the tradition of the Church. No one is going to accept a religion which says that every sentence in the Bible is a Divine revelation of historic or dogmatic truth. In pressing for the Creed we are only asking for the shortest possible summary of what *is*, according to the most universal tradition, the irreducible minimum of history and dogma which is taken for truth by all Christians within the Catholic Church. It is only with those who accept this for truth that we can discuss the question of Reunion into one Church. The Creed is not an addition to the Bible : it is a distillation of the vital essence of the more important teachings of the Bible. If anyone accepts the Creed, we ask no further questions as to the exact sense in which he " believes all the canonical scriptures of the Old and New Testaments." If he believes that they are a gift from the Holy Spirit to the Church, that is sufficient.

While dogmatic unity is the foundation of any real Reunion, and incomparably more important than any other condition, it remains true that the things which really have most to do with keeping us apart are differences of practice. It is therefore necessary to discover how many of these differences need really be a cause of division at all.

The points on which Anglicans would be compelled in conscience to ask for satisfaction are not many in number and ought not to create insuperable difficulties.

There is Episcopacy. In the question of validity of ministration the matter of Episcopacy bulks very large indeed.

We shall come to that later on.   But in what is in itself the more important matter of the acceptance of an Episcopal *régime* there is surprisingly little difficulty.   The Wesleyans have already titular Bishops in America (" titular " that is from the point of view of those who have a difficulty in accepting their Orders).   The Presbyterians have Moderators, and would probably be quite ready to have Bishops for the sake of unity.   Surprising as it seems, some of the Congregationalists profess themselves ready to adopt the Episcopate as distinct from the Presbyterate, and the same would probably be true of the Baptists.   The only difficulties raised under this head are on points where we should be ready enough to recognise that our practice is in some need of reform.   Nonconformists are inclined to tell us that our Bishops are too much like State officials : that they are appointed by the State, administer State-made laws, and occupy altogether too lordly a position.   What they object to is not Episcopacy as such, but Erastian prelacy, the State governing the Church by means of a group of autocrats.   It may be imagined that most Anglican Bishops would repudiate the portrait with indignation tempered by amusement.   So far from the Bishop being an autocrat, it is only by the exercise of consummate tact that he can get his way in anything, unless he chooses to act under sanctions which bind neither his own conscience nor that of his clergy.   But it is true that the theory of the Episcopate in the British constitution is feudal in character, the Crown having taken the place of the Pope as the Bishop's overlord.   We owe this to Henry VIII., and almost all of us want it altered, if for no other reason than because it has become unworkable. Most of us want free appointment of the Bishops and synodical government.   And we gather that that is very much what the Nonconformists want too.   The present system ought not to be defended.

Then there is the matter of Eucharistic practice.   In this matter Anglicans are probably very ignorant as to what is actually done in Nonconformist churches ; and are perhaps prone to take what is done in some churches as more characteristic of general custom than it really is. We should be obliged to ask, not indeed for a set liturgy, but for some recognised form of Consecration. We do not set up the Anglican Prayerbook in this matter as ideal : very far from it. We recognise that the doctrine as to what is necessary for Consecration, which seems to underlie the Anglican rite, exposes itself to the charge that the words of Institution are of the nature of a charm.[1]   But we should be obliged to press for the invariable use of these words of Institution at every Eucharist. Presumably there would be no difficulty about this. Nor could many of us feel satisfied of the validity of a rite in which anything other than real wine was used for the matter of the Sacrament. And we feel certain that Nonconformists would agree that some assurance might rightly be asked for that the whole of the consecrated Elements should be reverently consumed immediately after the service. That is perhaps all that could rightly be made a condition of intercommunion, though indeed there is one other Nonconformist custom which would make intercommunion almost a dead letter as far as many Anglicans were concerned. It is the custom of sitting down while receiving the Blessed Sacrament. Of course we are well aware of the venerable Example of the Upper Room : yet it is not unreasonable to urge that the experience of the Church has led us to a fuller insight into the mystery of the Eucharist than was possible at the Institution, and that those who have realised that the act of Communion is the pledged and covenanted coming of Christ to the soul would find it well-nigh impossible to remain seated, if they had not been always accustomed to receive the Sacrament in that posture. The result of the sitting posture would therefore be that most

---

[1] The reference is not to the Prayer of Consecration itself, in which the words of Institution do form part of a prayer ; but to the direction as to what is to be done if a second Consecration should be necessary.

Anglicans would in practice find it almost impossible to bring themselves to communicate according to the Nonconformist rite, in spite of the Reunion which we are imagining to have been safely accomplished. We think, therefore, that it might be possible to ask the Nonconformists to consider the possibility of adopting, in common with the Eastern Church, the custom of *standing* to receive.

Then there is Confirmation. By this we do not mean the confirmation of vows previously taken on our behalf at the time of Baptism. We mean the " Laying on of Hands." It is almost impossible to imagine how it can have come about that the purely Anglican and modern custom of exacting a renewal of Baptismal vows as a preliminary to Confirmation can have become confused with the Confirmation itself. Nor do we mean anything that has any essential and invariable connection with admission to Holy Communion. Historically Confirmation is the sequel to Baptism. The nature of the relation between them is a difficult and complicated question, but it is difficult to see how any scholar can fail to realise that Confirmation is simply that laying on of hands which was always administered after Baptism in the primitive Church. Now this is a " first principle of the doctrine of Christ " according to Holy Scripture, and it seems intolerable that we should be asked to count it as a matter of secondary importance. But it is impossible to believe that this could not be adjusted. Confirmation need not be administered by the Bishop himself, so long as it is done under his authority ; and there is no need to press the Anglican rules as to the age and occasion of the ceremony. There is no reason at all why it should not be added to the ceremonies of Baptism, if that would meet the wishes of the church concerned. Nor could we insist that it should be an invariable preliminary to Holy Communion. Thus it would perhaps be within the competence of the Bishop to dispense particular persons altogether from receiving it. All that we should press for would be that the scriptural rite of the laying on of hands should be in some recognisable way restored, and made the invariable accompaniment or sequel to Baptism.

And it must not be thought that we press for this unintelligently merely because " the Bible says so." Rather we infer that *because* the Bible calls it " a first principle of the doctrine of Christ " therefore it cannot be a mere outward ceremony. Whether it is *called* a Sacrament matters very little, but the sole reason for urging the restoration of it is that it is, as we believe, a channel of grace, in the same sense as that in which Baptism is a channel of grace. It is true that Confirmation is not explicitly mentioned in the Lambeth Appeal ; but Dr. Gore represents a very widespread feeling when he urges that on any historical showing the term Baptism must be taken to include or imply Confirmation. But it is not suggested that on Reunion all Nonconformists would have to be confirmed before they could receive Communion in the reunited Church. That is a matter of discipline which on our side it belongs to the Bishops to determine. There is no sacrilege from any point of view in an unconfirmed person receiving Communion. But there is from the Catholic point of view a very grave sacrilege in an *unbaptised* person so doing ; and as we are being candid it may be permissible to say that we on the Anglican side are uncomfortable about the general and indiscriminate encouragement to Communion given by non-Episcopal Ministers. (This, of course, does not apply to the Presbyterians, who probably consider that the Anglican Altars are made far too easy of approach. Perhaps they are right. Perhaps on the other hand they are not. It is difficult to say.) It is not suggested that elaborate security should be taken to enquire into the fact of Baptism : obviously it must be left to the conscience of the communicant, unless the fact that he is not baptized is notorious. What we are objecting to is the custom of issuing a general invitation to Communion to all " who love the Lord Jesus Christ," without any reference to the necessity of being already united to the

Church which is His Body. Of course if the Sacraments are mere forms all this insistence on receiving them in the right order is puerile in the last degree ; but the rules of the Church were not made for those who believe the Sacraments to be mere forms ; and if we thought that Nonconformists generally thought they were the prospect of Reunion would leave us entirely cold.

The real difficulty has been deliberately left to the end. It is the matter of the " validity " of non-Episcopal ministrations. This comes last, partly because it is superstructure not foundation, partly because if we can agree on the more fundamental things it will create a will to union on these practical points. It is no good disputing who is to navigate the ship till the engineers have made up their minds how the engines work.

Supposing then that we have agreed with some body of Nonconformists that there is nothing, either positive or negative, in our respective doctrine and practice such as forbids intercommunion, what is the next step ? We should all agree that the act of communicating together is the supreme expression of unity. What then is necessary before we can do this ? We shall want to be *morally sure* that it is really the Sacrament of the Eucharist that is being administered. It is probable that, put in this form, the difficulty will be almost incomprehensible to many people. Is not the Sacrament, they would ask, simply the doing of what Christ told us to do ? Yes ; but He did not give the command to individuals, but to that group of Apostles whom he had constituted the governing body of His Church. That, of course, is to use modern language, not altogether applicable to the situation ; but the point is that not any Christian can sit at home and carry out a Eucharist : it is the act of Christ and the Church conjointly. The Eucharist can only be celebrated by some one who *has a right to represent the Church*.[1]

[1] Cf. Ign. ad Smyrn. viii., " Let that be deemed a valid Eucharist which is administered either by the Bishop or by one to whom he has entrusted it."

It is essentially a public action in which Christ acts through a duly constituted minister. If there is to be intercommunion without heartburning both parties must be satisfied that the consecrating presbyter or priest is a duly appointed minister of Christ and the Church, and that in consequence we may expect verily and indeed to have given to us, to take and to receive, the Body and the Blood of Christ. Both parties must be satisfied. Otherwise Re-union will cause nothing but distress : it will be artificial and external, even if it does not merely cause another schism.

What then is the reason why some of us are *not* satisfied as to the validity of the ministrations of the Nonconformist Minister ? This is not primarily a question of doctrine, seeing that it is not seriously proposed to press for the acceptance of any particular theory of the ministry. But we cannot get away from doctrinal presuppositions. All are agreed that no one can rightly approach the ministry unless he believes himself to be called thereto by God, either through interior conviction or through human authority. All are agreed that our Lord gave to His Apostles authority to govern and to teach the Church. But there our doctrinal agreement stops. For some of us think that this Divine Apostolic authority was meant to continue in the Church, and is now held by the ministry of the Church, and is given to individuals in the act of Ordination. Others believe that the sole function of the Church in Ordination is to *recognise* a God-given call. Here is a fundamental difference in pre-suppositions which is at least likely to lead to a difference in ideas as to validity. All that can be said on this point here is that New Testament evidence seems decisive as far as it goes for the former view. We have evidence as to the way in which the Seven " deacons " were ordained, and the presbyters in Asia Minor, and S. Timothy. In each of these cases there was an apostolic gift, in none of them a mere recognition of a personal conviction of a Divine call.

Now in this matter we should certainly find the Presbyterians on our side (and of course the Swedish Lutherans) : the Congregationalists and Baptists would be against us : and the Wesleyan Methodists would probably be divided. If we can judge from the fact that the majority of the Wesleyans have voted for amalgamation with the other branches of Methodism which permit of lay administration of Holy Communion it seems probable that they would be against us also.

Again, whatever the meaning of Ordination may have been, it is hardly disputed that at the end of the Apostolic period there was probably, as Dr. Headlam says, " a fixed and universal custom of Ordination by the Church through properly appointed ministers " ; the only questions which can really be raised are whether this was *absolutely* or only *almost* universal, whether it was a matter of divine appointment, and who was the ordaining minister, and whether, if the ordaining minister were not properly empowered to act, it would render the whole proceedings null and void.

As regards the first point we can only take the evidence as it stands. There is nothing to suggest that anyone ever made himself a presbyter. It has been held that the ministry of the " prophets " was self-authenticated and " charismatic "; but few scholars now maintain this view. The difference between the prophetic and the ordinary ministry was rather that the one was peripatetic and the other local.

The matter of divine appointment is one of a group of similar questions. But if we believe that the Church has power to legislate and the assistance of the Holy Ghost in so doing, the only practical interest of the question is whether the ordinance of Ordination could be altered by the authority of the Church or not.

There is more to be said about the third issue. The only New Testament evidence that we have does restrict Ordination to an Apostle or else to an Apostolic delegate, as S. Timothy or S. Titus, each of whom seems to have occupied a position indistinguishable from that of the officer afterwards called a Bishop.[1]

On the other hand the Epistle of S. Clement (A.D. 95 or earlier) seems to imply that there was no " Bishop " at Corinth at that time, only the presbyters. The word " Bishop " is still used as the equivalent of " Presbyter." But in 110 S. Ignatius of Antioch uses language of extraordinary vehemence as to the necessity of every church having its Bishop. He certainly *thought* that monarchical Episcopacy was universal and had always been so. His evidence is cogent for Asia Minor, and is not without weight for the Church as a whole, when we remember the marvellous facilities for travel which were characteristic of the times. By 175, according to Dr. Headlam, the idea of the Apostolic origin of Episcopacy was universal.

What are we to make of these facts ? The view held very strongly by the Tractarians, of which Dr. Gore is now the most eminent upholder, is that the Apostles appointed Bishops in the modern sense in every city where they had founded a church, and that the position of S. Timothy and S. Titus is the universal prototype of ecclesiastical organisation. As time went on the *name* of Bishop became appropriated to the quasi-apostolic head of each local church, but this did not correspond with any change in his authority, and in particular it was always he who had the sole ultimate authority for Ordination. It must not be thought that this is an exploded view. In many ways it accounts for all the facts better than any other. The only real difficulties about it are that the Acts suggests that many places were left with only their college of presbyters (even Ephesus which S. Paul did not expect to visit again) ; and the case of Corinth mentioned above.

Secondly, there is what we may term the " Congregationalist " view, that the Ignatian " Bishops " were really

[1] It is well known that in the New Testament " Bishop " and " Presbyter " are synonyms.

not what we should call Bishops at all, but pastors of particular and independent congregations. Now it is, of course, quite true that the Diocese, as we know it, is a later invention. The Ignatian Bishops each presided over the Christians of one town and no more. The idea of a bishop as a person who presides over the Christians of a large tract of country has nothing to do with the essence of Episcopacy. But the Congregationalist view of the Episcopate does not really account for the existence of the threefold ministry in S. Ignatius' time at all, and it seems to assume what, as Dr. Headlam points out, is very unlikely, that there was only one congregation of Christians in each town. And it is precisely union with the Bishop which constitutes membership in " the *Catholic* Church."

Thirdly, there is the view now specially associated with the name of Dr. Headlam. On his showing the Bishop is simply the chairman of the local college of presbyters in each place. With extraordinary rapidity and unanimity it came to be held that the presbyters could do nothing anywhere without the consent of the chairman, nor he without theirs. This applied to Ordination as well as to everything else. In other words, there happened in many places at the same time a process which can best be compared to the gradual development of the idea of the Papacy. The Bishop was at first *primus inter pares* : then his consent became necessary to the validity of any action : finally he emerged as more or less independent of his colleagues, and monarch of his Diocese.[1] At the same time the Bishop as chairman of the local college of Presbyters became their representative in any action which

[1] It is easy to say, as of course is said, that the " Anglo-Catholic " insistence on Episcopacy, but not on the Papacy, is inconsistent, that we ought either to sit loose to Episcopacy on grounds of the appeal to the primitive Church, or, if we talk of development, we should submit to the Papacy. But the two cases are not parallel. In regard to Episcopacy this view is only one theory devised to cover a particular short period, whereas in the case of the Papacy we can actually trace the development. Further, if this *was* what happened in the case of Episcopacy, it happened universally and without question. In the case of the Papacy it split the Church.

concerned other parts of the Church. According to the
" Tractarian " view the Episcopate is the norm of the
ministry, and Presbyterate holds a delegated authority : on
the " Congregationalist " view there never ought to have
been any difference at all : in Dr. Headlam's opinion the
Presbyterate is the norm, and the Bishop's authority is a
concentration of what was originally diffused. The query
which seems to arise in considering this last view is that it is
much easier to suppose that a change which happened so
suddenly and yet so quietly as it is represented that this
change did happen is hardly thinkable unless it has apostolic
authority behind it. And if the Episcopate is an apostolic
institution, then we are almost, if not quite, back in the
Tractarian position. Moreover, there is the case of S.
Timothy, left in personal charge of a particular church with
instructions to provide for the continuance of the ministry
by means of the laying on of hands.[1]

But Dr. Headlam has combined with a perfectly tenable
view of the origin of Episcopacy a condemnation of the whole
idea of transmitted authority, as it was taught by the Tractarians. He asserts that the original and truly Catholic
doctrine was simply that the Church ordains. As a matter
of fact she does so by means of Bishops, but that is purely
an ecclesiastical arrangement. Then S. Augustine, wishing
to make room for the recognition of the validity of schismatic
ministries, started the theory that validity depends on
exterior conditions, not on the will and intention of the
church to ordain. The fact of being in separation, he

---

[1] Mention must be made of S. Jerome's testimony to the usages of
Alexandria. He states that until the middle of the second century,
i.e. about a century and a half before the date at which he is writing, the
presbyters of Alexandria used to " appoint " (*nominabant* is the word he
uses) their own bishop. But it is impossible to be certain of S. Jerome's
exact meaning, and *if* he means, as has generally been held, that their
Bishop-elect was not considered to need any Consecration, the statement is quite devoid of any contemporary support. In fact, the evidence
of Origen, who *was* a contemporary of the actual time when the change
to normal Episcopacy must have been made (if Jerome's story is true),
tells strongly in the opposite direction.

taught, did not interfere with the validity of the sacrament. What he ought to have taught, according to Dr. Headlam, was that the fact of being in separation did not interfere with being within the Church, and *for that reason* neither did it interfere with the validity of the Sacraments. The Sacraments are the acts of the Church : where the Church is, there are valid Sacraments. And, as we cannot unchurch the Nonconformists,[1] therefore their Ordinations and other sacramental or quasi-sacramental acts must be valid. The whole idea of *transmission* he asserts to be an Anglican invention. There is nothing in the nature of things to prevent any number of Christians, or any one Christian, acting with a serious intention of doing what the New Testament orders, from ordaining a minister. It is irregular, for the law of the Church requires that this should be done by a Bishop, but the question of validity does not arise.

This seems a very astonishing result. The view propounded of the origin of episcopacy is of fascinating historical and ecclesiastical interest : its truth is a question for scholars. But the theory of what is needed to make a minister is so paradoxical as to make criticism inevitable.

[1] This is the theory which lies at the root of the Lambeth Appeal. " We acknowledge all those who believe in our Lord Jesus Christ, and have been baptised into the name of the Holy Trinity, as sharing with us membership in the universal Church of Christ which is His Body." It has been subjected to very damaging criticism by Fr. Puller, S.S.J.E., and Dr. Darwell Stone in a characteristically learned pamphlet entitled, " Who are members of the Church ? " They seem to prove decisively that there is no precedent whatever for the idea that Baptism and faith are sufficient to ensure such membership. " So far as can be judged," they say, " from the writings of the Fathers, the whole Catholic Church of the third and following centuries would unanimously have rejected the statement concerning membership in the Church set forth in . . . the Lambeth Appeal." They do not even accept the statement of the Bishop of Nassau, " that each baptised member of these various denominations is *individually*, by virtue of his Baptism, a member of the one Catholic Church." It must, however, be said that they do not offer any proof of the statement on the title-page, that the sentence of which they offer such powerful criticism " is fundamental to all the propositions of that Appeal." It *is* surely possible to follow up the Lambeth suggestions without insisting on an answer to the question whether before Reunion the separated bodies are already in any sense members of the Catholic Church.

Beginning with the thesis that Orders are the gift of the Church, we find in the end that any Orders by whomsoever conferred are valid, provided that there is faith, a serious intention and imposition of hands. This conclusion is reached as the result of combining two premisses, one—belonging to naive primitive ecclesiasticism—that Orders are the gift of the Church, the other—purporting to be based on S. Augustine—that the Church consists of all baptized Christians who believe in the Lord Jesus. We cannot but be suspicious of a conclusion which wanders so far from the opinions of those who framed the premisses. For the pre-Augustinian view that the validity of Orders depended on their being administered within the Church was invariably held in combination with the opinion that to be in heresy or schism was to be outside the Church. And the idea that the Sacraments are operative outside the limits of the Church was certainly *not* held by S. Augustine to validate non-Episcopal ministries.[1] It is in fact to S. Augustine more than anyone that we owe the distinction between regularity and validity, which in the case of a Bishop is equivalent to the distinction between jurisdiction and order.

A little consideration will show that there are two things necessary for the function of a Bishop. He must be chosen—somehow : and he must have the authority of the Catholic Church. It is the latter which ratifies the former, gives to the office of a Bishop its mystical and supernatural side, and lifts the whole matter out of the province of the local and particular into that of the universal. The Consecration of a Bishop, like the Ordination of a priest or a deacon, is an act of the whole Catholic Church, and so an act of Christ. It is *unfortunate* that the method of choosing a bishop has so

---

[1] S. Augustine states, it is true, that heretics are " joined to the body of the Church " by Baptism ; but he teaches most clearly that neither heretics nor schismatics *belong* to the Church. They may have the Sacraments, but in Augustine's theory, they get no good from them. He would certainly not have accepted Dr. Headlam's statement, " The Church consists of all baptised Christians who believe in the Lord Jesus."

often been unsatisfactory, but if the diocese does accept him, in the end no irreparable harm has been done. But it is *disastrous* if there is any doubt as to his having received the authority of Christ, and that is why the Church has always insisted that those who ordain or consecrate shall have indubitable authority to do so. In practice this has worked out as an insistence that they shall themselves be *Bishops*, the power of Ordination being in fact the most conspicuous *differentia* of the episcopal office.

So we find that there are two senses in which the conception of " Apostolic succession " may be used. In early ages, before the distinction between order and jurisdiction had been made clear (as in the writings of S. Irenaeus) it means the succession from holder to holder of a particular see, and is employed to vindicate the teaching authority of a bishop as against heresy. He is the repository of the apostolic teaching by virtue of the traditions of his see. But the later use of the conception, which has been so prominent in all discussions as to the validity of Orders, is amply justified. The course of history and the stabilisation of Church doctrine makes the tradition of particular sees less important. What we do want to be certain of is that our ministers represent something more than human choice, and that they come to us with the Divine authority of Christ as embodied in His Church. This is secured by the line of succession from consecrator to consecrated all down the ages. To believe that this is a transmission of the authority once given by our Lord to His Apostles does not tie us to a particular conception of the origin of the threefold ministry : it only commits us to the necessity for making sure that the person who administers Consecration or Ordination has the authority of the Church to do so. The Episcopal office, whether created by our Lord, as we may reasonably believe, or evolved by the Church, is our security. There is nothing mechanical or materialistic in believing in the transmission of the grace of Holy Orders in this sense.

There is a saying of Dr. Gore which is worthy of bein repeated many times in this connection. " The opposite of secure or valid," he reminds us, " is not *non-existent*, but *precarious*." [1] What we ask for in all matters connected with the Sacraments is above all things *security*. If there is to be a reunited Church ever or anywhere one essential thing is that all members of it shall have a moral certainty that the Sacraments are administered according to the intention of our Lord, and also of the Church. For that reason our Bishops state that they would submit to a second Consecration if that were the only thing which stood between them and union with the Roman Church. But in the eyes of Catholics everywhere the Eucharist is only valid if it is consecrated by a priest : therefore to us it is of vital importance to have a moral certainty that the consecrator *is* a priest. And there are too many uncertainties about the priesthood of the ministers of the Free Churches for us ever to feel happy about communicating with them. They do not themselves claim to be priests, or to have any power in this matter of consecrating the Eucharist which is not shared by the laity. And the validity of their Orders depends on theories which are far from certain. It depends, first, on the idea that the Free Churches are corporately portions of the Catholic Church, in spite of the fact that they appear *prima facie* to be new and rival churches ; secondly, on the theory that the grace of Orders is *not* a transmitted authority first given by our Lord to His Apostles, and then handed down by them to their successors, in spite of a great deal in Holy Scripture and the writings of the early Church which might make us think this a very good way of describing the nature of Holy Orders.

This is the point at which all negotiations with the Free Churches hitherto have broken down, and it seems that there is no immediate prospect of much further progress being made. Perhaps we could hardly have expected any-

[1] *The Mission of the Church*, p. 26.

thing else at the moment. Quite certainly, as we have already had other reasons to think, the time is not ripe for Reunion with Congregationalists in this matter of the Ministry. Their whole conception of the ministerial office is different from ours. The belief that the Blessed Sacrament is even a channel of grace is far from universal among them. That being so, there does seem a certain unreality in asking or expecting a Minister with these convictions to submit to a rite which is believed by the ordaining Bishop to carry with it the pledge of the actual presence of the Humanity of our Blessed Lord. The difference of doctrine is too acute. Moreover, the whole theory of Ordination is different. Some Congregationalists still hold—and it is the logical and consistent outcome of their position—that Ordination is simply the appointment to a particular charge, and ought to be repeated if a minister is called to a new church. Others object to Ordination altogether in principle. Sometimes, according to the testimony of the apparently well-informed author of *Church and Chapel*, there is no pretence of Ordination at all. Usually there is no imposition of hands. Dr. Garvie tells us that any suggestion of " reordination presents an insuperable obstacle."[1]

The same remarks seem to apply to the Baptists, and the President of the Baptist Union has recently told us not to expect any encouragement at present in suggestions for Reunion.

As regards the Wesleyans, there is perhaps more hope. Doctrinally, as we have seen, they are very much nearer to the Anglican position ; and they have not definitely rejected the proposals of the Anglican Bishops. They have only said that they could not accept Episcopal Ordination as part of the scheme of union, " if it be interpreted as implying reordination." It seems just possible that they would be satisfied with an assurance that the object of such Ordination

[1] See the section on " Congregationalism," by Dr. Garvie, in *What the Churches Stand For.*

would be the satisfaction of Anglican scruples, and that it would not be taken to imply that they had themselves any doubts as to the sufficiency of their own commission. But the Primitive Methodists have shown themselves more uncompromising; so that it must be doubted whether a re-united Methodist body would really have any desire to come into union with ourselves on the only terms on which we could seriously consider the matter.

There remain, among the non-Episcopalian bodies, the Scottish Presbyterians, whose lead the English Presbyterians would probably follow.

Here the position is rather different. There is a long-standing desire in Scotland for Reunion. The names of Bishops Wordsworth and Wilkinson are well-known and honoured in Scotland for the part they played in trying to create a favourable atmosphere. Moreover, the Church of Scotland at any rate has far more of the " churchly " attitude than the English Nonconformists. The Scottish Presbyterian Churches have not committed themselves to any definite reply to the Lambeth Appeal, having been too closely occupied with their own plans for Presbyterian Reunion.

The Presbyterian is a sacramentalist in doctrine, meagre though his sacramental practice must seem to our eyes. If we are distressed at the rarity of Communion services in Presbyterian churches, we cannot but admire the devotion with which they are prepared for, and the care that is taken to exclude the obviously unworthy. Presbyterians claim to have in effect a threefold ministry, of Minister, Elder and Deacon; and although nominally Elders and Deacons are laymen, the fact that an Elder (but no one else) is occasionally permitted to celebrate the Communion may suggest that perhaps we are justified in thinking of the Ministers as corresponding to the Bishop and the Elder to the Priest. In that case, *apart from the question of validity*, it is merely a case of an abnormally numerous episcopate, as contrasted with the abnormally sparse one to which we in England are accustomed.

The Presbyterian Minister takes his position as an ordained man very seriously indeed : he is something of a sacerdotalist. An influential school holds a theory, for which there is considerable mediaeval scholastic support, of presbyteral apostolic succession. The theory as held by some of the schoolmen was that the three Holy Orders were not those of Bishop, Priest and Deacon, but of Priest, Deacon and Subdeacon : the difference between a Bishop and a Priest being one of jurisdiction and not of character. A possible result of this theory would be that though a Priest was forbidden to ordain, yet if he did so the action would be valid. The theory, which is identical with that held by John Wesley, is extremely difficult to maintain, and we could hardly be expected to commit ourselves to anything so uncertain, but in dealing with Presbyterians we have this great advantage, that the Catholic conception of Holy Orders does exist. Of course in one way this makes the situation even more difficult. In approaching the English Dissenter we are offering him something—the priesthood—which he does not claim to have ; but to the Catholic-minded Presbyterian his presbyterate and our priesthood are one and the same thing. The only question is as to whether he possesses it or not. To submit to a fresh imposition of hands does look like an acknowledgement that his claim has been without foundation. But it may well be believed that where the Catholic conception is already in existence it will be easier and not harder to make the sacrifice required in the interests of unity and security. We can only lay before our brethren in Scotland the considerations which have induced our Bishops to make their large-hearted offer to the Roman Church, and ask whether they do not apply equally to the relation of the great Scottish Presbyterian Churches to the little but noble Scottish Episcopal Church, and through her to the Anglican Communion and the Catholic Church. We do not ask them to repudiate their Orders ; only to " mak' siccar."

Presbyterians have been nobly active in the cause of Reunion lately in many parts of the world. May it not be that they will be the first to accept the Anglican Eirenicon ?

It is time to bring this long discussion to an end. It has been an ungracious task to suggest to our non-Episcopal brethren that some of them ought to be willing to take a step which seems to cast doubts on their own experience. We know well enough that it is no unworthy fear of humiliation which makes them hesitate to take the step to which they are invited, but a holy fear of being untrue to the Holy Ghost. But we can only repeat what has been said so often by responsible authorities, that no one on either side doubts for a moment the fact that God has blessed their ministry. All that we are doubtful of is whether a ministry separated from the Catholic Episcopate is really in accordance with the ultimate will of God. We know that we have much to learn from non-Episcopalians, and much to gain from union with them ; but we think that we have also something to give them, which they have not got : unity with the primitive stock and secure access to the covenant of grace. Might they not say to us, much as we hope one day to say to the Roman Church, " You are the primaeval body. We felt obliged to split off from you. Let there be no recriminations. Each of us has learnt our lesson : we wish to be reconciled. Unity is represented by *unquestioned* Orders ; these we can never have from the mere fact that you do question them for reasons which seem to you (not to us) sufficient. If we ask you to give them to us, will you make impossible conditions ? "

It would be easy in this connection to rewrite the parable of the Prodigal Son. But the son in this case would not be a prodigal at all, but a pious, even a saintly, person, whose exodus from his home was by no means altogether his own fault. And in this parable we can paint the character of the elder brother as black as we please ; we can lay on him all and more than all that he deserves of the blame. Still the home is the home ; and the moment it is tolerable for the younger it is his duty to return and see for himself the welcome he will receive, not from the Father alone, but from his penitent and rejoicing elder brother too.

XVIII

EPILOGUE

IT is difficult to avoid writing about the Reunion of the Church as though it were an affair of Plenipotentiaries, Concordats and Alliances, whereas, in fact, it is an attempt to make the outward unity correspond to the inward which is there already. And that is what we so often feel when we come face to face with those from whom we are separated as far as outward communion is concerned. There *is* an inner unity; only it is not corporately or outwardly expressed. This has always been the case wherever real Christians met together. The new fact in the situation is the growing sense that the outward unity matters. We are growing back into the old Greek idea of the importance of *form*. There have always been formalists of course, but a formalist is a man whose forms are mere hollow moulds : *form* as conceived philosophically is the defining of what would otherwise be chaotic. And the confusion of the chaotic with the spiritual is one of the most disastrous that can be made. When our Lord came to earth He came in definite form, not as an indefinite influence. And the Church which is to express Him on earth is also a *Body* ; it has definite outlines, it is a definite expression of an impression once made. Only it is a *living* Body, inhabited and *formed* by the Spirit of God, who is the Spirit of Jesus. Therefore its outlines, though definite, are not hard and rigid and unchanging. We may even, *as things are*, adopt whole-heartedly the words of Dr. Carnegie Simpson : " We must acknowledge that its visi-

274

bility is not definable with complete precision, and, therefore, we should not press the contour of its outline rigidly. . . .
There is the visibility of a house and there is the visibility of
a cloud. A house has distinct walls, and we can say of
anyone that he is outside or in. A cloud is quite clearly
seen, but the observer cannot draw in the sky a definite line
and say where exactly the cloud begins and where it ends.
The visibility of the Church is rather that of a cloud than that
of a house." [1] It must be acknowledged that it *is* very
difficult to say with confidence of so and so, " He is within,"
and of so and so, " He is without." Yet it must surely be
acknowledged that this is on account of the confusion we
have got ourselves into, rather than because of the Divine
ideal. If membership in the Church is really all that the
Scriptures represent it to be, it is really almost intolerable
that there should be any doubt as to who are the bene-
ficiaries of the Divine endowments.

It might be truer, as well as less metaphorical, to say that
the visibility of the Church and its unity are those of a
pilgrimage. The pilgrim band has its organisation, its
catering arrangements, its guides, its official route, its badges,
its human weaknesses. It has also its scrupulous followers
and its stragglers. All alike may have the free pilgrim spirit,
and we never want to say to anyone, " You don't belong."
The stragglers may be heartier pilgrims than many of the
docile and orderly, bead-telling, litany-reciting procession
which leads the way ; but abolish your " good " pilgrims,
and you have abolished the pilgrimage ! And when men
grow disgusted with the multiplicity of sects, and say, " Let
us join up," are they not really saying, " Let us go back to
the Catholic Church," as the stragglers might say, " Let us
get back to the main body " ? For we may never forget
that the primary outlines of the Body were impressed on her
by Christ Himself ; and even the secondary outlines have no
object except to express the indwelling Spirit of Christ. If

[1] *Church Principles*, pp. 33, 34.

they no longer do this they are idle : yet even so it does not follow that they are to be abolished. Why not consider whether they cannot be brought back again under the moulding power of the Spirit ? We are not likely at this time of day to devise a better outline than that of the historic Catholic Church. So long as everybody goes on saying, " All alike and equally we are parts of the Catholic Church," we are not even aiming at anything more vital than a federation, and the result is likely to be little better than a conglomerate. The return to unity wants a great deal more humility on both sides than the signing of a treaty, but how much the better shall we all be for that ! What raptured greetings ! What knitting severed friendships up ! And what a sense of security in our membership in the one Body fashioned by the King Himself ! And, if even that seems tinged with selfishness, there are our Lord's words to ponder again and again : " That they all may be one . . . that the world may believe that Thou hast sent Me." [1]

* * * * * * * *

Have we then come to the conclusion that there is nothing to be done ? Far from it. *We have to make ready for Reunion.* It is allowable to think, as we have been doing, what our neighbours on their principles ought to do ; but it is far more important that we should be considering what we ought to be doing ourselves.

There is a quotation from the late Dr. Gwatkin at the beginning of the preface to a book entitled *Towards Reunion*, by a group of Evangelical and Free Church Divines, which deserves every echo which can be made to ring for it. He cites S. John xvii. 23 (R.V.), " That they may be perfected into one," and concludes that perfection is the path to unity, not unity to perfection. We cannot put things right simply by joining up. But as we advance towards perfection we advance towards unity also. At the moment it is not clear that Christian men outside of the Church of England are

[1] S. John xvii. 21.

quite certain that it is so very important to join up with her. To the Romans she seems the City of Confusion; to the Orthodox a combination of three churches; to the Dissenters a Protestant body, culpably tolerant of Anglo-Catholicism. The comprehensiveness we boast of does not strike them as so very glorious. Yet within the Church of England there are few who would wish to make that comprehensiveness much less than it is. We sometimes read utterances which make us rub our eyes. But on the whole we *desire* to be comprehensive, and not to be too quick with charges of heresy. The national spirit and the critical spirit have their own dangers; but we believe that Anglican theology has been on true lines in letting them have their say in religious matters, and in trusting to the Holy Spirit to prevent their leading to the guilt of schism or of heresy. What then is the explanation of the unsatisfactory character which the Church of England bears with the outside world ? We think of our ideals and are proud of them : the outsider looks at our performance and refuses to take us seriously. It is quite true that we are always apologising for ourselves. These apologies are quite sincere, and are recognised as such. But we tend to overdo it, and perhaps we deserve to be taken at our word. Yet that is not the real reason why men seem to doubt whether the Church of England is worth uniting with. There are two reasons which are far more cogent.

One is that we will not proclaim our positive ideals. We criticise Rome, we cultivate a half-sentimental friendship for the Orthodox, we exasperate the Dissenters by using unreal language and refusing to carry it into official action : while all the time there is a splendid ideal of Anglicanism which might serve as a rallying-point for Christendom in the future, something which we dare not compromise, unless we would lose the very thing which justifies our existence.

The Anglican appeal is not to antiquity alone : *Ubique*, *Semper*, *ab Omnibus*, isolated from its context, is a fit motto for a fossilised ecclesiasticism, not for a dynamic faith. The

Anglican appeal is to a *true* development from antiquity, which shall not contradict the spirit of the antiquity from which it has sprung. This is what S. Vincent of Lerins really meant. These are his words : " It is right that these ancient dogmas of heavenly philosophy should be cultivated, dug out and polished : it is wrong that they should be changed, deformed and mutilated. The nature of development is this : that each thing grows while remaining in its proper nature, while the nature of change is that it is transmuted into something else." Or again, " This is the right and legitimate rule of progress, this the established and most beautiful order of growth, that mature age always develops in the full-grown those parts and forms which the Creator's wisdom has formed in them beforehand as children." [1] It could not be better put. Here is no pedantic attempt to set up an impossible antiquarianism, or to represent the growth of Church principles as the mechanical unwrapping of the contents of a parcel. The Church grows, organisation grows, dogma grows ; but its growth must be watched, pruned, criticised, harmonised with the growing body of secular knowledge ; it must be tested by the spiritual sense, by historical learning, by pragmatic experience. We need not be afraid for it ; the truth will stand the test.

It is not an easy ideal : it would be far easier to have a few clear-cut principles and get to work with them at all costs ; but it corresponds with the greatness of our subject-matter. You may call it Liberal Catholicism [2] if you will, so long as "Liberalism" bears its proper meaning of scholarly freedom.[3]

[1] *Commonitorium*, c. xxiii.

[2] The phrase was used as long ago as 1878 to express the " Gallicanism " of Dupanloup and his school.

[3] Near the end of his life Newman could maintain that through all his changes of opinion he had consistently contended against what *he* called Liberalism. By his definition " Liberalism " is " a false liberty of thought on matters in which, from the constitution of the human mind, thought cannot be brought to any successful issue, and is therefore out of place." But Newman's own theory of Development is a Liberal theory ; it is the attempt of a scholar to free himself from the shackles of the older theories of a doctrinal development which was either mechanical or else dialectical. Compare Tyrrell : *Christianity at the Cross Roads*.

For the phrase " Liberal Catholicism " has sometimes been used to express what the late Fr. Tyrrell called " Modernism," which was, to be precise, an attempt to combine the teaching of Schweitzer with the dogmas of Roman Catholicism.[1] That is an attempt which has come to an end with the disappearance of the purely Apocalyptic school of exegesis. " Liberalism," then, must not be taken to mean that we are prepared to give away what does not belong to us. We have nothing to give away, not the Episcopate, nor the Sacraments, nor the open Bible, nor the marriage law, nor our national character, nor the disciplined freedom which is the ideal of our theology. We hold these things in trust for the future : if we give them away we shall have done our best to destroy the hope of final unity. We have a wide field in which to develop. The British Empire and the United States extend over more than a quarter of the inhabited world. And within the sphere of the English-speaking races at least there is nothing to hinder the establishment everywhere of a " reformed and scriptural Catholicism,"[2] such as might form a model for the reorganisation of the Church some day on true and constitutional lines. Our principles enable us to face all the facts : those that have created Protestantism as well as those that have developed Catholicism. There is a great future before the Anglican Communion if she will but proclaim her principles.

The second reason for the poor figure we sometimes cut is our unbrotherly behaviour. Here in the Anglican Communion we have already that principle of unity in diversity which is the only hope for Reunion in the future. It is true that a genuine and final unity must be a unity in the faith ; true also that our differences within the Church of England go beyond those differences in mere opinion which would necessarily exist in any church so long as human nature is

[1] What is now called " Modernism " Tyrrell would have called " Liberal Protestantism."

[2] Dr. Darwell Stone's phrase.

opinionative. But we have deliberately and on principle been more than loth to exclude from our communion any who seriously think they have a place within the borders of the Church. We may have been too lax, but hatred of heresy-hunting is very deeply engrained in us, and our national love of truthfulness over every other virtue makes our sympathies take sides at once with a man who is saying what he thinks, even though our deepest convictions are that truthfulness and the truth are in his case ranged against each other.

In all these circumstances it is surely a principle of Anglicanism when it is true to itself to seek for unity of heart within its own borders. If we think a man ought to be excommunicated, then no doubt it is no good trying to be brotherly with him in the things of the Spirit ; but if we do not go so far as that, if we are willing to remain in communion with him, then surely that includes all lesser degrees of charity, kindness and toleration.

It is not easy to be a good Anglican ! All of us probably have moods in which we react wildly in one direction or the other. Some are only kept where they are under the stress of forces which are equal and opposite : occasionally someone breaks loose and talks wildly : we need a great deal of patience with each other, and a firm faith in the Divine plan and in our Living Head : then some day the Anglican Church will have its reward.

INDEX

Abbot, Archbishop, 107, 109.
Abyssinians, 38, 205, 240.
Acacius, Patriarch, 43, 44.
Acts of the Apostles, 25.
Agatho, Pope, 42.
Alexandria, 31, 37, 43, 58, 65, 107, 133, 193, 206, 207, 264 n.
America (United States), 21, 22, 91, 126, 167, 182-184, 190-192, 196, 202, 255, 279.
Anglican Orders, 84-88, 166, 179, 180, 226, 227, 238, 242 n.
Anglo-Catholicism, 102, 110, 174, 212, 235, 263 n.
Anicetus, Pope, 26, 27.
Anti-Christ, 48, 92, 95.
Antioch, 32, 35, 37, 38, 43, 58, 65, 154, 185, 193, 206, 207.
Antony of Kiev, Metropolitan, 180 n, 192 n, 196, 217.
Apostolicae Curae, 84, 85 n, 166.
Arianism, 16, 17, 31, 44, 47 n.
Armenians, 38, 179, 204, 239, 240.
Arminianism, 144, 146.
Arnold, Dr., 151, 175.
Arnold of Brescia, 55.
Articles, XXXIX., 80, 137, 152.
Assyrians, 35.
Athanasius, S., 31, 32.
Augsburg Confession, 70, 78, 152, 240.
Augustine, S., of Hippo, 13, 34 n, 42 n, 71, 72 n, 73, 160 n, 264-266.
Australia, 190, 204.
Austria, 6, 138, 159.
Avignon, 18, 59.
Azymites, 49, 62, 206 n, 207.

Baptists, 114, 115, 149, 200, 201, 202, 251, 252, 255, 269.
Baptists, General, 105, 139, 148, 149.
Baptists, Particular, 105, 139, 148.
Barbarossa, 56.
Barlow, Bishop, 87, 88.
Bartlet, Dr., 188, 189.
Basel, Council of, 61.
Batiffol, Mgr., 33, 34, 54 n, 217, 218, 231.
Baxter, Richard, 122, 123.
Belgium, 6.
Bernard, S., 10.
Bible Christians, 149.
Bishops, 14, 29, 30, 37, 68, 75, 81, 146, 157, 172, 188, 189, 220-222, 254, 255, 261-269, 271, 279.
Bohemia, 52, 60, 61, 139, 161, 162, 196.
Boniface VIII., Pope, 59.
Bonn Conference, 162, 163.
Bonner, Bishop, 79.
Boris, of Bulgaria, 52.
Bryce, Lord, 31, 54 n.
Bulgaria, 51, 52, 57, 58, 65, 134, 154, 194, 195.
British Church, 39.

Caesaro-Papism, 43, 78.
Callixtus, S., 28.
Calvin, John, 72-74, 79, 82, 104, 105.
Calvinists, 19, 21, 79, 93-95, 97-104, 107, 108, 113, 117, 123, 129, 138, 139, 144, 146, 148, 197.
Canada, 189, 190, 203, 204 n.

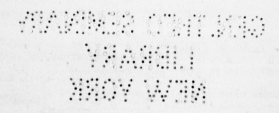

PRINTED IN GREAT BRITAIN BY ROBERT MACLEHOSE AND CO. LTD.
THE UNIVERSITY PRESS, GLASGOW.